DATE DUE

JUL - 8 1994	
MAR - 7 1995	
MAR 21 1995 *A3*	
DEC - 1 1995	
auc 545	
Sept. 16/96	
MAR - 4 1997	
MAR 1 8 1997	
APR - 3 1997	
JAN 2 9 1998	
FEB 25 1998	
APR 1 3 1999	
NOV - 2 1999	
MAR 2 9	
JUL 2 0 2001	
NOV 2 8 2003	

BRODART   Cat. No. 23-221

THE MERRY-GO-ROUND
OF SEXUAL ABUSE:
IDENTIFYING AND TREATING
SURVIVORS

William E. Prendergast, PhD

SOME ADVANCE REVIEWS

"An absolutely essential manual for anyone who wants to work with or who is already working with survivors/perpetrators of sexual abuse. A powerful, clear, and well-documented guide, illustrated with numerous case studies. All who try to find their way around the pitfalls, landmines, and cesspools in treating the survivors and perpetrators of sexual abuse without studying this book are doing their clients a grave disservice."

Robert T. Francoeur, PhD
Professor of Human Sexuality and Embryology
Fairleigh Dickenson University

"A mine of information for all who work in the field of sex offenders. . . . From a law enforcement perspective, understanding the processes of victimization is vital when attempting to discover the truth about a cycle of offending behavior and when interviewing both victims and offenders. This book offers an extensive insight into those processes."

Michael Hames
Superintendent, Obscene Publications Branch
New Scotland Yard, London

"Defines and addresses every aspect of the training and supervision of professionals diagnosing and treating molesters and survivors of sexual abuse. Case histories, imprinting, survivors as molesters, and vice-versa, are particularly significant."

William E. Hartman, PhD
Co-Director, Center for Marital and Sexual Studies
Long Beach, CA

"Deals comprehensively with the vicious circle that traps survivors. Vividly written by an international trainer in this field, [this book] offers visionary ways of recovery and treatment, reducing the escalation of effects which would otherwise be passed on to later generations."

Vera Diamond, MNCP, MBAFATT
Psychotherapist, Secretary of Cornelian Trust

"Here is another must read book for all therapists, victims, and molesters as well as the general population–all of whom could understand the problems related to sexual abuse."

Marilyn Fithian, PhD
Co-Director, Center for Marital and Sexual Studies
Long Beach, CA

NOTES FOR PROFESSIONAL LIBRARIANS AND LIBRARY USERS

This is an original book title published by The Haworth Press, Inc. Unless otherwise noted in specific chapters with attribution, materials in this book have not been previously published elsewhere in any format or language.

CONSERVATION AND PRESERVATION NOTES

The paper used in this publication meets the minimum requirements of American National Standard for Information Sciences–Permanence of Paper for Printed Material, ANSI Z39.48-1984.

The Merry-Go-Round of Sexual Abuse

Identifying and Treating Survivors

HAWORTH Criminal Justice,
Forensic Behavioral Sciences
& Offender Rehabilitation

Nathaniel J. Pallone, PhD
Senior Editor

New, Recent, and Forthcoming Titles:

Treating Sex Offenders in Correctional Institutions and Outpatient Clinics: A Guide to Clinical Practice by William E. Prendergast

The Merry-Go-Round of Sexual Abuse: Identifying and Treating Survivors by William E. Prendergast

The Merry-Go-Round of Sexual Abuse
Identifying and Treating Survivors

William E. Prendergast, PhD

The Haworth Press
New York • London • Norwood (Australia)

The Haworth Press, Inc., 10 Alice Street, Binghamton, NY 13904-1580

Library of Congress Cataloging-in-Publication Data

Prendergast, William E.
    The merry-go-round of sexual abuse : identifying and treating survivors / William E. Prendergast.
        p.   cm.
    Includes bibliographical references (p.   ) and index.
    ISBN 1-56024-387-2 (acid-free paper).
    1. Sexual abuse victims–Rehabilitation. 2. Sexual abuse victims–Psychology. I. Title
RC560.S44P74   1993
616.85′822390651–dc20

                                     93-17364
                                          CIP

To all the victims of sexual abuse everywhere, male or female, infant, child, adolescent, or adult, who belong to the world family of survivors.

Contents

ILLUSTRATIONS, GRAPHS, AND TABLES

About the Author

WILLIAM E. PRENDERGAST served as Director of Professional Services at the Adult Diagnostic & Treatment Center in Avenel, a specialized unit of the Department of Corrections of the State of New Jersey statutorily charged with the diagnosis and treatment of repetitive, habitual, or compulsive sex offenders from the Center's opening in 1976 to his retirement in 1991. Prior to that appointment, Prendergast had served for nine years as Director of the Rahway Treatment Unit housed at Rahway State Prison, the predecessor to ADTC, and as a staff clinical psychologist at the New Jersey State Diagnostic Center at Menlo Park. Prendergast is presently engaged in lecturing, teaching, and training sex therapists and correctional psychologists, social workers, and administrators and also maintains a limited private practice in sex therapy and serves as a consultant at the Center for Health Psychology and Evaluative Medical Services, both in New Jersey.

A native of Connecticut, Prendergast was educated at Fairfield University and the University of Detroit and received his Ph.D. from Walden University. He is certified as a sex therapist by the American Association of Sex Educators, Counselors, and Therapists (AASECT) and holds the Diplomate as Certified Sex Therapist and Clinical Supervisor of the American Board of Sexology. In 1991, he was presented the Distinguished Service Award of the New Jersey Child Assault Prevention Project for his contributions to treatment and the training of other professionals in the specialized techniques of treating sex offenders in correctional institutions and outpatient clinics.

This is Prendergast's second book in a trilogy on the sex offender and his victim. His first book was titled *Treating Sex Offenders in Correctional Institutions and Outpatient Clinics: A Guide to Clinical Practice*, published by The Haworth Press, Inc. It is currently being used as a training manual by therapy groups as well as police training academies and as a text in several universities, including New York University.

Preface

I began working with the survivors of sexual abuse during my internship at a reformatory for boys, ages seven to eighteen. Shortly before my arrival there, there had been a serious scandal involving both the physical and sexual abuse of some of the inmates. As a result, my caseload consisted of a large number of these survivors.

While my graduate work at the University of Detroit was specifically in child psychology, little, if anything, was ever covered on the subject of sexual abuse. I was therefore unprepared and had to learn on the job, the worst possible way to work with survivors. Fortunately, I had one of the toughest and most brilliant supervisors that an intern could ever hope for, Dr. Bohdan Cymbalisty. We worked together either six or seven days a week, spent many hours after work discussing cases and, little by little, I began to get a "feel" for this specific group.

After completing a year's internship, I transferred to what was then called the New Jersey State Diagnostic Center (D.C.) where I wanted to work with one of the foremost forensic psychiatrists of that period, Dr. Ralph Brancale who was like a "father" as well as mentor to all of the staff. I learned more in these two years with these two great teachers than in all the years of my formal education and this brought me to the realization that *specialized training and supervised experience* were a sine-qua-non for working in either the field of sexual offenders or in the field of the survivors of sexual abuse, whether child, adolescent or adult.

During my seven years plus at the D.C., I specialized in diagnosing and treating children and adolescents, mostly males, who were either sexual offenders or the survivors of sexual abuse or both. The connection between sexual abuse and future offending soon became quite apparent.

In my 30 years of working with both sex offenders and their victims of all ages, it is still unfortunate that it is possible to find professionals who use both of these groups as experimental learning tools, by choice, not by necessity. The primary reason for this fact appears to be that there is too little specialized training *required* on the academic level. Professional schools issuing degrees from the bachelor's level to a Ph.D. are too often lax in providing the necessary background courses and the practical supervised training experiences that are necessary to prepare counselors and therapists alike to treat either offenders or survivors. Both groups require specialized handling as well as specialized treatment techniques in order to produce even minimal positive changes.

To this end, during the last almost thirty years, I have been traveling around this country and to England as well to different professional and para-professional organizations attempting to provide a minimal to moderate level of training in these two areas. The effectiveness of the training is dependent on the time afforded me. It is obvious that a one-day training seminar will not produce the benefits of a full-week's intensive training, with roleplays and case discussions.

When I first began working with survivors in 1961, no such training or help was available and, therefore, for the first several years I floundered about, making mistake upon mistake. Fortunately I had the expertise and support of two great mentors, mentioned above. Gradually, I was forced to develop my own techniques for treating survivors (and also the offenders who abused them) and began to see successes, measured through confirmed behavioral changes. The development of these specialized techniques continued for more than five years before I felt comfortable enough with my success rate to believe that I might be able to help others who were just beginning in this field. My framework was: *Why should they go through the same mistakes and developmental frustrations that I did?* Would they be as fortunate as I was to have two great mentors in my formative years as a therapist? The probabilities were that they would not.

During these training experiences, I discovered a large number of counselors, therapists, and supervisors, who were already involved in treating either offenders or survivors or both, who could not pass even the simplest test covering topics such as *what were the characteristics specific to each of these groups, what specific needs did they have, and what treatment techniques were necessary to promote change.*

Additionally, I discovered that many of these professionals had their own problems and hang-ups where sexuality was concerned, including *personal prejudices, prejudgments, phobic-reactions, rigidly moral convictions about sexual preference and behaviors, or, in several cases, sexual dysfunctions or pathology of their own.* Most of these problems were based on either a defective or nonexistent sex education background and/or unresolved sexual issues stemming from their own childhood — often including their own sexual traumas and victimizations. (Was this one of the reasons that they chose to become counselors or therapists for these two groups?)

Additionally, I discovered a serious lack of training in interviewing techniques, a vital skill where survivors (and offenders) are concerned. Quite frequently, the whole basis of the pathology or trauma is missed and therapy continues in a meaningless and frustrating manner for both the therapist and the client because inadequate or incomplete interviewing techniques were utilized.

Next, I discovered many counselors and therapists who kept survivors in treatment for many years, supporting their practices and funding their world-wide vacations but leaving the survivor in pain and depression, often to a degree that could eventually lead to suicide. At the minimum the damage was that this long-term weekly therapy convinced the survivor that he/she was sick and defective in some way.

Last but not least, in all of the training experiences I conducted, I found an ego-defensive factor. Professionals, in groups with other professionals (and possibly their supervisors), were reluctant to ask questions that they felt they should know the answers to or that might provoke laughter and ridicule from their peers. To overcome this barrier, I incorporated a 3x5 card system in all sessions, where participants were encouraged to write questions in disguised handwriting, either before the training began or during the breaks. These cards provided the real direction for the training sessions which then could be focused on specific areas of concern and/or deficiencies in the group.

For this last reason, as well as for all the others mentioned above, I decided to incorporate *all* of the material that I had accumulated over the years and that comprise the content of a full-week's training seminar into a manual-type book. The chapters closely equate with each of the training sessions and the order of presentation is identical. The length, however, is greater since the book has been augmented with many more case histories than time allows during training seminars.

Concerning the case histories, each one represents either an actual case that I have treated or worked with in an ancillary modality over the many years, or a compilation of several cases molded into one persona. However, in compliance with the federal regulations on patient's rights, each case has been carefully altered in order to prevent identification. Names, ages, family constellations, locales and even offenses have been altered without changing the basic dynamics of the pathology.

If this work becomes an aide in the positive and successful treatment of even one *survivor*, then all of the years of frustration and the daily *swimming in the cesspool of sexual deviations and offenses* will have been worth it.

For those more interested in the sexual offender and his/her dynamics, personality, treatment techniques, etc., I have already published a work, reflecting my personal experiences in that area, titled *Treating Sex Offenders in Correctional Institutions and Outpatient Clinics: A Guide to Clinical Practice* published in 1991 by The Haworth Press.

This second book in a trilogy on sexual offending and the survivors of sexual abuse would not have been possible without the invaluable support and assistance of so many wonderful people. To name a few: MY WIFE MILDRED, whose support, patience and tolerance as well as her suggestions were invaluable; MY SON SHAWN, who again pushed me into continuing when I wanted to quit and who was always a friend as well as a terrific son of whom I am incredibly proud; Nathaniel J. Pallone, Ph.D., of Rutgers University whose persistence, knowledge, experience and friendship made this second book possible; to my colleagues and co-workers over the course of the years at the Rahway Treatment Unit and at the Adult Diagnostic & Treatment Center, Avenel, of the New Jersey Department of Corrections, who contributed to the development and refinement of many of the ideas expressed in this manuscript; and to the thousands of sex-offenders and survivors of sexual abuse who taught me so much.

William E. Prendergast

Distinguishing Characteristics of Survivors of Sexual Abuse

The Who of Treatment

As incredulous as it may seem today, there are still parents, professionals in all the sciences and arts, politicians, states and even countries who continue to suffer from the *"Ostrich Syndrome."* Regardless of the publications, programs, T.V. talk shows, newspaper headlines and articles, etc., these groups still refuse to believe that *sexual abuse not only exists but continues to increase in frequency and severity and that sexual abuse, when left undiscovered or untreated, continues to affect the survivors for the rest of their lives.*

This phenomenon, in my experience, results from the need to deny the existence of sexual abuse. Adults, especially parents and law enforcement agencies, still feel (and rightfully so) that protection of children is one of their primary mandates. If they accepted the fact of and the constant increase in sexual abuse of children and adolescents, then all of the above groups would in some way have to feel responsibility and the resulting guilt.

Since children's charges and allegations are so easy to discredit and attribute to *fantasy, nightmares, games, revenge, etc.,* it should not be surprising to learn that there are still many professionals (psychiatrists, psychologists, social workers, counselors, etc.,) and many well-meaning parents who do not know — and may not want to know — *WHO* the large number of divergent *survivors* of sexual abuse really are.

Additionally, there are parents, who due to their own feelings of responsibility and guilt, minimize or ignore the pleadings of their children who tell them they are being molested, especially when one of the parents, a relative or a person in authority is involved. These individuals even punish and admonish the child for *"making up such vicious lies about . . ."* (A case that clearly demonstrates this condition is that of KYLE, whom we will discuss in Chapter 11.) These parents convey the implied message to their children that the abuse is *acceptable* and that the child should cooperate and not complain. A typical statement illustrating this reaction might be *"Daddy is so good to us, just be a good boy or girl and do what he wants."*

These forms of ignorance or denial only aid the abuser in his/her quest for victims. They also help to explain why the public and the *"powers-that-be"*

⇨ *SURVIVOR TRAINING PRE-TEST*

Before proceeding further, it is recommended that the reader take this training pre-test. Answers to the questions will be found in the ensuing chapters. However, if an immediate answer is required, the correct response to each question is provided in the Appendix, along with a reference to the chapter(s) where the answer, subject or material is covered

DIRECTIONS: Answer each question to the best of your present knowledge *before* reading the appropriate chapters in the text. Allow 10 points for each correct response. If you cannot find a specific answer in the text, please refer to the Appendix.

☐ 1. What is the most important personality trait in a prospective therapist needed to qualify for work with the survivors of sexual abuse?

☐ 2. What is the ONLY really effective type of group therapy that works with the survivors of sexual abuse?

☐ 3. What is the FIRST major factor that must be dealt with in therapy when dealing with the survivor of sexual abuse?

☐ 4. What is the major prerequisite to DISCLOSURE in the survivor of sexual abuse?

☐ 5. Name the major BLOCKING-FACTOR to treatment in the survivor of sexual abuse!

☐ 6. Of all the elements in a sexual molestation, name the one that is most often overlooked and yet can be the MOST-DAMAGING one!

☐ 7. Name the BEST indicator, in non-reporting children or adults, of either present or past sexual abuse.

☐ 8. Name the FIRST and MOST IMPORTANT consideration with survivors before any real treatment can take place.

☐ 9. In INCEST, name one of the most frequently-overlooked problems.

☐ 10. Define IMPRINTING and its effects on survivors of sexual abuse.

too often refuse to either morally or financially support professional training or to make treatment available for the survivors. Their common cry is that *"We don't have a problem! Therefore, we don't need a treatment program or training!"* During the first International Conference on Incest and Related Problems, held in London, England in August of 1989, the authorities did everything they could possibly do to prevent the conference from ever being held. Their constant cry to the American presenters was "Child sexual abuse is an American problem! We don't have problems of that type in England." This is a direct quote from a political leader to a group of presenters, including myself.

FOUR GROUPS OF SURVIVORS

For purposes of this work, survivors will be divided into four distinct categories that coincide with the perverted needs and desires of the abusers These definitions and distinctions will be consistent throughout the book and the reader is advised to keep them in mind..

Pedophilic Survivors

This group includes all young children from birth to pre-adolescence, male or female. The pedophiles, as child molesters, exclusively prefer this type of innocent, pre-sexual child whom they can initiate, train and program to their specific needs. When these survivors enter adolescence, they are no longer desirable to this group of molesters.

Hebophilic Survivors

This group includes emerging adolescents, both male and female. The hebophiles, as molesters, almost exclusively (since there is a group that vacillates between pre-adolescent and post-adolescent victims) prefer this age group since they are looking for a sex-partner who is post-orgasmic and who knows about sex. Part of their delusional rationalization is that they are simply "having an affair" and that they are in no way perverted. Their other rationalization is that they are "teaching sex education, by example."

Incestuous Survivors

From my lengthy experience, I have come to the conclusion that incestuous parents are different in many dynamic ways from the pedophiles and the hebophiles. Therefore, I limit these survivors to those who have been abused by biological parents, siblings or relatives. Foster-parents and adoptive parents or live-in significant others are all included either under the pedophilic or hebophilic categories.

Adult Survivors

This group ranges anywhere from 18 to 21 years old, depending on the local laws where they reside.

DEFINITIONS AND ELEMENTS OF SEXUAL ABUSE

Another frequently encountered problem in this field is the *definition error* as to how broad and complex the groups that contain the survivors of sexual abuse are. The general thrust is that this is strictly an adult-child crime/offense and that is far from the truth. There are also: brother-sister, brother-brother, cousin-cousin, playmate-playmate, schoolmate-schoolmate (big vs. little) offenses, and in institutions: adult-adult, resident-resident, supervisor-child, supervisor adult-resident, clergy-child, clergy-adult, teacher-teacher as well as teacher-student, etc., in an infinite variety.

This work will attempt to identify the *survivor* as completely as possible and to suggest specific techniques that work in treating these individuals, whether children, adolescents, or adults; whether male or female; whether in a private practice, in a clinic setting, or in a mental health or correctional institution.

However, before we can begin to discuss *"Who"* survivors are, there are several definitions and elements of sexual abuse that must be considered. At this point, a brief outline-form coverage will be provided with extensive amplification as the work progresses.

DEFINING SEXUAL ABUSE

Any definition of sexual abuse must include the following factors:

- That a bigger and more powerful person used his/her strength or authority over a smaller, weaker and more vulnerable individual.

- That force, implied force or deliberate deception was utilized to sexually talk to, touch, fondle, or engage in any type of sexual behavior.

- That the victim was too frightened, inadequate or intellectually and emotionally immature to either realize what was happening or to resist and, therefore, that there was no real or true choice in the matter.

An Outline of the 20 Factors and Elements Involved in Sexual Abuse

Each of 20 areas delineating the elements and special definitions involved in sexual abuse will be presented first in outline or schematic form. Each will then be covered in the following chapters with multiple examples of actual cases that I have seen or treated throughout the 31 years of my experience in this field with both sex offenders and their victims.

1. That, at the very minimum, something unwilling and unwanted of a sexual nature occurred.

Regardless of the existence or nonexistence of resistance on the part of the survivor, sexual abuse by older youths or adults is an *unwanted* act and the full responsibility of the abuser. This factor is extremely important where the survivor's residual guilt is concerned when he/she did not resist or fight off the abuser.

2. That there is a difference between a one-time and a long-term case of sexual abuse.

In *long-term* sexual abuse, *severe guilt* is usually found arising from several factors:

- That the survivor never reported the molestation. This factor applies in incest, as well, where either minimal or no choice was involved.

- In seductive molestation, a more damaging guilt factor arises, that is, *that at least on one occasion* the survivor either initiated the behavior in order to maintain the relationship and all of the attached benefits (love, acceptance, companionship, gifts, a sense of belonging, etc.,) or made himself/herself easily available to the molester. I have *never* treated a survivor of long-term, seductive sexual abuse where one of these factors did not *eventually* surface as a primary cause of sustained guilt.

- In one-time sexual abuse, while guilt from not reporting *may* exist in a few cases, it will be to a lesser degree. (Chapter 2 deals with Survivors Who Did Not Report.) The second factor is nonexistent in the majority, if not all of these cases.

3. That there is a great difference between cases of forced sexual abuse (assaultive) and seductive sexual abuse.

In *forced* sexual abuse (kidnapping, physical restraint, use of a weapon or other threat) while guilt will exist regarding the behavior or the role the victim was forced to play (e.g., boys raped (sodomized) as girls, girls treated as whores, prostitutes) it usually is a lesser degree of guilt and more easily treated and resolved by *trained* counselors, therapists, etc.

In *seductive* sexual abuse, there is an element of implied or real cooperation (limited by age and maturity factors) that results in *perceived sharing* of the responsibility and guilt for the behavior, often in a co-conspiratorial role.

4. That force can be either implied or direct.

Direct threat or force, involving brute strength, weapons, death threats to the individual, his/her family, siblings and even his/her pets is obvious, even to children as young as five years old. (Good examples of different types of force can be found in the cases of RYAN in Chapter 11 or JESS, in Chapter 9.)

Implied threat or force is much more insidious. Incest fathers are experts in this area. The use of questions like the following predominate.

- "If I'm arrested, what will happen to you, Mommy, and the kids?"
- "If you don't do what I want, I'll leave and then what will happen to you and the family?"

Pedophiles and hebophiles often use *photographs, videotapes, and letters* from the victim to accomplish their implied threats. Several examples of these threats follow.

- "If you tell anyone and I'm arrested, the police will find *our pictures* or the letters (inspired by or requested by the molester) that you wrote me about *our games and how much you liked them.* They'll show them to everyone: your parents, your teachers, your friends. Then how will you feel?"

- "If I'm a fag, queer, pervert, sickee, etc., *so are you!* You came back again and again and never complained or told anyone, that must mean that *you liked it!* Isn't that right?"

- "I can always find another *special friend* if you don't want to play our games anymore. He/she will get everything that you're getting now. Is that what you want?"

5. That in seductive sexual abuse, it is not uncommon for the survivor to enjoy the physical act (sexual stimulation or orgasm).

Children are sexual beings. Today, children are maturing physically and mentally earlier than ever before and are being exposed to sexual material as early as the second and third grades. Sexual experimentation also begins earlier, including masturbation and "playing doctor." Initial intercourse may begin as early as ten years old.

Sex offenders are "experts" at sexually pleasing their victims. This is especially true of adult males molesting young boys. They are more than familiar with the male body and know *exactly* how to produce pleasant feelings and even first orgasms. Where girls are concerned, heterosexual pedophiles/hebophiles are also experts at performing physical behaviors that "feel pleasant" (although "strange") to the little girl.

6. That society is preoccupied with sex and uses sex to prove everything, especially manhood.

Both boys and girls are affected by this factor, especially as they enter adolescence. Boys develop the need to prove their manhood. What they see and hear on T.V. (especially from soap operas, M.T.V., and commercials) portrays *sex* as the ultimate proof of reaching adulthood and being accepted as *normal and healthy.*

- Girls similarly want to be seen as women and of being capable of winning their man. Here again society teaches that beauty, seductiveness, and sexuality *earn* love, gifts, success, employment, and ultimately *happiness.*

7. That, in sexual abuse, arousal and orgasm are more common for boys than for girls.

As a result, *boys,* once seduced and initiated into sex for the first time, often become *"willing partners"* who enjoy the sexual pleasures and all the *"extras"* (benefits) that come along with it.

Girls, usually have more communication with their mothers or mother substitutes about physical changes, sexual development, and maturity. They also are more *cautious* than boys where intimacy is concerned. When they are vulnerable, however, the same danger applies and they *learn* to like sex or to allow it for all the personal gains, rather than for the physical pleasure.

Caveat: *"Willing"* must be understood in this context to *only* mean that there was no physical threat or force, as in the assaultive cases. It should not be construed to mean an informed, mature, free will choice on the part of the survivor. The survivor's free will is affected greatly by his/her mental and maturational status, perceived personality deficits, physical concerns (perceived or real unattractiveness, lack of desirability, feelings of peer rejection, especially from the opposite sex), psychological needs, and environmental circumstances (family problems, loneliness, etc.,).

The abuser's use of seduction and manipulation, using personal knowledge of the child's needs, using his authority position over the child, using purported friendship, love and concern, all greatly decrease the level of freedom of choice and, therefore, influence the purported *"willingness"* of these child victims as promulgated by offenders and offender support groups.

8. That many child survivors of seductive sexual abuse become available to the molester, over and over again, very often due to parental neglect.

The need for love, acceptance and attention are *natural* for all human beings and are magnified in all *normal* children. Pathological conditions such as schizophrenia, psychosis, mental retardation, brain damage, etc., alter these needs, either positively or negatively.

When these needs are not satisfied in the child's home and the child sees other children receiving these forms of love, affection, and concern, he/she tends to look for and finds fulfillment elsewhere. *At that point, he/she becomes vulnerable to and potential prey for the always searching pedophiles and hebophiles.*

9. That submission to the molester becomes a payment for the needs of the child.

This includes needs for:

- Acceptance,
- Love (LUV),
- Gifts (clothes, toys, games, money, trips, etc.),
- Attention, especially when none exists at home,
- A parent substitute (especially boys looking for a father), etc.

10. That labeling is a major factor in sexual abuse.

The physical act is frequently not as damaging as the:

- words of the molester,
- judgmental labels of the survivor, or the
- labels of parents, police, friends, even therapists.

11. That feelings of being secondhand, soiled or used occur and need to be resolved.

12. That perceiving the abuse as the whole relationship rather than one aspect of the relationship may damage interpersonal relationships throughout the remainder of the survivor's life.

Statements such as "All men want is sex," "All fathers sexually hurt their children," "All mothers are seductive," have all been heard from survivors of sexual abuse.

13. That generalization by the survivor is a danger and may be damaging to all future relations.

Statements such as "All authority figures lie and should not be trusted," "All priests or ministers are hypocrites," "All mothers are on the side of their husbands and don't really care about their children," have all been made by survivors that I have treated.

14. That memory of the abuse is an important and essential element for the recovery of the survivor.

- "Forget about it!" is the worst possible advice to give to a survivor.
- Survivors must remember the facts but let go of the feelings.
- Survivors need to communicate about the abuse to at least one friend or relative that they trust and who will not reject or denigrate them.

15. That today, survivors will never be the same as before the abuse.

Compared to their pre-abuse personalities, they can now be:

- Stronger.
- More choosy.
- More assertive.
- More in touch with their needs, especially from others.
- More price conscious where relationships are concerned.

16. That Imprinting (discussed fully in Chapter 5) does occur and needs to be explained before it happens.

17. That fears will occur of:

- Being used.
- Failing in their own sexuality.
- Transmitting their perceived deviant tendencies genetically to their children.

18. That readiness (which will be discussed fully in Chapter 7) is an essential consideration to all therapeutic efforts.

19. That value problems are involved including:

- Blind obedience toward authority figures.
- Sex = Luv (Love) values.
- Obedience = Luv (Love) values.
- Sexual arousal or orgasm = cooperation and equal guilt.

- Reporting = Betrayal.
- Being a survivor permits breaking rules.
- Undoing/Normalizing is necessary by victimizing others in the same manner.

20. That there are remote factors involved. These include:

- Family disharmony resulting in:
  - Runaways from home.
  - Runaways *to* a substitute parent, home, etc.
- Lack of communication at home.
- Lack of others, especially adults, to talk to (before, during or after the abuse).
- Lack of adequate treatment or the means to obtain it.
- Lack of support groups, especially peer groups.

By now it should be obvious that the extent and complexity of the above 20 factors is equivalent to the extent and complexity of the problem of sexual abuse. The professional, choosing to become involved in this field, needs to become thoroughly conversant with each of the 20 factors and their sub areas. As will be stated continuously throughout this work, the best way to accomplish this task is through extensive training with an experienced expert in the field of child/adolescent/adult sexual abuse.

TWELVE INDICATORS OF ONGOING SEXUAL ABUSE IN CHILDREN AND ADOLESCENTS

Quite often, the excuse is used by parents, teachers and others involved in the life of the sexually abused individual (survivor), that there was no way for them to know what was happening and, had they known, that they certainly would have stopped the abuse or acted differently. To alleviate these alibis, the following indicators of ongoing sexual abuse are offered. These are the 12 most frequently seen warning signs in my experience. Taken alone, each individual indicator, by itself, may not indicate sexual abuse but in groups or combinations, parents and other caretakers should become wary and begin investigating the cause(s) of the symptoms.

- 1. Isolation and withdrawal in a normally sociable individual (dropping sports, friends, parties, after school activities, etc.).
- 2. Escape through T.V. and stereo earphones or a 'Walkman' (often at the same time).
- 3. Eating pattern changes: anorexia or bulimia being the most common.
- 4. Sloppy dress and hygiene used to cause social and physical avoidance from others in order to provide safety.
- 5. School grades often dramatically drop as does interest in studying or future goals. Achievement then withers. An exception to this indicator may occur when the abuser is a teacher that the child/adolescent holds in high esteem. In cases of this type, the survivor may actually excel in the abusive teacher's class/subject.

- 6. Regression to a former age or behavioral level may occur. In young children, this may manifest itself in bed wetting, thumb sucking, nightmares, crawling into their parent's bed at night, clinging to mother's body, etc.

- 7. Instant fear and withdrawal reactions to any physical contact, even from parents and relatives.

- 8. Becoming extremely private often occurs. The survivor then shares little or nothing with anyone.

- 9. Explicit sexual drawings, language or behaviors are common. Drawing graffiti in bathrooms, notebooks, texts and elsewhere is not uncommon and is often a "cry-for-help" or the child's/adolescents's only means of telling someone that something has occurred.

- 10. Refusing to change their clothing before or after gym classes or to shower with peers is common. (The fear is that if their peers or adult supervisors see him/her naked, they will know about the abuse!)

- 11. A visible lowering in self-esteem and self-confidence almost always occurs.

- 12. Communication becomes nonexistent or extremely limited.

It is important to remember that a cessation of former communication patterns is a good test that the therapist can use to determine the extent of the trauma and the progress of the therapy. The more resistance there is to communication, the more damage that has occurred. The more that the survivor reinstitutes communication with parents, friends, associates, and the therapist the more positive effects the therapy is producing.

Caveat: All of these changes in behavior are *sudden and abrupt* with no obvious reason or causation. Parents must *understand* the above enumerated changes but do not have to *accept* them. They can express their concern about any of these areas directly to the survivor and offer their help, even if it is rejected. This should be done often, consistently and with true sincerity.

The above list of 12 indicators is certainly not intended to be all inclusive or exhaustive. These 12 indicators are the ones I have seen most consistently in the abused survivors that I have treated or had ancillary contact with. Just as individuals differ, so can the reactions of survivors to ongoing abuse. The main characteristic, however, attached to all of the possible indicators will always be: *A dramatic change in normal behavior for the worse.*

An unusual example, from my early experiences, will help to clarify.

- *During my internship experience at a reformatory for boys under the tutelage of one of the most intelligent, dynamic, demanding and thorough mentors I have ever met (Bohdan Cymbalisty, Ph.D.), I was assigned to see a young, 12-year-old boy,* PAUL *who had suddenly displayed the following symptoms:*

  - *The sudden onset of shame at nudity and subsequent refusal to change or shower in the presence of his peers which he had done for more than six months.*

  - *Sleep disturbances including nightmares and night terrors that neither he nor anyone else could explain.*

  - *A break in all of his social behaviors and contacts.*

- *A change in clothing choices from fitting and attractive outfits to dull, oversized, baggy clothing.*
- *A fear of therapy or any other interpersonal communication on a one-to-one basis.*
- *A fear of being alone with any authority figure.*

The one major characteristic of each of these behavioral changes was that they all occurred with a rapid and sudden onset and with no observable or reported cause.

After seeing "Paul" no less than three times per week for several weeks, there was still not the slightest clue as to what had caused the sudden changes in his behavior.

During this same time period, a major scandal erupted at the institution involving the staff clinical psychiatrist molesting a large number of boys during sodium amytal hypnotic therapy sessions. All of the boys were slim, well built and good looking, like "Paul." One boy, due to a faulty injection, was not completely under the influence of the drug and was conscious of what was done to him. He later reported it to his parents who insisted on some form of immediate remedial and punitive action. The administration began an intensive investigation.

On a gut feeling, I checked the list of boys that this psychiatrist had "treated" and there was "Paul's" name on several different dates, listed for sodium amytal hypnotherapy sessions. The sudden onset of "Paul's" behavioral changes occurred the morning after his last sodium amytal session.

Very slowly and cautiously, I discussed the scandal with "Paul" and, one day, crying and sobbing for about 20 minutes, he asked if I thought he might have been one of the kids that was molested. I honestly told him that I didn't know but that it was a possibility. Then, the real therapy began, with a special focus on distancing between the boy who may have been molested and the boy sitting in my office. Within three sessions, behavioral changes, with a visible return to "Paul's" old personality, began. In the following six months, "Paul" returned almost to his old self but with less trust, a great deal of anger toward authority and a need for continued treatment once he returned to the community. "Paul" was given a special release based on his victimization before he was able to consciously remember his victimization (admitted to by the psychiatrist). I lost all contact with him.

PEDOPHILIC ORGANIZATIONS

Sexual abuse absolutely does not *improve the character and behavior* of the survivor as some pro-child/adult sex groups ridiculously maintain. Child molesters, especially the fixated pedophiles, are the most prone to make these claims through organizations that support their molesting such as NAMBLA, the North American Man Boy Love Association or PIE, the Pedophile Information Exchange, based in London, England.

In order to justify their deviant behavior, these groups look to anthropology, especially the Greek myths, to support their sexual behavior with boys. They also publish a multitude of pamphlets, journals, books, etc., containing alleged letters from boys, now men, who were involved in long-term sexual relationships with older men and who purport that *"these experiences helped them to mature and become better adult lovers, both heterosexual and homosexual."* Nowhere is there validation that former victims actually wrote even one of these letters and these groups conveniently use *confidentiality* as a barrier to any confirmation studies.

THE SCOPE OF THE PROBLEM OF SEXUAL ABUSE

Recent statistics state that:

- Only 4% of survivors of sexual abuse ever tell anyone before adulthood.
- One out of six boys are abused before age 18.
- One out of four girls are abused before age 18.

Source: Finkelhor. 1992. *Parent to Parent: Talking to Your Children about Preventing Child Sexual Abuse.VHS.*

A 1991 study at the FBI's Behavioral Science Unit in Quantico, Virginia reported that:

- 41 serial rapists were studied
- 837 rapes were committed (20.4 per rapist)
- 400 attempted rapes were committed (9.75 per rapist)

A 1991 study by Gene Abel for the National Institute of Mental Health reported that:

- 453 child molesters were studied
- 67,000 victims were admitted to (147.9 per molester)

The molesters who chose girls averaged 52 victims each.
The molesters who chose boys averaged 150 victims each.
This is certainly a different trend than normally reported.

NBC's *Today Show* with Bryant Gumbel and Katie Couric on July 9, 1992 reported that:

- There are 300,000 cases of child sexual abuse reported each year.
- 80% of all child sexual abuse is committed by someone the child knows.
- One in three girls and one in six boys will be molested before they are 18 years old.

Finally, a 1992 report published by the National Center on Child Sexual Abuse Prevention Research [NCPA, 1992] offered the following statistics: Estimated Number of Reported Child Victims:

- 1985 = 1,919,000
- 1986 = 2,086,000
- 1987 = 2,157,000
- 1988 = 2,243,000
- 1989 = 2,407,000
- 1990 = 2,537,000
- 1991 = 2,694,000

A breakdown of the 1991 2.7 million (rounded number) children victimized was also included in the report.

- Physical: 28% (756,000)

- Sexual: 16% (432,000)

- Emotional: 5% (135,000)

- Neglect: 43% (1,161,000)

- Other: 11% (270,000)

If these are the published statistics, it obviously follows that *these* abuses were reported. From our contact with many adult survivors in correctional facilities and also in private practice, less than five percent of those I have worked with ever reported their abuse to anyone. Thus the reported statistics merely scratch the surface of the real numbers of children who are abused annually. [*Note 1*]

It is also interesting to note that 90% of the seductive pedophiles that I have treated over the last 30 years were themselves sexually traumatized or abused and either never reported or, if they did, were not believed. The majority of the sex offenders I worked with were all convicted and in a prison treatment facility, and were a special group diagnosed as repetitive/compulsive types.

I still strongly feel that the reported statistics are ridiculously low. The problem that results from low incident statistics is less funding and support for treating survivors and for training programs for the counselors and therapist who want to become involved with these survivors. The attitude that predominates by the powers that control these funds is that people like myself are making a mountain-out-of-a-molehill.

Before continuing our discussion of the sexual survivor, it is necessary to briefly discuss the abusers, both the convicted sex offenders and those who are still in the community continuing their deviant behaviors. It is this group that produces the disturbed and damaged children and adults that are the concern of this work.

NOTE

1. It must be noted that the author was more than frustrated when in late December of 1992 he made 12 calls to statistic agencies involved in Child Sexual Abuse work in several states including Washington, Virginia, Colorado, Texas, Illinois, etc., and discovered that no updated statistics were available beyond those cited in this chapter. Excuses ranged from money problems, to states not cooperating, to general lack of interest. It appears that we are dealing with an "out of sight, out of mind" phenomenon and this is extremely disturbing since the number of victims continues to rise at an alarming rate, *in spite of the reported statistics.*

2

The Offender

The most important fact to remember about the offender is that *It Can Be Anyone!* Of all of the thousands of sex offenders I have met, either diagnostically or therapeutically, the most imposing factor has been that *they do not look like sex offenders* (whatever that is supposed to mean). Society has always had its own conception of the sex offender, especially the image of a *"dirty old man in a long coat waiting to expose himself or to steal children for his own deviant purposes."* The available literature and television dramas often add to this misconception as did the misinformed press until the late 1970's and early 1980's.

In my over 30 years of experience in treating these individuals and their victims, I have found no common demographic trait that these individuals share, *except* that of their *inadequate personality.* The only other commonality I encountered was that a majority of them had experienced some form of past *sexual trauma,* active or passive, conscious or repressed.

- *Physically,* they come in all sizes, shapes, colors, nationalities, etc., and for the most part fit the *"boy next door"* or *"good neighbor"* profile.
- *Education-wise,* their profiles span the gamut: ranging from those who never completed grammar school to those with Ph.Ds.
- *Employment-wise,* their profiles range from simple laborers to work supervisors, professionals of every category, to individuals who own and successfully operate their own businesses, etc.
- *Economic-wise,* the range spans from indigent to very wealthy.
- *Social-adjustment-wise,* they range from social misfits to social giants who are often perceived as the pillars of the community, as well as all ranges in-between.
- *Religion-wise,* all denominations are represented, including clergy from most of the different denominations.
- *Marital status* appears to have no bearing on the problem. Both single and married females and males sexually abuse.

Due to the above mentioned inadequacy, the sex offender is repetitively looking for a victim who is *inferior to him/her in every way possible.* Since he/she cannot deal with equals (peers), the potential victim is too often a child or adolescent with characteristics that pose no threat to the offender and who offers more than one opportunity for the offender to become involved with. A list of some of these characteristics, gleaned from sex offenders can be seen in the table titled: *Traits Offenders Seek in Potential Victims.*

THE ROLE OF SEXUAL TRAUMA IN THE FORMATION OF THE OFFENDER

A major area of controversy among individuals involved in the field of sexual abuse is that of the role of *sexual trauma* in the formation of the sexual deviate. While some professionals in the field insist that *all* sex offenders were themselves victims, others disagree, myself included.

While in my experience, approximately 90 percent of convicted child molesters were themselves sexually molested, the opposite is not true, that is that 90 percent of the children who are molested become child molesters as adults.

Not All Children Who Are Molested Become Adult Child Molesters

I have met many, many adult males and females who were molested as children who, today, are happy, well-adjusted, productive, good parents, and sexually well-adjusted.

I have also met hundreds of adults, mostly males, who were molested as children who, today, are unhappy, maladjusted child molesters or sexually assaultive personalities.

- *A perfect example of this involved two brothers who were masturbated and fellated, on a weekly basis, by a granduncle who supported the family, treated them well and always brought them gifts. They went to their mother and reported the sexual abuse and were told: "Do what he wants you to because he's so good to us." (She also feared him since he was allegedly crime-connected.)*

    The molestations continued for four years or more until the granduncle disappeared. Years later, one of the brothers married, had three children and was an excellent husband and parent while the other became a child molester, repeating the granduncle's rituals exactly. He is now serving a lengthy sentence in prison.

⇨ *TRAITS OFFENDERS SEEK IN POTENTIAL VICTIMS*

☐ 1. Low self-esteem.

☐ 2. A lack of loving and caring individuals in their lives.

☐ 3. A strong need to be told consistently that they are acceptable.

☐ 4. Loners and individuals who tend to isolate.

☐ 5. Individuals who are handicapped either physically, emotionally, or mentally.

☐ 6. Institutionalized children and adolescents ("Caretaker Abuse").

In interviewing some 125 adult survivors of sexual abuse who did not become abusers themselves, *ten factors* were found that do not exist in the sexually abusive adult offenders that I have had contact with.

The confusion as to whether a sexually abused child will become an adult sexual molester appears to result from a *misunderstanding* of the concept of sexual trauma and its effects. Two concepts need to be discussed which may resolve this confusion.

IDENTIFICATION OF PASSIVE SEXUAL TRAUMA VERSUS ACTIVE SEXUAL TRAUMA

Active sexual trauma is well known and easily identified. It occurs when there is a real, direct, sexual molestation involving sexually explicit behavior on the part of the molester and also on the part of the child.

Passive sexual trauma, on the other hand, is more insidious and too often missed.

When a therapist suspects a case of sexual molestation due to presenting behavioral symptoms and asks the child or adult if they had ever been molested, the passive sexual trauma group spontaneously and honestly replies that they had not. The therapist, if he/she believes the client, then usually looks for other causes of the presenting problem and may use the wrong treatment methods. Too few therapists that I have supervised were able to ask specific questions that would elicit *passive sexual trauma*, due to lack of training in this area and lack of the initiative on the part of postgraduate therapists to seek out specialized training and supervision before attempting to treat survivors.

The definition of *passive sexual trauma* that I use is: *Passive sexual trauma occurs when sex, itself, in some indirect way has a profound and traumatic effect on the child's life, without the child ever having been directly sexually molested.* A few examples may clarify.

- RALPH *(whom we will meet in greater detail in Chapter 3) was severely sexually passively traumatized when his mother came home from work early one day, due to illness, and caught his father in bed with his secretary. She threw them both out of the house (which was exactly what they wanted) and the father was never seen again. This changed the economic base of the family and totally changed "Ralph's" life for the worse. The most visible effect was "Ralph's" rage toward his mother, projected onto all women, that resulted in his referral for treatment. While "Ralph" was never physically sexually molested, he was well on his way to becoming a sexually assaultive person and only identification and treatment prevented it.*

- HERB *came from an incestuous family where he was the only boy. He had four sisters, all of whom were repeatedly molested by their father over a period of 12 years. In about the third year, "Herb's" oldest sister (the first to be victimized) revealed to him what was going on but swore him to secrecy. "Herb" later found out that the rest of the girls were being molested as well and, in fact, walked in on one occasion during the father's incestuous molestation. The father threatened to kill "Herb" and the whole family and also to use "Herb" as a girl if he ever said a word to anyone.*

Some ten years later, "Herb's" oldest sister committed suicide and he went into a deep depression, exacerbated by a deep personal guilt since he had never interfered with or reported the problem to his mother or to the authorities.

As an adult, "Herb" was a loner, never dated and when he attempted his first intercourse, was impotent. When he finally tried therapy, none of these facts were elicited and he was treated for the impotence alone. Nothing worked. He became more and more depressed and eventually attempted a feeble suicidal gesture. With a new sex therapist, well trained in this area, the whole story emerged in a little over a month and "Herb" then began to respond.

This type of passive sexual trauma may be as severe in its effects as active or direct sexual trauma and may even, at times, be worse!

➡️ ## *TEN FACTORS FOUND IN SEXUALLY ABUSED MALES WHO DID NOT BECOME ADULT SEXUAL OFFENDERS*

☐ 1. Their *self-esteem* was strong and positive.

☐ 2. They had a fairly good sexual knowledge at the time of the molestation/seduction.

☐ 3. There was an important adult in their lives with whom they could discuss anything without fear of repercussion.

☐ 4. Their religious education was along positive and forgiving pathways rather than the "sin and damnation" models.

☐ 5. They had several real friends in their peer group with whom they could discuss anything without fear of being rejected or put-down.

☐ 6. Their personality structure was stronger and more positive than the usually quite inadequate sex offender personality.

☐ 7. They were successful in either school, sports or some other area that produced pride, both from their parents and, more importantly, from themselves.

☐ 8. Their parents were more regularly involved in their lives and activities, attended P.T.A. meetings and other school functions and spent as much time as possible with them on weekends, etc. They also traveled and vacationed with their parents.

☐ 9. They believed in themselves and had enduring self-confidence.

☐ 10. They were *long-term goal-oriented* as opposed to the living day-by-day orientation of the sex offender.

PATTERNS OF CHILD MOLESTERS WHO WERE THEMSELVES SEXUALLY MOLESTED AS CHILDREN

There are several distinct behavior patterns that child molesters, both pedophiles (who choose pre-pubertal victims) and hebophiles (who choose adolescent or post-adolescent victims) employ that need to be recognized and dealt with in treatment.

1. The Molester Projects All Responsibility on the Victim.

In seductive molestation, this is especially true of the *incest fathers* but also applies to authority figures who molest their charges (scoutmasters, priests, big brothers, foster parents, etc.). They make statements such as:

- *"If you weren't so cute and seductive, this wouldn't have happened."*
- *"If you hadn't made your mother (or father) leave us this wouldn't have happened."*
- *"If you didn't dress so seductively and sexually, it wouldn't have happened."*
- *"You don't have to do this, even though I do so much for you. It's your decision!"*

In incest, the abusing parent *cons* the child into believing that she/he is protecting the family, siblings, other parent, etc., — Then, after the second time, the abuser puts all blame on the victim as *wanting it!*

2. The Molester Creates Insurance.

Child molesters frequently take Polaroid pictures or make home videos of the child performing sexually or posing in the nude in a sexually excited state (e.g., boys with erections, girls masturbating or touching their genitals) or make audiotapes of the child talking about how much they enjoyed having sex with the abuser and how they want to continue both the acts and the relationship. Of course, all of these methods of blackmail are carefully prepared and scripted in advance of the first molestation.

3. The Molester Also "Psychs-Out" the Potential Victims.

Great care is taken by these offenders to assure their own personal safety. They choose passive-dependent type children who either are in conflict with their parents or who have demonstrated that they want or need the molester's attention and acceptance.

The groups that both pedophiles and hebophiles prefer include: loners, needy kids, missing-parent kids, shy and timid ones or, conversely, popular and outgoing ones (to become the kid he/she never was, his/her ideal self) or himself/herself as a child by role reversal.

The molester makes sure that he/she has them *well hooked* in wanting and needing the relationship and the benefits that the relationship provides (gifts, trips, 'LUV', acceptance, etc.) *before* making the first, simplest test, sexual advance, or suggestion. In this regard, the offenders have infinite patience.

While the above three patterns of the molester apply to *all* sexual abuse, there are several distinct differences in cases of assaultive sexual abuse. In Assaultive Sexual Molestation the sexually assaultive molester hurts the victim in many ways, not just physically.

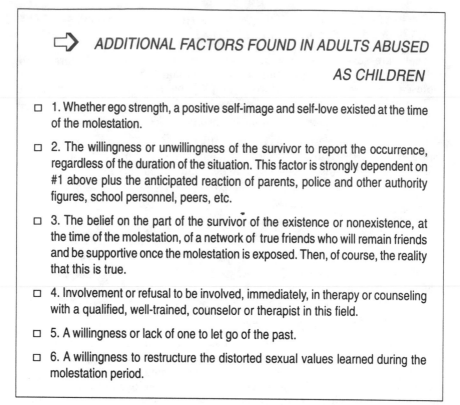

☐ **ADDITIONAL FACTORS FOUND IN ADULTS ABUSED**

AS CHILDREN

☐ 1. Whether ego strength, a positive self-image and self-love existed at the time of the molestation.

☐ 2. The willingness or unwillingness of the survivor to report the occurrence, regardless of the duration of the situation. This factor is strongly dependent on #1 above plus the anticipated reaction of parents, police and other authority figures, school personnel, peers, etc.

☐ 3. The belief on the part of the survivor of the existence or nonexistence, at the time of the molestation, of a network of true friends who will remain friends and be supportive once the molestation is exposed. Then, of course, the reality that this is true.

☐ 4. Involvement or refusal to be involved, immediately, in therapy or counseling with a qualified, well-trained, counselor or therapist in this field.

☐ 5. A willingness or lack of one to let go of the past.

☐ 6. A willingness to restructure the distorted sexual values learned during the molestation period.

Of extreme importance in treating survivors of assaultive sexual trauma is the need to be sure that ***all*** aspects of the assault are exposed including a step-by-step account of the attack but only when the survivor is ready to deal with this issue (Chapter 7 will discuss Readiness in detail). Quite often, a survivor tells the police and the therapist *only what she/he feels is necessary for prosecution.* This is most often true in cases of rape, regardless of whether the survivor is a female or a male.

Associated behavior, preceding or following the actual rape behavior, is often more important than the forced intercourse, itself. A detailed case example will clarify.

• JAY, *a 50-year-old psychologist, was a self-referral to my office for severe depression and sexual dysfunction. After the usual initial resistance and when he stated that he was ready to discuss the real problem, "Jay" related that while at a conference he had been raped in his hotel room. His story was that he had made a special presentation and when finished had offered to discuss his paper and it's new therapy technique with anyone who so wished that evening. A young man, identifying himself as a graduate student at the local university, asked if he could see him in private and "Jay," without thinking of the potential danger, invited the man to his room late that evening. When the man arrived, he appeared grateful and pleasant and, after the usual chitchat, asked if he could use the bathroom. When he came out, he was naked and wielding a large switchblade knife. "Jay" was shocked and asked what was going on. The demeanor of the friendly young man changed to an angry, ordering and threatening one. "Jay" was ordered to undress and lie on the bed or die! "Jay" complied and the young man sat on his chest, reached back and placed the knife point at the base of "Jay's" penis and told him he would definitely castrate him slowly if he did not do as he was told. After being forced to fellate the young offender, he was ordered to roll over and was raped with sadistic force and extreme pain.*

Throughout the ordeal, the assailant kept telling "Jay" that this was all his fault, since he had looked at him in a sexual manner during the paper presentation and had offered the invitation to his room in a seductive manner. Also, the attacker had continued stimulating "Jay" through the two hour ordeal and brought him to a climax. The intruder's immediate and mocking interpretation of this was that "Jay" was enjoying the sexual assault and that he, the offender, was correct in interpreting "Jay's" attitude towards him. When the two hour ordeal was over, the young man told "Jay" that he knew his name and address and, if "Jay" made any mention of the assault, he would report to the police that "Jay" had raped him after seducing him to come to his room, allegedly to discuss the paper. Since he was younger and a student at the conference, he assured "Jay" that he would be believed. He even boldly offered "Jay" the telephone, daring him to call the authorities.

"Jay" was traumatized and fearful of his colleagues' reactions and the reactions of his family as well so he told no one. He left early the next morning, feigning illness to one of the leaders of the conference and to his family when he arrived home two days early.

For the next year (before calling for an appointment) "Jay" lived a life of fear and paranoia, anticipating a call from the assailant or possibly blackmail or extortion attempts. His coworkers sensed something was wrong but he continued to place the blame on physical problems. Sex with his wife ended and she accepted the fact that he was physically ill.

The above *facts* took over nine months of therapy to elicit. There was almost a *peeling* process, layer by layer (like the rings of an onion). Each time the incident was discussed, *something new was added.* Eighteen months into therapy, "Jay" *remembered* being sexually molested at age 12 by a scoutmaster, over a three year period, and then admitted, *for the first time,* that while his fear and shock were real, that there was an element of sexual excitement in the recent rape and that he was now masturbating to the sexual incident with the young man but changing the fantasy to one that was friendly and compliant. *Guilt* was incredible at this point and therapy became a real challenge.

No real progress occurred from that point on until "Jay" accepted the fact that he had a *bisexual imprint* from the time of the scoutmaster's three year period of sexual molestation. He gradually came to the realization that he never had to act out homosexually because of his bisexual orientation and that he could *choose* to function exclusively in a heterosexual manner. In other words, he did not lose the ability to choose his present or future sexual preference.

4. The Molester Uses Any Means Possible to Project the Blame and to Place the Responsibility for his (the Offender's) Behavior Onto the Survivor.

"Jay's" rapist did a really good *con job* on him, projecting all the blame on "Jay" because he had an orgasm. What the offender was unaware of was

"Jay's" past sexual molestation and it's connection to the fact that "Jay" did enjoy parts of the sexual attack.

Also in "Jay's" assault, the issue of *control*, on the part of the offender, is more than apparent. What the offender was unaware of was that the control would last for years after the attack. Too often, new therapists dealing with a case of this type *miss* the fact that even though the incident is over, the feelings of *control* persist ("Jay's" fears of being discovered, contacted or black-mailed).

Almost all of the rape survivors that I have dealt with still feel the fear that the offender will find them again and that the rape will recur. There are even cases where this fear appears to cause the survivor to set themselves up to be assaulted again. This then becomes a self-fulfilling prophesy.

5. The Next Major Damage the Offender Produces by his Assault is to Alter the Survivor's Values About Sex.

Where the distorted value *sex = love* is taught in seductive molestation, then *sex = hate, = fear, = pain, and = degradation* are the distorted values taught in sexual assault. These distorted values must be continually dealt with in the treatment of the survivor and changed to more positive and realistic values.

6.The Final Major Pattern that the Offender Uses in his Sexual Assault that Severely Damages the Survivor is the Choice of Words he/she Uses, Before, During and After the Act.

There are cases where what the offender *said* during the attack was more traumatic and damaging than the actual physical act. Several examples from my own experiences with survivors will clarify.

- The boy who is raped and then told that he was *"better than any girl"* that the abuser had been with can be damaging for life where self-image and self-esteem are concerned. Therapy will aid the survivor to understand and accept these *words* as part of the pathology of the offender and not the survivor's problem.

- JOEY (who will be discussed in Chapter 3) is an appropriate example of this type of damaging pattern. His father, during the sexual assault on him, referred to "Joey" as his *"boy pussy!"* That phrase stayed with "Joey" into adulthood and into his marriage. Needless to say, he was sexually dysfunctional with women.

- The young girl who is *blamed* by her abuser for causing the abuse because she was either *"too pretty"* or *"too sexy"* is similarly affected until treated.

- The rape victim who is told that since she/he had an orgasm or became obviously stimulated that she/he *"wanted to be raped and enjoyed it!"*

- The boy who has his first orgasm with a male abuser who then tells him *"I knew you were a queer; I can spot them a mile away!"*

- The survivor, male or female, who is told by the police or his parents that *"You must have given him some signal that you were interested or wanted sex with him!"* or *"You must have acted seductively or done something that stimulated him!"* and on and on and on, ad infinitum.

For more in-depth information on the sex offender, his etiology, dynamics and treatment, the reader is referred to my first book: *Treating Sex Offenders in Correctional Institutions and Outpatient Clinics — A Guide to Clinical Practice,* The Haworth Press, 1991.

For a differing viewpoint, the reader is referred to the instructive volume *Rehabilitating Criminal Sexual Psychopaths: Legislative Mandate, Clinical Quandries* by Dr. Nathaniel J. Pallone (Transaction Books, 1990). Dr. Pallone presents an excellent survey of both standard and aggressive methods of treatment for sex offenders and their legal constraints that includes such aggressive treatment modalities as bioimpedance measures, including surgical and chemical castration, and aversive modalities, including aversive behavior therapy, revulsion, electroshock and pharmacologically induced aversion (nausea). Examples and studies are included for each type of therapy.

3

The Survivor

The "Who" of survivors is both simple and complicated. Anyone can become a survivor for the following reason. While some sexual offenders choose a specific age, sex, body-build, behavioral characteristic, etc., (as discussed in Chapter 2), others find their victims strictly by chance or by opportunity.

Many survivors, male and female, young child and senior citizen, become victimized simply because they were in the wrong place at the right time. Predictability and prevention thus become extremely difficult, although not totally impossible due to this latter factor.

Survivors can become either *Denyers,* who tend to repress the event, *Adjusters,* who place the blame accurately on the abuser and therefore usually have little or no negative effects, or *Accepters,* who take full responsibility for their own molestation and are often the most seriously damaged. The accompanying illustration graphically indicates the negative reactions of all three types of survivors in a general way. As our discussion progresses, these effects will become more specific to each of the different types of sexual molestation.

A second general consideration regarding survivors is the problem of their becoming *judgmental* rather than analytic or curious about their abuse. When the focus of the survivor, especially the *Accepter,* becomes judgmental, a series of consequences occur. These *consequences of judgmentalism* are also graphically displayed in an accompanying illustration and again are a general rather than specific list of reactions to sexual abuse.

Prior to beginning any treatment, it is the therapist's task to first delineate the type of survivor that he/she is treating and secondly to determine the extent of the general negative effects of the survivor's abuse. Once these two factors are clearly defined, an understanding of the specific type of sexual abuse that was involved, specific effects of that type of abuse and specific treatment techniques to utilize follow.

In general, survivors (my preferred term to "victims") of sexual abuse can be divided into the following categories: Pedophilic, Hebophilic, Incestuous, and Adult. Each of these categories will be discussed separately and in some detail.

SURVIVORS OF PEDOPHILIC MOLESTATION

This group of survivors includes children, male and female, who are prepubertal, anorgasmic and therefore "virginal" where sex is concerned. They

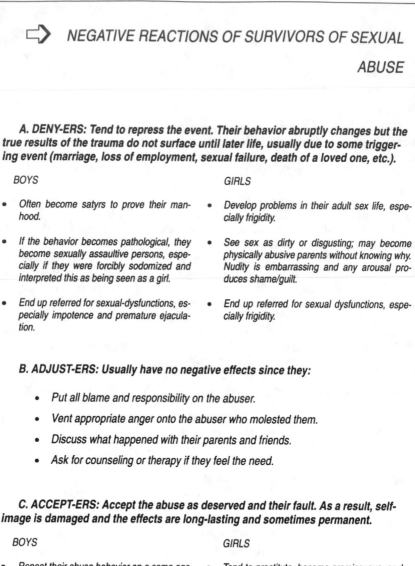

⇨ *NEGATIVE REACTIONS OF SURVIVORS OF SEXUAL*

ABUSE

A. DENY-ERS: Tend to repress the event. Their behavior abruptly changes but the true results of the trauma do not surface until later life, usually due to some triggering event (marriage, loss of employment, sexual failure, death of a loved one, etc.).

BOYS

- Often become satyrs to prove their manhood.

- If the behavior becomes pathological, they become sexually assaultive persons, especially if they were forcibly sodomized and interpreted this as being seen as a girl.

- End up referred for sexual-dysfunctions, especially impotence and premature ejaculation.

GIRLS

- Develop problems in their adult sex life, especially frigidity.

- See sex as dirty or disgusting; may become physically abusive parents without knowing why. Nudity is embarrassing and any arousal produces shame/guilt.

- End up referred for sexual dysfunctions, especially frigidity.

B. ADJUST-ERS: Usually have no negative effects since they:

- Put all blame and responsibility on the abuser.

- Vent appropriate anger onto the abuser who molested them.

- Discuss what happened with their parents and friends.

- Ask for counseling or therapy if they feel the need.

C. ACCEPT-ERS: Accept the abuse as deserved and their fault. As a result, self-image is damaged and the effects are long-lasting and sometimes permanent.

BOYS

- Repeat their abuse behavior on a same age child, almost ritualistically in order to reverse roles with the abuser.

- They now feel that they are the adult aggressor in control rather than being controlled.

- May show no other visible problems in their employment or social lives.

GIRLS

- Tend to prostitute, become promiscuous, or develop other self-punishing behaviors. Attempt to undo the abuse.

- Tend to marry aggressive, battering type (dominant) husbands.

- Tend to lose all goal motivation; isolate socially.

are selected for that specific reason so that the abuser can "train" them in sexual roles and behaviors that satisfy his/her deviant fantasies. Ages range from birth to early teens, depending on body size, physical and mental maturation, etc. The choice is based mainly upon the needs and perceptions of the molester. The pedophiles, being the most inadequate of all of the sex molesters, usually choose slightly built, nonassertive and nonaggressive children whom they feel they can easily control and who pose no physical or emotional threat to them.

A second choice-factor in the selection of a potential victim involves the child being perceived as either the abuser's *ideal self* i.e., the child he/she always wanted to be and never was; or the abuser's *identical self* when he/she was a child i.e., the child who most closely resembles the pedophile himself/herself as a weak and inadequate, lonely, and rejected child. Most molesters in the pedophile group are *fixated* sexual abusers. This designation simply means that he/she stopped developing on a psychosexual level at either a prepubertal or early pubertal level and never had an adult sexual experience. The majority of them consider themselves "virgins" where sex is concerned.

Etiology of Pedophilia

In the most simplistic terms, these individuals simply never grew up. Developing along normals lines, at some point prior to adolescence they suffered some form of emotional, physical, or sexual trauma that *froze* their

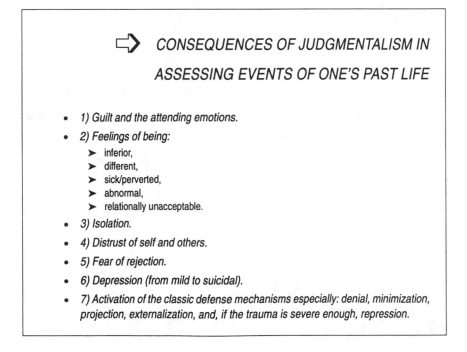

> ⇨ *CONSEQUENCES OF JUDGMENTALISM IN*
>
> *ASSESSING EVENTS OF ONE'S PAST LIFE*

- *1) Guilt and the attending emotions.*
- *2) Feelings of being:*
  - ➤ inferior,
  - ➤ different,
  - ➤ sick/perverted,
  - ➤ abnormal,
  - ➤ relationally unacceptable.
- *3) Isolation.*
- *4) Distrust of self and others.*
- *5) Fear of rejection.*
- *6) Depression (from mild to suicidal).*
- *7) Activation of the classic defense mechanisms especially: denial, minimization, projection, externalization, and, if the trauma is severe enough, repression.*

emotional and psychosexual development while physically their bodies continued to grow and develop. Most of them (more than 90%) were seductively-sexually molested and never reported. They then began having sex with other pre-adolescent peers. Upon entering adolescence, the trauma from the pre-adolescent sexual abuse was fully activated. Psychosexually they remained pre-adolescent and looked for other children, mostly same-sex, to molest in the same manner that they had been molested. Thus, *undoing and/or normalizing* became a primary motivation in all of their sexual activities. An example will clarify.

- BUDDY *was sexually molested from age nine to ten. While walking alone in a neighborhood park, he stopped in the men's room. Standing at the urinal, he began to play with his penis in preparation for masturbating and did not hear the stranger enter. Suddenly, while lost in his own pleasures, a hand reached around him and grasped his penis. The man then said: "Don't waste any of it!" He then turned "Buddy" around, pulled his shorts down to his knees, knelt and fellated him. "Buddy" never felt anything so good and thoroughly enjoyed the act that resulted in the most pleasurable orgasm he had ever experienced.*

  When he finally took note of the man, he noticed that he was fairly young, well-dressed, and obviously a well-to-do individual. When he finished, the man smiled, thanked "Buddy" and pressed a ten-dollar bill in his hand. He then asked "Buddy" to meet him again next week, at the same time, and left. His new "friend" never asked "Buddy" to reciprocate in any way nor did he ever expose himself to him.

  Lying in bed that evening and "replaying the tape" of his adventure in the park, "Buddy" was excited, got an erection and masturbated to thoughts of the man fellating him. He decided he would meet the man again and did on many successive Wednesday afternoons. This pleasurable and profitable adventure continued for approximately six months and then the man disappeared. "Buddy" faithfully showed up in the park for the next several weeks but the man never again appeared.

  "Buddy" missed his weekly adventure and began looking for other boys in the park to have sex with. Within a week, he followed another boy, his age, into the men's room and almost ritualistically repeated the incidents with his "friend" but added reciprocation to the program. These adventures continued until "Buddy" reached adolescence. His masturbation fantasies, however, remained focused on his adult male friend in the park.

  "Buddy" now began hearing about the sexual adventures of his peers in the gym, in the locker room and on the way home from school. All of his peers bragged about their heterosexual conquests and "Buddy" began to realize that he was different. He had no interest in what he was hearing about girls and the wonders of his peers' newfound heterosexuality and continued to masturbate to fantasies of being fellated by his adult friend in the park.

  At age 16, "Buddy's" sexual behavior abruptly changed. He was no longer interested in trying to find age-peers to have sex with in the park but began looking for nine-year-old boys (the age of his first molestation). He followed one nine-year-old boy into the men's room, waited for the boy to stand at the urinal, walked over quietly, reached around the boy and grasped his penis saying: "Don't waste any of it!" The boy pushed his hand away and ran out of the men's room. "Buddy" stood there in shock and a few minutes later the boy returned with a policeman and "Buddy" was arrested for sexual molestation. An enlightened judge listened to his story and gave him probation with the mandate of therapy and I met him in my practice.

SURVIVORS OF HEBOPHILIC MOLESTATION

This group includes adolescents, male and female, who are post-pubertal and fully orgasmic and are selected for that specific reason. The fact that these victims have been sexually active, decreases the *guilt* that the hebophile experiences. By rationalization, since they (the survivors) were already sexually active, he/she (the offender) is not responsible for teaching them sexual behaviors. Ages for the hebophile group range from early teens to late teens, again depending on size, development, appearance and both physical and mental maturation. As in all cases of sexual abuse, the needs, fantasies, and perceptions of the offender control the choice.

Etiology of Hebophilia

The development of the hebophile appears to be as follows: having progressed through childhood and adolescence into adulthood, these individuals then experience some form of severe trauma (active or passive) that results in a *regression* to a former developmental stage. Hebophiles usually regress to a former age bracket where they were the most happy, content and satisfied both with themselves and with others in their lives. For the majority, this age of satisfaction occurs in adolescence, usually somewhere in the age range of 12 to 16 with 14 an often preferred age.

The majority, if not all, of the hebophiles are *regressed* sexual abusers. This designation simply means that this group developed along normal psychosexual lines, had adult sexual encounters (many of them are married with children) and then *regressed* to a former psychosexual stage due to some form of trauma.

An example of this type of regressed offender will clarify.

- DON *is the sixth grade teacher in an elementary school, where the sixth grade is the last and highest grade. From there, the children go on to a junior high school across town. During the first week of each semester, "Don," a longtime hebophile, begins the selection process of his victims for that school year. In his mind, he is looking for a specific type of boy: one who is cute and good-looking, friendly and somewhat assertive, has a minimal closeness to his father, is popular with the other students and, most importantly, will probably need extra help during the school year. He finds five or six boys of this type each school year.*

  Slowly, over the next several months (no fewer than three) "Don" develops a special relationship with each of the boys, independently of the others. He assigns them special jobs in the classroom, finds excuses for them to stay after school and makes sure that they know he is their friend and that his interest in them is strictly motivated by a desire to help them. When he feels comfortable enough with any of them, he offers them tutoring at his apartment. One of the most shocking elements of these molestations is the ease with which "Don" and others like him are able to get the parents' permission for this type of activity, simply because he is a teacher — even though the parents have never met him.

The first session at the apartment is legitimate and very positively and supportively oriented. "Don" suggests that several more sessions would be beneficial and the boys each agree. Don makes sure that the second or third session lasts until dinner time and then calls the parents, telling them how great things are progressing and suggesting that he be allowed to take the boy to McDonald's for supper. He says that it would also be beneficial if they continued the tutoring after dinner since things were going so well. If the parents sound pleased, he then suggests that the boy be allowed to sleep over and that he will bring him to school the following morning. Surprisingly, he never had a parent refuse!

After another half-hour or so of tutoring, "Don" suggests they need some fun and suggest card-playing, which eventually leads to strip poker. He makes sure he loses the first game to test the boy's reaction to nudity and, if the boy reacts with interest, laughing, etc., he makes sure the boy loses the next game. Next in the well-planned scenario is Polaroid picture-taking, followed by tickling when both he and the boy are nude, and mild groping. If all goes well, that ends this night's adventure for "Don."

Over the next few tutoring sessions, "Don" begins asking questions about sex and masturbation and begins to teach a sex education course, sometimes bringing his five or six chosen boys together for the first time. "Don" extols the joys and need for boys to masturbate to become normal, healthy men and from here on the progression is predictable: "Don" and the group of boys self-masturbating to mutual masturbation to contests of speed, first ejaculator, etc. All during this process the Polaroid picture-taking continues and now becomes both "Don's" security and a pressure tool to advance the deviant behavior even further to fellatio, etc.

"Don's" behavior went on for several years, lasting only with each group of boys for one school year. "Don" felt that this practice would provide safety for him since his was the last grade in his school and the following year the boys would transfer to a junior high school across town. Each year he seduced a new group of boys (usually about five or six) and this behavior continued for four years before he was exposed.

*How this occurred was interesting. One day, one of his boys acted up in class and became openly defiant. "Don" kept him after school and the parents then threatened to severely punish the boy for his behavior since it embarrassed and shamed them. In anger and in defense, the boy related what "Don" had done to him and connected it to the school punishment. Subsequently "Don" was arrested and confessed to the true number involved: **a minimum of 40 victims over a period of ten years.***

The school authorities were shocked as were his fellow teachers. All insisted that there "wasn't the slightest clue or hint of 'Don's' secret life or deviant tendencies." Part of this was due to the fact that for several years of his teaching career, "Don" had been married and appeared to be the typical middle-class person in his neighborhood and at all school social functions, which he usually chaired. "Don's" wife reported normal sexual behavior and a good marital relationship for the first year or so, but then his work and devotion to the school and his kids overshadowed their lives. What she did not know was that even during their sexual relations, "Don" was fantasizing being with one of his boys.

SURVIVORS OF INCESTUOUS MOLESTATION

This group includes a special category delineated by the *biological* connection of the offender to the victim. Stepparents, adoptive parents, grandparents, aunts and uncles, live-in boyfriends/girlfriends, etc., all, in my experience, belong in the pedophile/hebophile categories, although legally they may end up charged with incestuous crimes. Their own statements and rationalizations support this stance. "After all, it wasn't as if she/he were my own child. She/he isn't my own flesh and blood, so it can't be incest." The victims may be male or female as may be the offender. Two main categories of incest need to be delineated: parental and sibling.

Parental Incest

In *parental incest* the main characteristic is that due to their biological connection, the offender(s) develops a perception that he/she *owns* the children and that the child/children *owe* him/her something in return for bringing them into the world, feeding and clothing them, etc. By their rationalizations, the abuser therefore has a *natural right* to use them in any way he/she chooses, including sexually.

Caretaker Incest

While in most states foster parents, adoptive parents, common-law parents, live-in parents who abuse children in the home are charged with incest, the hundreds of sex offenders I have known or worked with who fall into this category have all used rationalizations that since he/she (the survivor) is not their natural (biological) child, they were not guilty of incest. As interviewing and treatment progress with these individuals, the dynamics and characteristics of pedophiles or, more often, hebophiles emerge. The traits and characteristics of the incestuous parent are not elicited.

Sibling Incest

Three different types of *sibling incest* behaviors need to be included in our discussion.

1. The Normal, Developmental, Experimental Sex-Play Group

There are two groups of children that fall within this category. Firstly, there are the young children, close in age, who share the same bedroom, change in front of each other and who often bathe at the same time. Normal curiosity about difference in body structure, especially in the genital area occurs *normally* and no trauma results from this "checking each other out" or from a child's form of "playing doctor." Trauma, however, may result if a parent or other authority figure catches the children in these behaviors and reacts angrily, hysterically, judgmentally, and punitively.

A second group is usually composed of young children and prepubertal or barely pubertal adolescents. The young adolescents tend to be impressed with the braggadocio of their peers regarding their amazing and frequent sex conquests. Being themselves "virginal," they feel "different" and need to catch up in order to join the bragging and shared locker room discussions. With a sister at home, close in age (younger or older does not matter), they may experiment with her. These occurrences are usually consenting and nontraumatic unless the children are caught in the act and judged, punished, or labeled. Trauma may also occur should some unfortunate result occur such as a sexually transmitted disease (STD) or pregnancy. An unbelievable case will clarify.

- PHILIP, *age 7, returned home from a Sunday visit to his next door neighbor and caught his mother and father in bed nude and in the midst of having intercourse. He stood there and watched, unnoticed for several minutes. When the mother glanced over and saw him, she simply said something like "Oh, hi!" and asked why he had come home so early. After explaining that his friend's parents had to go shopping, young "Philip" asked what his parents were doing and was told "We're making love, but it's private so would you please leave and close the door." "Philip" left.*

  The following day, "Philip's" mother heard a commotion coming from the children's bedroom with a great deal of laughing and giggling and went to investigate. It should be no surprise to learn that she found "Philip" and his six-year-old sister (Rachel) nude and "making love." Mother screamed, became hysterical, began beating "Philip" and called him derogatory names including 'pervert', 'sickee', 'bastard,' etc. Nothing was said to his sister. When his father came home, "Philip" was severely beaten on the buttocks and on his genitals and, once again, called every derogatory name and four-letter word that the father could think of. All of this for "making love," like he saw his parents doing. The effects lasted through adolescence when I first met "Philip," following his arrest for an attempted rape on a schoolmate. More on these cases later in the section on treatment.

2. Adolescents Sexually Abusing Their Younger Siblings Group

This reactive behavior appears to be a method of undoing or normalizing their own abuse by their parent(s) through abusing their younger siblings, both girls and boys. Boys predominate and rationalize that "If Dad can do it to me or my sister(s), then I can do it to them too!" They identify with the male, even though a deviant one. Most boys in this category were sodomized at one time or another in their abuse and perceived the father's action as *"using them as a girl or woman substitute."* They then may victimize their female siblings in an attempt to *regain their lost masculinity.*

This growing group remains highly underreported. One reason is that families do not want this "secret" known since an investigation would eventually lead to the parent(s). This group is also undertreated since families do not want relatives and neighbors to know that one of their children is seeing a "shrink" and especially do not want the reason known. One case of this type that I am presently treating lives over 70 miles from my office but the family travels this distance weekly to ensure that no one in their local area will find out.

3. Parent Provoked, Encouraged, or Taught Sibling Incest

A large number of the incestuous parents that I have dealt with involved their children as co-offenders in incestuous abuse on other children in the family. This most often, in my experience, occurs with male incestuous abuse survivors. An active case will clarify.

- JIMMY *was incestuously molested by his father from age 9 to 16. His father promised him that, if he cooperated, he would eventually be allowed to have sex with his mother. In order that "Jimmy" practice and become good enough to sleep with his mother, he was taught and encouraged to have sex with his younger siblings, both male and female. I met him at the sex offender unit where both he and his father were serving sentences for sexual abuse.*

Note: In the last two groups of sibling incest, undoing or normalizing appears to be the major dynamic and motive of the behavior, even when it is introduced or encouraged by the abusing parent. The need to not be the "only one" who is victimized appears critical in these cases. Not infrequently, in multiple child families, the incestuous father forces the other siblings to "witness" the abuse of their siblings and thus makes them co-conspirators. Treatment in these cases is therefore very difficult due to this form of a *double trauma*. Treatment techniques for these survivors will be discussed in Chapter 11.

Adult

This group could begin at 18 years of age or 21 years of age, depending on local laws for age of majority. The offender's need here is to rationalize that he/she is dating or having sex with a peer partner who has the full ability to make a choice or decision about his/her life and behaviors.

In most of the offenders' minds, the molestation/attack will *always* be projected as the victim's fault, in one way or another. He/she was either *"too pretty, too seductive, too sexual, too inviting,"* etc. *If he/she reached orgasm, that confirmed the molester's distorted perception that the victim really wanted him/her to do what he/she did and enjoyed it.*

These reactions occur in other forms of sexual abuse as well and appear to be one of the common denominators in sexually abusive parents.

All three categories of survivors may be involved in either a seductive or assaultive molestation and effects of the incest will vary accordingly.

TYPES OF SEXUAL TRAUMA

There is an important need, at this point, to again distinguish between two very different types of *sexual trauma:* active and passive. This differentiation was first discussed in Chapter 2.

Active Sexual Trauma

These are the highly visible and easily discovered traumas, wherein an actual seduction, sexual assault or other form of sexual molestation occurs, including any sexually motivated physical contact: touching, patting, fondling, etc. Sexual harassment is included in this category. It does not matter whether the molestation was reported or whether the victim ever told another human being; the effects, in general, will be the same.

Passive Sexual Trauma

These are the traumas that are the most frequently overlooked, ignored or minimized. In fact, in my years of supervising both new and experienced counselors and therapists, these are the traumas that are most often missed. My working definition is: *Passive sexual trauma occurs when sex, itself, in some indirect, conscious or unconscious way has a profound and lasting unconscious effect on a child's present and/or future life.* (See Chapter 2 for an expanded explanation of this concept.)

An example of a *passive sexual trauma* is necessary to clarify this very important distinction.

- RALPH, *whom we briefly met in Chapter 2, is a 13-1/2-year-old emerging adolescent who had just recently discovered his own sexual nature and begun masturbating. "Ralph" came from an upper-middle-class family, who lived in an expensive, upper-middle-class home, belonged to the country club, traveled extensively and, in general, lived fairly well-to-do lives. "Ralph" was president of his junior high school class, captain of the basketball team and a junior champion dirt bike racer.*

  One day, his mother, who volunteers at the local community hospital, came home early with a touch of the flu and found "Ralph's" father in bed with his secretary. In an angry rage, she ordered them both to leave and told her husband never to come back. Unknown to her was the fact that her husband had fallen in love with his secretary and was planning to leave the family when he could find a way out. He, therefore, gladly packed his clothes and left, never to return.

  With no financial support from his father and with his mother able to find only secretarial work with a local accountant for very small wages, a financial crisis occurred and the family lost their beautiful home. With the help of a family counseling agency (where I was employed as a part-time consultant) "Ralph's" mother found a "flat" in a poor and rundown area of town. The apartment was dirty, the walls were damaged and "Ralph" now had to share a bedroom with his younger sister. The children were transferred to a local school that in no way compared with their former one. "Ralph" was assaulted by school bullies on his first day of school and robbed of his lunch and bus money. He was also told that he had to "pay a fee" (protection) daily or that he would be beaten again. His sister was also harassed and the family, in general, was miserable.

  A few weeks later, the mother came to the agency and stated that she was in "fear of her life." "Ralph" had turned on her. He had replaced her expensive perfume with his own urine and had punched holes in the walls over her bed in obvious rage. His language was threatening and disrespectful and the mother stated that she "no longer knew her own son." "Ralph" was added to my caseload on an emergency basis.

  Using a very directive and confrontational approach, (he obviously did not want to be there and was belligerent from the moment he stepped into the office) immediately brought the anger and rage to the surface. "Ralph" paced around the room, kicked chairs and cursed profusely. When his outburst subsided, he finally sat down and began to cry. He then offered the following comments.

  "Why couldn't she just ignore the whole thing?"

  "It was only a little sex!"

  "Why do I have to suffer for their problems?"

  "I didn't do anything to deserve this!"

  "Ralph" then admitted that he had begun masturbating to rape fantasies and that, more often than not, his mother was the victim in the fantasy. This frightened him and he realized that he needed help.

  Fortunately, through the agency and some friends in the community, we were able to improve the family's situation including finding the mother a better place to live and a better-paying job. "Ralph" was given a job as evening receptionist at the agency which served a dual purpose: he earned some extra money and he was available for me to observe and talk to on an informal basis. We also were able to get a variance from the local school board to permit both children to return to their original school even though they were out of the district.

Had this interruption in his developing pathology not occurred, there is little doubt in my mind that "Ralph" soon would have become an adolescent rapist and then an adult rapist as he physically grew and became more self-confident and aggressive.

"Ralph" was never *overtly sexually molested* by anyone and would not, in many clinics and practices, be seen as a sexually traumatized boy, but he certainly was a classical example of *passive sexual traumatization.* "Ralph" was definitely a survivor of sexual abuse.

Lack of adequate and specific training in identifying and handling this type of survivor results in poor interviewing techniques, especially in family or local mental health clinic counseling situations, with the result that these cases are too often missed.

This too frequently *missed-case-scenario* also occurs in inadequately investigated incest cases. Several of the survivors we have treated in our private practice were *unreported/undiscovered male victims of incest* in cases that were reported to the police by their sisters. However, in a majority of the cases, *no one questioned the boys in the family, only the girls.* The boys were certainly not going to volunteer the information that their fathers had sexually abused them as well. More on this later.

UNREPORTED AND UNTREATED SEXUAL ABUSE

At this juncture, let us look at the different reactions that survivors have when the sexual molestation/assault is not reported or treated.

Forced Sexual Assault

Deny-ers constitute a group of survivors who cope with their molestation by denying that it occurred and through *repressing* the event. As in all cases of repressed sexual trauma, their behavior abruptly changes, usually for the worse and in later life the full results of the trauma surface.

Since repression is a major defense mechanism in all cases of Deny-ers, we need to first define the concept.

"Repression can be best understood as an unconscious exclusion from the consciousness of objectionable impulses, memories, and ideas. The ego, as it were, pushes the objectionable material down into the unconscious and acts as if the objectionable material were nonexistent" [Wolman, 1989, p. 292].

In forced sexual assault, the reactions of *male* survivors differs from that of *female* survivors and needs to be discussed.

Boys often become *"satyrs"* to regain the manhood that they feel they have lost as a result of the sexual assault. Feelings that they should have been able to protect themselves and thereby prevent the assault produce severe ego damage and self-doubt. Feelings of inadequacy and inferiority often result. Besides all of the expected reactions discussed previously, if their behavior becomes pathological, they often become sexually assaultive persons, especially if they had been sodomized and perceived that act as having been *used as a girl.*

A striking example will clarify.

- JOEY, *whom we met briefly in Chapter 2, now an adult rapist, came from a family of marital conflicts. When "Joey" was around 12 years old, the following set of circumstances occurred.*

  "Joey's" father began to take him out every Saturday, explaining to "Joey's" mother that he and his son needed more time alone to become friends and to get to know each other better, especially since "Joey" was entering adolescence. "Joey's" mother believed the story.

  In reality, "Joey's" father was using him as an alibi to visit his secret paramour. After a quick lunch at McDonalds or Burger King, "Joey" would be given a game or some comic books to read and instructed to sit on the porch of the paramour's home while the father visited upstairs.

  "Joey" was quite streetwise by age 12 and knew (or fantasized) what he felt was going on upstairs. However, as long as his father treated him well and bought him gifts and later took him somewhere, such as an amusement park, swimming or bowling, he really didn't care. He also wanted and needed the individual attention he was getting from his father and was unwilling to upset the applecart.

  These Saturday excursions continued for more than six months and then a dramatic change occurred. One day, as "Joey" was reading a comic book on the front porch of the paramour's home, his father came down in his underwear and took him by the hand, leading him upstairs.

  Upon entering the bedroom, "Joey," now quite frightened, became aware of two things immediately: **a naked woman, quite large, lying on a frilly bed and a strong odor of cheap perfume.**

  "Joey's" father ordered him to undress and when he hesitated, the father undressed him, stating **"It's about time you became a man, if you're good enough!"** *"Joey" was then ordered to lie on top of the woman and to* **"Show me what kind of a man you are!"** *"Joey" knew about sexual intercourse but was a* **virgin** *and, under the circumstances, was so frightened and confused that he could not get an erection. The woman (he never was told her name) put her arms around him, held him tightly and whispered in his ear* **"Be a good boy for daddy, "Joey" and don't cry."**

  "Joey," more frightened and confused than ever, felt his father climbing on top of him. The next thing he felt was terrible anal pain as his father forcibly and without lubricant penetrated him. "Joey" now was in shock and the woman kept trying to calm and comfort him. When the father was finally finished, he said **"Boy, you've got the best and tightest pussy I've ever had!"**

  "Joey" was never to forget this phrase, which to him meant that his father had **used him as a woman.**

  When they left the mistress' house, not a word was spoken between them throughout the ride home. Upon arriving home, "Joey's" father simply dropped him off and left. As he entered the house, "Joey" obviously was in pain and his short pants were wet since he was bleeding quite a bit. His mother took him into the bathroom and treated his bleeding by forcefully packing cotton up his anus — a second rape. She never asked him a single question as to what happened. "Joey," therefore, assumed that she knew what his father had done to him and that she really didn't care. When she was through tending to his injuries, his mother sent "Joey" to bed telling him that "You'll be all right in the morning."

Lying in bed but unable to sleep, "Joey" replayed the tapes of being sexually assaulted by his father over and over again. He had to have an answer to his paramount question "Why?" He suddenly remembered that whenever he showered, his father found an excuse to come into the bathroom and to open the shower curtains. Since he was often erect (especially if he had been masturbating), "Joey" would turn toward the wall so that his father could not see his erect penis. Each time, then, what his father did see was his bare buttocks. Maybe, thought "Joey," his naked behind turned his father on. If that were true, then the assault was his, "Joey's," fault.

From this point on, "Joey" became a real behavior problem both at home and in school. He was constantly disrespectful to his mother and to his teachers. Also, he was always getting into fights and doing all sorts of daring feats to prove his strength but more to prove his masculinity.

Less than a full year after his own rape, "Joey" committed his first sexual assault on a high school girl whom he so terrified and threatened that she never reported it. "Joey" was on his way to becoming a compulsive sex offender and by the time he was finally apprehended, some eight years later, he had sexually assaulted more than 25 women, inflicting some type of severe physical injury on each one.

*During his first year or more of therapy, there was no conscious memory of his own rape. "Joey" had **repressed** the entire incident. He had rationalized his rapes on his difficulties in all female relationships and the resulting anger and rage he felt at being ridiculed, rejected or putdown by females, regardless of age.*

One of the most difficult problems faced in treating the survivor is to discover whether there are any repressions and, if there are repressions suspected, to bring them to the conscious level.

I have developed the following rule or guideline in determining whether a *repression* exists or not in a particular case. *Whenever a compulsive behavior is discovered that has no logical explanation or etiology, I look for a repressed trauma.*

Girls, who have been sexually assaulted, usually have problems in their adult interpersonal relationships, especially where sexual behavior is concerned. They often see sex as dirty, disgusting, repulsive, etc. They usually end up being referred for a sexual dysfunction, the most frequent ones being *frigidity, vaginismus, and sexual aversion.*

An example here will clarify.

- JULIE, *a 29-year-old nurse, referred herself for severe depression resulting from a "screwed-up and unsatisfactory sex life" (her words). She had accumulated seven failed relationships, all due to sexual difficulties. While she insisted that she "liked sex," in each sexual encounter that she had experienced since she began dating, she would become "frightened, uncomfortable and then nonresponsive," although each occurrence began willingly, happily, and excitedly. When asked to recall the latest "failure" in minute detail, the following picture emerged.*

  "We returned to his apartment from an absolutely wonderful and enchanting evening. We dined at a new and marvelous restaurant, went to see the greatest top-hit play on Broadway and then went for a romantic ride in a surrey in Central Park.

  At his apartment, we talked over after-dinner drinks and one thing led to another. The next thing I knew we were in bed, naked. The moment I realized that he was going to eventually penetrate me, I began to get frightened, started sweating profusely, and stopped responding to him. I just laid there like a mannequin as stiff as a board. He realized something was wrong and stopped. The rest of the evening was an embarrassing disaster. I haven't dated since."

"Julie," by this time in the story, was sobbing with her head down. Her shame and embarrassment were quite obvious and painful for her. I waited for several minutes until she had calmed down and was more composed. I then asked her to tell me about her childhood sexual molestation. She immediately began to deny that anything had ever happened, protesting that *"that's always what therapists attribute sexual problems to."* She appeared angry and quite upset by my inference. When she calmed down, I explained the need to remember what had happened to her as a child and we ended the session, without her making another appointment.

A month later, "Julie" called and asked for an "emergency" appointment, as the depression had worsened and she was now *willing to do whatever it took to get better since she feared becoming suicidal.* In the next session, after some small talk and time to relax, "Julie" recounted the following.

- *"Julie" had been sexually molested and raped by her maternal* UNCLE LOUIE *who lived with and supported her and her mother after her real father's desertion. The first molestation occurred when she was nine years old and further molestations/assaults continued until she was 12.*

   In a typical seductive child molester pattern, "Uncle Louie" first befriended her, taking her to parks and amusement areas and buying her gifts almost daily. Her mother enjoyed watching the two of them developing a father-daughter relationship and trusted her brother implicitly.

   Within a month of his arrival, the mother had to work late one evening and asked "Uncle Louie" to arrange for "Julie's" bath and to put her to bed. Instead of arranging for her bath, he gave her a bath, fondling her genitals and attempting digital vaginal penetration until she cried from pain. "Uncle Louie" then threatened to leave the family if she told her mother what he had done. He also assured her that her mother would believe him and not her (a typical caretaker abuser ploy).

   "Julie" was devastated. She had begun to see her uncle as her father and trusted him enough to allow him to give her the bath. She concluded that "it had to be my fault that all of this occurred. God must be punishing me, just like he did when my father left, which was also my fault."

   "Uncle Louie" continued his fondling at every opportunity and slowly but surely progressed. The next phase was to have "Julie" fondle and then masturbate him. In less than three more months, he completely lost control one night and raped her. The pain was terrible; she bled and was sure that she was going to die. The threats now heightened to include the promise that "he would have to kill both her and her mother if anyone found out what he had done, since he was not going to prison for anyone."

   From then on, "Uncle Louie" used "Julie" whenever he felt the urge. Her life became a constant frightening nightmare. At age 12, her uncle was arrested for molesting another girl in the neighborhood but "Julie," when questioned, denied that he had ever touched her, remembering the death threats against her and her mother that "Uncle Louie" had made.

By age 14, "Julie" had successfully *repressed* the entire period of time that her uncle lived in her home until I triggered the memories with the inference that she had been molested. Once the repression was brought to light, therapy was rapid and successful, with "Julie" experiencing her first really happy sexual encounter within a month. The man was someone she had always cared for and whom she brought to two of her last therapy sessions. They are now happily married but "Julie" still needs an occasional *booster session*, as the nightmares sometime recur.

Seductive Sexual Abuse

Accept-ers justify their sexual molestation/abuse and continue the learned behavior, resulting from the abuse, on a peer level until they eventually fail *sexually* as an adult. They then revert to the original, learned behavior. Through a process of *"role reversal"* they attempt to justify their behavior in their own original abuse.

Additionally, once they have sexually molested another child, they no longer need to deal with the obsessive fear that "I'm the only one!"

Here again, the reactions of male survivors differs from that of female survivors and needs to be delineated.

Boys tend to repeat the behavior on a child who is the same age as they were when they were molested, almost ritualistically, to reverse the roles so that they are now the aggressor, the adult.

An example will clarify.

- GARY *was 18 years old when he molested his first young child, an eight-year-old boy. In tracing his own sexual molestation, the following story emerged.*

  At age eight, his 26-year-old UNCLE PAT *used to take him on outings, bowling, or playing catch in the nearby park. He began his seduction by teaching "Gary" how to wrestle (another typical pattern in child molesters). His uncle would lay on top of him, moving around in what "Gary" termed a "dry humping" fashion. This excited "Gary" and he got an erection and sometimes an orgasm. While it felt good, he still felt guilty about it but didn't try to stop his "Uncle Pat" since he was the only male friend and father-figure that "Gary" had. His own father deserted the family when "Gary" was only five years old.*

  The sex play progressed when he stayed overnight at his uncle's house. Since "Uncle Pat" slept nude, "Gary" also slept nude, at the uncle's suggestion. They began wrestling and once they were both erect, "Uncle Pat" fondled "Gary" and "Gary" fondled him in return. From this beginning, they graduated to mutual masturbation. After an hour or so of sex play, "Uncle Pat" carefully sodomized "Gary" and "Gary" learned to "like it a lot." Their sexual relationship lasted until "Gary" was 12 and had just fully entered puberty.

  "Gary" cannot remember why the relationship ended. (It is quite possible that "Gary" was now too developed and too old for the uncle's tastes.)

  From age 13 on, "Gary" had sex with girls and enjoyed it. However, he never stopped masturbating to fantasies of "Uncle Pat" sodomizing him. In fact, he now had to digitally penetrate his own anus to enjoy his masturbation and to reach orgasm.

  Eventually "Gary" became impotent with girls and at age 18, he initiated sex with his eight-year-old male cousin. "Gary" repeated the identical behavior pattern with his cousin that had occurred between himself and his uncle. Eventually, after molesting 12 or more young boys, "Gary" was arrested.

"Gary" was treated successfully using the techniques described in Chapter 11 under *Homosexual Abuse Techniques*.

Girls who are Accept-ers tend to prostitute, become promiscuous, marry aggressive, battering (dominant) husbands, and tend to lose their personal goal motivation. An example will clarify.

- JANE *is a 23-year-old college student who has earned the reputation of being the "dorm slut." She was a self-referral for what she termed "an obsession with penises and wanting oral sex with males who treat me nicely." While, at first, denying that she was a victim of sexual abuse, she later revealed the following story.*

  "Jane's" early childhood was fairly normal. Her mother and father treated her and her three brothers equally. She had several close friendships with girls in the neighborhood who were her own age. The problems began when she and her friends entered adolescence, around age 11. All her girlfriends became interested in the boys in school and in the neighborhood, while "Jane" did not. Part of the problem was that "Jane" was "plump and pimply" (her description) and boys tended to "avoid her."

  Living next door to "Jane's" home was a retired teacher who befriended all of the neighborhood children and maintained an open house policy. He was known to all as UNCLE JACK, *although he lived alone, had never married and was unrelated to anyone in the community. "Uncle Jack" was a good listener and also a self-proclaimed "counselor" for everyone: children and adults alike.*

  *One day, lonely and depressed, "Jane" sat on the swing in her backyard and "Uncle Jack" called her over to his yard. He was able to get "Jane" to tell him what was bothering her and soothed her feelings by telling her that "she would always be his special little girl and that he would be proud to be her boyfriend." "Jane" felt much better and in the next few weeks spent a great deal of time in "Uncle Jack's" house, often sitting on his lap while they watched television. "Uncle Jack" slowly and carefully went about his seduction and eventually convinced "Jane" that she was ready for sex education. He would teach her the **real way,** by "show and tell (and Do!)." He undressed to teach her about a man's body and how it functions and then had her undress, fondling her during the lesson. Next came a lesson on childbirth and in explaining reproduction, "Uncle Jack" masturbated to erection and then asked "Jane" to bring him to orgasm "so that she would see what sperm are like and what makes babies." From here, "Uncle Jack's" speed of teaching increased and within a week, he carefully and gently had his first intercourse with "Jane." "Jane" felt that "something was wrong," especially when "Uncle Jack" insisted that this had to be their secret or "he would have to go away and leave her."*

  *The sexual abuse continued until "Jane" was 16. The only reason it ended was that "Uncle Jack" suddenly moved out of the neighborhood. (Unbeknownst to "Jane," he was involved with other neighborhood girls and was under investigation by the local authorities.) "Jane" felt abandoned and betrayed, and blamed herself for losing "Uncle Jack." Her reasoning was that she must not have pleased him, especially since recently he had been complaining that "Jane" wouldn't **orally** satisfy him often enough. From this time until college, "Jane" lost herself in her studies and had few if any social contacts or experiences and remained sexually inactive.*

  "Jane" won a scholarship to a college, some 400 miles from home. With trepidation, she moved into a nonsegregated, unisex dormitory and was introduced into the "world of pleasures that college is all about," according to her roommate, BRENDA. *"Brenda" was a typical 21-year-old young lady, quite world-wise and*

liberal in all areas including sex. After each date, "Brenda" would relate to "Jane," in explicit detail, what had transpired, emphasizing the sexual aspects. Concerned about "Jane's" lack of social life, "Brenda" encouraged "Jane" "to loosen up and give the guys what they want." "Brenda" arranged a date for "Jane" with one of the dorm "hunks" and "Jane" reluctantly accepted.

After a movie and something to eat at a local eatery, the "hunk" took "Jane" to his room in the dorm. He undressed, revealing an erection, laid back on the bed and said "O.K. baby, time to pay up if you want to see me again. Let's see how good you suck!" "Jane" immediately thought about "Uncle Jack" and fearing another lost relationship — she really liked "Mr. Hunk" — complied. When "Jane" told "Brenda" what happened, "Brenda" congratulated her on becoming "one of us," a phrase that meant a great deal to "Jane."

By the time of "Jane's" return from classes the next day, the whole dorm had been told of her performance the night before by the "hunk." Soon the guys were lined up at her room wanting dates. Thus began "Jane's" life as the "dorm slut." Very quickly, "Jane" realized that the guys really didn't care about her and only took her out for the sex. She felt the same bad way she had, after an encounter with "Uncle Jack." Still, "Jane" felt she had no real choice, since anything was better than the loneliness. She continued being used for two full years of college before coming into therapy, depressed and pre-suicidal.

Therapy will be a long and difficult restructuring of her self-image and self-esteem as well as restructuring a new personality. Emphasis will have to be on positive traits. Assertiveness training will be essential. The fact that she referred herself for therapy indicates that there is a good probability of a positive outcome. Only time will tell.

Incest

Girls who survive incest typically:

- Stress being adult (this is of sudden onset and not necessarily age appropriate).
- Put on too much makeup and overdress to give the impression of being seductive (especially true where teenagers are concerned).
- Start *using* their looks and body for gain (learned from their incestuous father).
- Become a *tease* to other boys and older men.
- Become outrageous *flirts*.
- Lose interest in school — want gifts, job, travel, etc.
- Consider their father their *secret boyfriend and lover* (an idea that he implanted).
- Become physically, *but not sexually,* abusive parents in later years.

Boys, while displaying many of the victim traits and some of the incest traits, tend to:

- Repeat the offense either simultaneously with their own molestation or in the distant future in a ritualistic manner.
- If forced sodomy was involved, they can easily become rapists to deny feelings of femininity and to project the rage they feel for their mothers for not protecting them (identical to forced sexual assault cases).
- Display a projected, generalized rage at females throughout their lives that they cannot justify or explain. Often this rage is sudden and explosive.

- Tend to be aggressive in their sexual behavior and often cause pain to either sex that they are involved with. Again, they cannot explain or justify this behavior.
- Often have unresolved *bisexual* thoughts, feelings or tendencies that disturb them greatly since they do not understand these thoughts and feelings and have always considered themselves heterosexual.

An example of all of these reactions will help.

"Joey," whom we met earlier is a perfect example of the incestuously-damaged male. His rapes were all motivated to "prove his masculinity," deny his feminine feelings and traits (including wearing his wife's underwear) and were usually "triggered" when he experienced urges or fantasies of being sodomized by a male that he was attracted to.

COMMON SURVIVOR TRAITS

In summary, all *survivors* of sexual abuse have several traits or effects of the abuse in common that need to be carefully identified and treated.

- 1. They all experience *guilt* ranging from mild to severe, which may produce self-punishment in the form of failure, feelings of unworthiness and low self-esteem and may even lead to prostitution on the part of both females and males.
- 2. They tend to look for and find inappropriate mates and become completely submissive to them. *Girls* tend to find controlling and battering males (similar to their abusers, especially in incest) and *boys* look for mother-figure lovers/wives or the opposite: weak and submissive women to control and dominate.
- 3. They often develop a poor to defective self-image and lose all goals or the desire to change. This becomes a severe resistance problem in therapy.
- 4. If they repressed the event, it will surface in later years in their relationships and particularly in sexual affairs or marriage. When a sexual dysfunction results it usually manifests itself in *girls in frigidity* and in *boys in impotence*.
- 5. Sex, for them, becomes either disgusting, dirty and to be avoided or remains a *payment* for love, acceptance and delusional belonging.
- 6. They feel *strange,* scared, anxious, etc., and don't know why. They then become convinced that they are abnormal, sick or *crazy* (emotionally disturbed).
- 7. They fear therapy since they see it as a betrayal of the abuser, about whom they often retain highly *ambivalent* feelings of both love and hate. This causes confusion and indecision. In therapy, this is an extremely important consideration. Should the therapist, out of sympathy, talk down about the abuser, rapport may be permanently damaged.

4

How Survivors Deal With Sexual Trauma, Conscious or Unconscious

Prior to obtaining therapeutic intervention, either due to having reached the limits of tolerance of their problem or due to being caught at their deviation, survivors find a surprising number of *ingenious* methods of dealing with the effects of having been sexually traumatized. At this point, let us consider several of these methods and specific cases to illustrate them.

UNDOING OR NORMALIZING

One of the most frequently used methods of handling a past sexual trauma that is causing emotional pain and ego damage is that of *undoing,* an attempt to *normalize* the situation. The following case is a classical example of this defense mechanism.

- LEON *was a weak, inadequate and passive-dependent young boy who was physically abused by his father and nonsupported by his weak and frightened mother. Beginning in grammar school, "Leon" began acting out to get attention from both the teachers and also from the other pupils. As he grew older and bolder, this acting out increased to the point of his being charged by the school authorities with being **incorrigible**. Finding no support from his parents, the court had no choice but to send him to a state reformatory. "Leon" was 12 years old at the time.*

  From day one of his arrival at the "school," "Leon" was victimized by the older and more aggressive youths (known as "dukes") in residence there. The older boys found him physically attractive and easy to dominate and so fought over who would get to make him their "kid," which implied almost complete ownership in return for protection, gifts of food and clothing, prestige, etc.

  *Within a week, "Leon" found a friend and protector, who was the "duke" of his cottage. For a week or so, "Leon" really enjoyed the new friendship and the protection it offered but he soon learned the price. One night he was awakened by his "duke" and taken to the basement shower room where he was forcibly and brutally sexually assaulted, while the "duke's" gang and their "kids" from the cottage looked on cheering. From that day on, **on-cue,** "Leon" was used sexually, not only by his "duke" but was often **loaned** to other "dukes" from other cottages for their enjoyment and pleasure. From "Leon's" perspective and current memory, the staff cottage parents knew what was going on and made sure they were conspicuously absent during his molestations, leaving the "duke" in charge of the cottage for hours at a time.*

➡️ *METHODS SURVIVORS USE TO DEAL WITH SEXUAL*

TRAUMA, CONSCIOUS OR UNCONSCIOUS

☐ 1. Undoing to Normalize the Abuse

☐ 2. Ritual Repeating of the Sexual Abuse

☐ 3. The "I'm The Only One" Phenomenon

☐ 4. Miscellaneous Highly Subjective Methods of Dealing With the Abuse

☐ 5. Denial

☐ 6. Repression

Some years later, after having been through yet another older-level reformatory and again made a "kid" to a "duke" there with the same results, "Leon" entered the world of adulthood, angry, resentful, distrustful, and frightened of everyone who tried to befriend him. He found a menial job as a dishwasher in a rundown diner. He also found a room in a boarding house, complete with cockroaches and a filthy bathroom at the end of the corridor. Several older men tried to seduce him and he either ran or, if the man looked weaker and more inadequate than he felt, "Leon" would beat him up.

After living like this for almost a year, now 22 years old, alone and miserable, "Leon" approached a woman on the streets for sex and was humiliated by loud laughter and being called a "young squirt." Feeling intense rage, he cautiously followed her to a deserted area, pulled her into an alley, beat her severely and committed his first sexual assault. As his luck would have it, he was immediately apprehended and sent to the sex offender unit, then housed in a separate building of one of the state prisons. All therapy attempts with "Leon" failed and he simply sat passively in group, answering only direct questions, usually with one word answers or vague replies.

*Almost six months to the day after his arrival, he requested an emergency session with me, both as his therapist and as director of the unit. "Leon" proceeded to tell me that he had **raped** one of the younger and more passive-inadequate inmates in the dorm the night before. His whole demeanor and attitude had changed. He was more assertive, had excellent eye contact, sat upright instead of his usual slouched position and seemed almost **proud** of what he had done. He then related his sexual victimization history in the other institutions and stated the following — "I couldn't live with myself the way I was. I couldn't stop thinking of those guys (the 'dukes') using me for their 'woman' and my doing nothing about it. While it was going on, even though there were other guys who were 'kids' to other 'dukes,' I always believed* *that I was the **only one** who was letting another male use him as a woman. Then, lying in bed last night, I knew that the only way the pain would stop was if I **passed it on** and stopped being the only one. I had to convince myself that any young, weak and skinny, frightened kid would have to let it happen. I then looked over and saw* JEFF *lying in bed and looking so much like me when I was in those other places. I knew what I had to do. I even used the same con-job on him that was used on me, promising him protection and favors and that I would be his 'Daddy' (protector) if he didn't scream or resist me. Then I raped him and **it was like everything that happened to me was being transferred to Jeff**. When it was over, I kissed him and thanked him. I felt great! No guilt or shame, just great! **Now I'm not the only one!**"*

From that day on "Leon" was a new person. He became a leader in his group, was more assertive in the institution and at his work assignment and appeared happier than anyone had ever seen him. I could not convince him that what he had done was wrong or that it would not work.

In therapy, it took almost a year before "Leon" was willing to confront what he had done to "Jeff," to realize it was wrong and that he had become the same as the "dukes" he hated and resented. He had created another victim like himself. Once this admission and responsibility took place, his real therapy began.

RITUAL REPEATING OF SEXUAL ABUSE

I have met many other sex offenders who used *undoing* as a means of dealing with a past sexual trauma that made them feel *unique* but in a *negative way*. Most of them were child molesters, repeating *ritualistically* what had been done to them on a child of the same age and general personality that they were when the abuse occurred. A classical case of undoing by role reversal and exact repetition of the original abuse will illustrate.

- ROGER, *like so many other sex offenders as children, was an inadequate, lonely, shy, inhibited boy who desperately wanted a relationship with his father but always felt rejected by him. His mother, realizing that he needed a relationship with a man and that he would never have one with his father wanted to do all that she could for her son. She enrolled him in the boy scouts at age 12. Almost from the **first** week, the scoutmaster was sexually attracted to "Roger" and deliberately found little things for him to do after their meetings. While putting supplies away in a back room, he began, on the **second** night, to tickle "Roger" and then to mock wrestle with him. "Roger" enjoyed the attention as well as the physical contact.*

  *After the **third** meeting, "Roger" again was asked to stay and help with cleaning up and in the same back room, the leader again began wrestling with "Roger" but this time groped and fondled him. "Roger" became erect and, although embarrassed and a little frightened, said nothing and allowed the leader to do what he wanted.*

  *After the **fourth** meeting, the leader suggested they strip to their underwear to wrestle ("to protect their uniforms from getting dirtied or damaged") and "Roger" reluctantly agreed. Again the fondling occurred but this time the leader took "Roger's" underpants off and **masturbated him to orgasm**. This was "Roger's" first sexual experience (a critical factor) and he enjoyed it.*

After the *fifth* meeting, the leader introduced "Roger" to fellatio and also to the necessity of reciprocating if their relationship was to continue. "Roger," frightened of losing his newly acquired "father" agreed.

Their relationship continued and "Roger" was made an assistant to the scoutmaster with great ceremony in front of all of his friends. He was as proud as he could be and grateful to his newly found "father" and friend (his perceptions).

Almost a year passed and then suddenly, without explanation or farewell, the leader literally disappeared, moving out of town overnight. "Roger" was crushed. He felt betrayed, used, rejected and lost. (What I subsequently learned was that "Roger's" father overheard him talking to another boy scout on the phone and discussing his relationship with the leader. The father then went to the leader's home, threatened to have him jailed and suggested that the leader leave town. The leader agreed but "Roger's" father never discussed this event with his son.)

"Roger" reverted to his old behaviors: isolation, loneliness and feelings of unworthiness and guilt. That was his last year of grammar school and he transferred to junior high school the following September. Here he met new friends and eventually had his first heterosexual experience, trying unsuccessfully to forget what had happened between him and the scoutmaster, although remaining uncomfortable in gym and shower room activities with the other boys.

"Roger's" life continued in an almost normal manner although he always felt that something was missing and that he was not like his peers, that is, he was not normal. Relationships with other boys began normally but soon he would become uncomfortable and find a way to end them. At age 17, he joined the Navy and began a new life, of sorts. He fit in well and did what all of the other young sailors did, including drinking and carousing in every port and getting the usual number of STD's (sexually transmitted diseases). Two factors remained with him throughout this period: his discomfort in nude situations with other men and his inability to continue in any relationship for a long period of time. He continued to feel that something was missing in his life.

When he was finally assigned to port duty in the western part of the United States, "Roger," now age 22, met a divorced woman who worked on the base and began dating her. She had three children and he enjoyed "having a family" once again, so he married her. The marriage only lasted nine months when she divorced him. He decided not to re-enlist but rather returned home to New Jersey to live with his mother.

Being home only a week or so, he returned to the sponsoring organization for his old scout troop and volunteered to be the scoutmaster. They gratefully accepted him since they knew "Roger" and were desperately looking for someone to run the troop, which had not met in several months.

During the *first* scout troop meeting, "Roger" noticed a young boy **who reminded him very much of himself as a youth** and asked him to stay after the meeting to help clean up and put supplies away. In the same back room, he ritualistically followed the same pattern he had experienced.

The *first* night, he checked the boy's home situation and discovered that the boy had little to do with his father.

The **second** night, he **tickled him and wrestled** with him.

The **third** night, during their wrestling, "Roger" **groped and fondled** the boy who got an erection but did not complain.

The fourth night, he suggested they strip to their underwear ("like the Sumo wrestlers") and during this wrestling, he took off the boy's underpants and masturbated him to orgasm.

The fifth night he fellated the boy and taught him that reciprocation was necessary, if their relationship was to continue.

"Roger" was sure that following this ritual would make him feel better and more normal since he had always believed he was the only one who would do these things with his scoutmaster and now wanted to prove to himself that "any scout would do these things with a leader he liked and respected." Unfortunately, it did not work. Not only did "Roger" not feel better, but, in fact, he felt worse. Rationalizing that he had picked the wrong scout, "Roger" chose a new victim and again failed. However, he did not stop but continued molesting one boy scout after another. Following each molestation his guilt became unbearable but he could not stop until he was arrested after molesting more than 40 scouts in the exact same ritualistic way.

It should be noted here that only *one* of the 40 boys ever reported the incident; the others were either afraid or too concerned about the reactions of their parents and peers to dare report. If "Roger" had not been arrested, the other 39 victims would never have been identified and the whole process could have been repeated some years later. The eventual numbers would have been astronomical.

In therapy, "Roger" was extremely resistant regarding the homosexual side of his personality. He insisted that "as long as he performed these acts with young boys and not with adult men that he was not a homosexual (a very frequent rationalization of pedophiles and hebophiles) nor could there be any homosexual component to his personality." It was not until more than two years into his treatment that he began to admit that even when he had sex with his wife, he was fantasizing about boys, and that he was physically and sexually attracted to several of the men in the treatment unit.

When these admissions were seen as positive by the therapist and by his peer group, and the anticipated rejection, name-calling and hurt did not occur, "Roger" became less frightened of the concept of being *bisexual* and was more open to accepting the responsibility for his behavior with the boys. A year after these admissions took place, "Roger" had his first adult homosexual relationship and related it to his group in their next meeting. He stated that he finally *"knew who he was"* and that *"for the first time in his life felt that he had a choice in his future behavior."* Concurrently, his masturbation fantasies changed from involving former boy scouts he had molested to men he was attracted to in the treatment unit. At the time of this writing, "Roger" has been released and is currently pursuing a bisexual lifestyle. He no longer needs pedophilic-homosexual fantasies to have intercourse with a woman and is able to openly admit his attractions for men that he either works with or with whom he has social contact.

Let me add a note about why I have chosen to use several examples of sex offenders in a book on survivors is to clearly show the connections between the two and to vividly demonstrate the concept of the "Merry-Go-Round of Sexual Abuse" and how it can become self-perpetuating when not discovered or not treated. *Ninety percent* or more of the seductive pedophiles and hebophiles I have encountered in almost 30 years, were themselves survivors of sexual abuse but never reported it and were consequently never treated. The results are clearly seen in the preceding cases and many more to come.

THE "I'M THE ONLY ONE" PHENOMENON

One of the most frequently seen and common factors in a majority of survivors of sexual assault is the *"I'm the only one!"* phenomenon. Both during and after the abuse child survivors do not perceive their peers, friends and even siblings (in incest) as ever having been sexually molested nor is this topic discussed in their daily lives. When they are chosen by a molester and are abused, they intrinsically feel that they are the only ones who have ever had this type of experience and, therefore, are *negatively unique.* The molester defensively implants this idea as well as the blame and responsibility for the sexual behavior onto the victim. Some of the offenders' rationalizations and projections are difficult to believe.

- "If you weren't so cute, this wouldn't have happened."
- "You know you wanted me to do this to you."
- "You came back for more, didn't you?"
- "If you weren't such a bad little girl/boy, I wouldn't be doing this."
- "If you weren't dressed like that, I wouldn't have raped you."
- "You smiled and gave me the come-on and then refused, so it was all your fault."
- "I know you had an orgasm and that means you wanted and enjoyed what happened."

The projections and blame go on forever. Unfortunately, the survivors, both children and adults as well, too often believe the offender's rationalizations. Being traumatized already, these survivors tend to easily assume the guilt for the offender's behavior and this becomes a major resistance factor to reporting. When in therapy, this guilt becomes a major barrier to any therapeutic progress. The therapist must always be wary of this factor and deal with it as soon as possible in the treatment process.

The real danger when these survivors do not report or receive treatment is that they may use "undoing" to deal with the abuse as "Leon" did or "ritual repeating of their abuse" as "Roger" did.

MISCELLANEOUS METHODS OF DEALING WITH ABUSE

There is no limit to the number of ways in which survivors can cope with the facts and the after effects of sexual abuse. An unusual example will clarify.

- *One of the most difficult and unusual cases I treated was that of a 14-year-old boy,* MEL, *who was referred to the psychological services center of a reformatory (where*

I interned) for **aphonia,** *the inability to speak. The onset was sudden and could be traced to a particular night at his cottage, sometime after the boys had all returned from supper. Cottage personnel and the other boys in the cottage denied that anything had happened to "Mel" that could have produced the aphonia. Everyone was baffled.*

After several weeks of trying to find a way to help "Mel" and being able to communicate with him only through written notes, sufficient rapport and trust was finally established for "Mel" to relate the following story.

On the night in question, after showering, "Mel" was assigned to mop the shower area and changing room. Since everyone in the cottage took turns doing this chore, "Mel" did not suspect anything unusual. He waited to shower last and with only a towel wrapped around his waist began his work. Suddenly a group of the older boys, all "dukes" (leaders in the cottage) came down to "inspect his work" and called him into the shower room to allegedly point out something he had missed. When he walked in, a coat was thrown over his head from behind and he was restrained in a bent over position. The next thing he knew, his towel had been removed and the first "duke" sodomized him viciously without concern for his pain. Then the five or six other older boys took their turns sodomizing him while calling him derisive names and suggesting that he was finally getting **"what he had been asking for."**

When they were through, "Mel" was in shock and bleeding quite profusely. Since the boys knew he would be taken to the hospital and asked what had occurred, they **threatened to kill him and his family if he told anyone what they had done.** *Frightened and in shock, "Mel" was taken to the hospital where the cottage supervisor told the doctor that "Mel" had inserted a mop handle into his rectum (the story the older boys and he, the cottage supervisor, had concocted). When the doctor asked if this was true, "Mel" could not speak and had not spoken since.*

The trauma was twofold: not only was "Mel" gang-raped in a brutal and demeaning manner but the cottage supervisor (to protect his job, since he had left the cottage illegally) had lied. In "Mel's" mind, this meant that the cottage supervisor, an authority figure, had **known about and condoned the rape.** *It was amazing to me that he ever took the chance of telling anyone but thank God he did.*

"Mel" was released from the institution immediately. An investigation was instituted that resulted in the older boys being transferred to a maximum security facility and the cottage supervisor being fired and referred to the prosecutor's office for indictment. "Mel" continued therapy in the community with a trained sex therapist and was able to recover but only after a long period of time.

"Mel's" case fits into a large number of *institutionally sexually abused males and females* who perceive authority figures as permitting the abuse, whether prison guards are *conveniently unavailable* when the attack occurred, or dorm and cottage supervisors leave an older "trustee-type" in charge while they absent themselves from the premises. These negligent and indirectly involved supervisory types then must cover for the transgressions of their charges in order to save their own skins.

The therapist in these cases must be sure to uncover all of the *feelings* that the survivor has for those involved in the actual abuse and also for those that the survivor holds ultimately responsible for allowing the situation to exist or to occur. This requires a great deal of trust on the part of the survivor since the therapist, himself/herself, is an authority figure.

Double Traumas

These forms of sexual abuse involve a *double trauma* that will pose long-term, serious problems for the therapist, especially where gaining the above mentioned rapport and trust is concerned. A great deal of patience and the ability to tolerate becoming the substitute authority figure, where their anger and mistrust is concerned, is vital.

Double trauma can occur in all forms of sexual victimization and will usually involve the trauma of the sexual abuse, itself, and then a second trauma involving the survivor's perception of who is ultimately responsible for his/her victimization. In *caretaker sexual abuse and incest,* the parental figure is perceived as condoning the abuse through inactivity, convenient absence, not believing the survivor when they relate what occurred, etc. Any of these instances can constitute the second trauma.

Survivors often blame the following "parental figures."

- In caretaker abuse, the judge or social service agency that placed him/her in the foster home or institution.

- In institutional abuse, the supervisors, administrators and the "system" that did nothing to protect him/her from the abuse (as in "Mel's" case).

- In incest, the mother who did nothing to protect him/her from the abusing father (or vice versa).

- In sexual assault, the husband who does not believe his wife or blames her for the assault and then rejects her.

- In seductive child abuse, the parent(s) who will not believe that he/she was or is being abused by a priest, minister, scoutmaster, big brother, teacher or other authority figure.

DENIAL AND REPRESSION

Two additional defense mechanisms need to be discussed — denial and repression. Both of these defenses are responsible for the majority of the resistance found in the survivors of sexual abuse (as well as in the sex offenders who committed the abuse) and for making the treatment of survivors a very difficult undertaking. A great deal of *patience* on the part of both the therapist and the client (either offender or survivor) is needed and too often one or both can't handle the frustration and quit. In either instance, *disaster* is a very possible outcome. Denial and repression, as defense mechanisms, will be discussed separately.

Denial

Denial may be defined as: ". . . the weak ego rejects not the past but the present. When its actual current life becomes too painful to accept or too difficult to cope with, the infantile ego withdraws from reality, breaking away from the truth, and refusing to acknowledge painful facts. Memory and perceptions prevent an unlimited escape from reality; but in some pathological cases, the hard-pressed ego gives up reality-testing and simply denies facts. [Wolman, 1989 p. 87]."

Where the sex offenders are concerned, this definition fits perfectly and *denial* is probably the most frequently used defense mechanism by this group to avoid accepting *responsibility and guilt* for what they have done to their victims.

Where survivors are concerned, the definition needs some explanation and possible expansion. Rather than a "weak ego" or "infantile ego" causing the denial process, the *trauma* resulting from the sexual abuse appears most often to be the culprit. No one expects to be sexually molested — neither child or adult, female or male. The *shock* of the abuse and the intense feelings of violation, filth, disgust, anger, shame, subjective guilt, etc., all produce an intense pressure that some individuals cannot bear. One frequent result is *denial.*

This *denial* takes many forms and has many degrees.

- 1. In some survivors, the *entire incident* is denied, even in the face of witnesses or incontrovertible evidence.

- 2. In some survivors, certain *specific details* are denied, e.g., pleasure, orgasm, fantasies, words the abuser used, etc.

- 3. In long-term seductive sexual molestation, *the excitement, the desire to repeat the behavior, the fact that the survivor may have initiated the behavior on some occasions,* etc., are all elements in the denial.

As in all other elements of sexual offending and sexual abuse, *each case is individual and different.* There are as many varieties of denial as there are survivors, acts or effects. The therapist, counselor, parent, investigator, etc., must be trained to differentiate denial from reality and then to aide the survivor in facing the denied facts, memories, judgments, feelings or other elements of the abuse situation. If the denial remains in effect, many of the emotional and behavioral aftereffects of the sexual abuse will also remain unresolved.

A specific case of *denial* will clarify.

- JOSH, *a 12-year-old boy whom I treated, was involved in a three year sexual relationship with his* UNCLE CARL *until it was discovered by his mother.*

   At first "Josh" denied any sexual behavior or involvement at all (even though his mother saw them in an act of mutual fellatio). Slowly, as rapport, trust and a promise that I would not disclose whatever he chose to share with me with his mother or the authorities developed, he admitted first to his "Uncle Carl" having fondled him on several occasions. Three sessions later, he volunteered that his uncle had masturbated him but that "It hurt, something awful!" Two sessions later, he volunteered that "It really didn't hurt, it tickled but I didn't like it!" A week later, he volunteered that "I sometimes liked how he made me feel.' After two months, "Josh" admitted to having reciprocated and that he enjoyed masturbating his "Uncle Carl's" much larger penis and would fantasize that it was his.

When asked by his blundering social worker (who had never been trained) why he never reported the sexual abuse during the three year period during which it had occurred, "Josh" again went into denial (a regression from his therapeutic progress seen above) and insisted that "Uncle Carl" took me up on a hill outside of my house and told me that if I ever told anyone, he would tie up my parents and my little sister and then set fire to the house and make me watch them burn to death and listen to their horrible screams!"

It took several months to once again develop sufficient trust and rapport (destroyed by the social worker's premature confrontation over his not reporting). Eventually, "Josh" admitted that he enjoyed both the sex and the rest of the relationship with his uncle and did not want it to stop.

Had "Josh's" therapy ended with the social worker's confrontation, no one knows what would have happened to him. It is highly likely that, at the minimum, he would have been sexually dysfunctional as an adult and, in the worst case scenario, he could have become a ritually repeating sex offender with boys around 10 to 12 years of age — the ages of his victimization.

The need for thorough training of the counselor or therapist again becomes one of the major determinants of how these cases will turn out.

Repression

In both sex offenders and the survivors of sexual abuse, *repression* is a more serious and much more difficult defense mechanism to deal with. By definition: "Repression is an unconscious exclusion from the consciousness of objectionable impulses, memories, and ideas. The ego pushes the objectionable material down into the unconscious and acts as if the objectionable material were nonexistent" (Wolman, p. 292)

Survivors with repression problems are usually self-referrals or medical referrals for unwanted sexual impulses, fantasies and/or behaviors. The unwanted occurrences cannot be explained by any conscious memory of being sexually molested or by any other logical reasoning. An example will clarify.

• DENNIS *(whom we will meet in Chapters 6, 10 and 15) was a self-referral, complaining of an unexplainable and extremely disturbing* **obsession** *with seven-year-old boys. He would go into either his or an adjacent neighborhood, schoolyard, playground or park and then search for young boys playing there who had to meet several specific requirements. The boys had to be "thin, friendly-looking, wearing no shirt, and have a small protruding stomach." After staring at them for long periods of time, he would return home and masturbate, fantasizing that "an older boy was punching the younger boy (his chosen victim) in his bulging stomach." Without this fantasy, he was unable to reach an orgasm. It should also be mentioned that his masturbation, itself, was unusual in that he had to "fuck a towel" to masturbate and not use his hand. According to "Dennis" there was never any sexual content to either the watching or the fantasy and he vehemently insisted that he was not interested in seeing the boys nude nor was he interested in either their genital or anal areas. As will be discussed in Chapter 6, as therapy continued for more than two years, "Dennis'" fantasies progressed to include actual sexual contact.*

"Dennis," age 29, has no memories for ages five to nine and insists that he has no memory of being sexually molested or, like the boy in the fantasy, being punched in the stomach. All the clues for a repression exist in "Dennis."

1. Unwanted and disturbing obsessive preoccupation with specific type seven-year-old boys.

2. Unwanted, guilt and fear producing masturbation that is compulsive and "makes no sense" to "Dennis" since it contains no sexual material.

3. Unexplainable fear that his fantasies will eventually turn into overt behavior (he predicted well), resulting in imprisonment, although in the original pre-therapy fantasies, he did nothing that was criminal or for which he would have been arrested.

4. A lengthy five year blank memory period in his childhood which is significant since it contains the preferred child age group for his obsessions and compulsive masturbation.

5. An inordinate fear of discovering what might have occurred in the missing years.

Whether a survivor or a sex offender, clients who utilize repression as a defense mechanism are difficult to treat and must be considered potentially dangerous either to themselves (suicide often occurs) or to others (fantasies becoming overt behaviors).

Treatment techniques that *may* help with these individuals will be discussed in Chapter 10.

DEPERSONALIZATION AND MULTIPLE PERSONALITY DISORDER

The American Psychiatric Association in DSM-III-R, 1987, defines *depersonalization disorder* as:

- Persistent or recurrent experiences of depersonalization as indicated by either: (1) an experience of feeling detached from and as if one is an outside observer of one's mental processes or body or (2) an experience of feeling like an automaton or as if in a dream.

An example will clarify.

- TARA *today is a 48-year-old, married woman with four children. "Tara" grew up in an incestuous family where she was one of eight children, six girls and two boys, all sexually and physically abused by their tyrant father. "Tara" was sexually abused from age five to ten, usually at night. Whenever she heard her father walking down the hall towards her room, she would become terrified and depersonalize. She left her body and hovered above the bed, looking down on poor* MOLLY, *the frightened little girl in her bed. Throughout the father's forced and painful sexual abuse, "Tara" remained floating over the bed, crying in sympathy for little "Molly" but at the same time being glad that it was happening to "Molly" and not to her. She felt no pain, no fear, nothing, only pity for "Molly." These depersonalization experiences were the only way that she could survive those years since there was no one to go to for help and she was terrified of the "monster" (the name she called her father). As time went on and the sexual assaults increased both in frequency and degree of trauma, "Tara" developed additional personalities and became a multiple personality (MPD).*

Multiple Personality Disorder is defined in DSM-III-R as:

- The existence within the person of two or more distinct personalities or personality states (each with its own relatively enduring pattern of perceiving, relating to, and thinking about the environment and self).

In my 30 years of experience, I have met both types of survivors, especially in cases of long-term incest. What I theorize occurs is that during the long-term sexual and physical coercion or abuse, in order to survive, *the young child first depersonalizes during the act.* Many child survivors of incest, both girls and boys, have described *"being on the ceiling looking down on what daddy was doing to that little girl/boy"* and, while feeling sorry for the victim, did not physically or emotionally feel or experience the sexual abuse. Many of them even gave a different name than their own to the child being victimized. These types of experiences appear to fit the APA's definition just cited. However, the survivors' descriptions of their lives outside of the home, appear to fit more closely the definition of multiple personality disorder. As opposed to the submissive, frightened (often terrified) youngster in the abuse situation, in outside relationships many of them function exceptionally, appear totally normal and give no indication of being a survivor of ongoing sexual abuse. How this occurs appears to explain the development of the multiple personality disorder (MPD). Several distinct personalities form as the necessity arises and each appears to have not only different strengths and weaknesses but also different functions: the planner, the manipulator, the seducter/seductress, the passive compliant one, the defender, etc. MPDs can have as few as two personalities and as many as 160 different personalities.

In one family I am presently involved with (and will be for many years to come), all eight children were victimized by a controlling, Jekyll and Hyde personality father — a monster in the home and the ideal father in the community. The incest was repressed by all of the eight survivors for more than 40 years, until **triggered** by one of the siblings, JENNIFER, who was forcibly placed in treatment for drug abuse. Under hypnosis, she eventually began remembering her own sexual abuse. Communicating her memories to her other seven siblings unleashed their repressed memories and each of them began having their own individual panic reactions. (This story will be discussed later and may become a book of its own.) The important point here is that during the many years of sexual abuse (each child averaged about five to six years of ongoing molestation), all of the children were ideal students, had positive and normal relationships with friends and adults in school and in extracurricular activities, including sports, debating societies, community groups and organizations, etc. The majority of the survivors were honor students and all of them continued their education through college. Today all eight are degreed-professionals of one type or another. The ones I have had contact with all describe a minimum of two distinct personalities functioning in their lives, beginning with the one at home and the one outside the home. As therapy with these adult-survivors progresses, more and more distinct personalities are coming to the surface, each with its own behavioral characteristics and its own name. "Tara," as of this writing, has now discovered five distinct personalities, each with her (they are all females) own *control* needs and devices. The entire case has become so convoluted and massive that a separate volume will be devoted to this one family.

For more in-depth information on Multiple Personality Disorder, the reader is referred to the literature and especially two excellent recent articles:

- Joan A. Turkas, MD Psychotherapy and Case Management for Multiple Personality Disorder: Synthesis for Continuity of Care. *Psychiatric Clinics of North America* — Vol. 14, No.3, September 1991.
- Colin A. Ross, MD & Pam Gahan, M.S.W. Cognitive Analysis of Multiple Personality Disorder. *American Journal of Psychotherapy,* Vol. XLII, No. 2, April 1988.

PAIN

The poetry of "Katherine," one of the abused daughters in the case discussed in this chapter, bears eloquent testimony to the deep scars that result from undiscovered, untreated incest.

UNNATURAL DISASTER

Devastation along the Jersey shore / And major inland waterways / Hurricane George hit / Twenty five years ago / Or yesterday
Leaving in his wake / The following injuries:
At least one / abortion / venereal disease / severed thumb / fractured ankle / concussion / crushed car / head injury / speech impediment / drug addiction / alcohol addiction / divorce / aborted career / thwarted ambition / slaughtered dream / sex addiction / night terror / proliferation / breathing cessation / emotional amputation / social humiliation / psychotic hallucination / suicidal ideation / delayed maturation / epileptic annihilation / asthma / food addiction / hunger addiction / nausea / cervical cancer / tipped uterus / ulcerated colon / duodenal ulcer / thyroid malfunction / spiritual alienation / migraine affliction / relationship dysfunction / sexual compulsion / clinical depression / memory suppression / imagination suffocation / Jesus Christ fixation / penis obsession / self-revulsion / joy repression.
The damage reported thus far has been validated / verified / cross-referenced / witnessed / testified / notarized.
All estimates of destruction / Must be considered Preliminary, and / Authorities warn that More may yet be revealed.
In the interim, God has declared a State of emergency, / And is Standing by In Case.

ME

My mind screams / I'm not enough / Not enough
Not enough for normalcy / For real jobs / Real friends / Real family
Not enough / For God and country / And Recovery
Not enough / For fun and love / And sexuality
Not enough / For healing and warmth / And serenity
A massive mistake / Of a life / Stunted, shrunken, / And deformed, / Is my kismet, / My piece of the pie, / My portion of fate.
Failures feel like friends, / Familiar;
And faults, / As comfortable as home!
Because they're so / Well-worn /
They're so / Everyday
They're so / Fitting
To my massive Mistakeness / My shroud of shame
Where / "I'm not enough" / Is all there is.

WHY I AM THE WAY I AM

Because / Before I could talk / Or walk,
I could trust, / And feel.
That was enough / To be damaged
Maybe (and maybe not) / Beyond repair
By someone who could / Rip the darkness / And bite it into two,
And hand my trust / And feelings / Back to me
Bloody, / And torn, / And bitten, / And blue.

Copyright by the author; reprinted by permission.

5

"Imprinting" as a Result of Early Sexual Seduction/Molestation

The *American Heritage Dictionary* [1982] defines an *Imprinting* as: A learning process occurring early in the life of a social animal in which a behavior pattern is established through association with a parent or other role model. By extension, I use *Positive Sexual Imprinting,* to mean that when a child (male or female), who is prepubertal and anorgasmic, is sexually molested and that molestation results in the child's *first* orgasm (with or without ejaculation), and the child perceives both the sexual experience and the relationship with the abuser as *positive,* a *lifelong imprint* will occur. Even when the abuse later becomes traumatic and is totally repressed (due to negative reactions of parents, authority figures, peers, etc.), the imprint remains and will surface at some future time when *triggered* by an event that, in some way is associated with elements of the original abuse. In these resurfacing events, the *content* of the abuse may (and often does) remain repressed while the *effects* (physical, sexual, emotional) are experienced vividly and to a disturbing degree. These are the *positive sexual imprints*.

Imprinting may also be *negative,* especially when a sexual assault occurs with accompanying fear, pain, threat, humiliation, degradation, etc. These assaults may also produce *lifelong imprints* resulting in sexual dysfunctions, characterized by aversions, frigidity, panic reactions, impotence, punishing behaviors, etc. In the last 30 plus years of treating individuals with sexual dysfunctions, there have been literally hundreds of clients who have reported instances of *unwanted, disturbing and guilt-provoking thoughts, fantasies or behaviors* that could not be explained by the client's present values or attitudes or that could be logically seen as the result of consciously remembered sexual traumas. There are several different ways in which these imprinting phenomena can become manifest. I suspect the presence of an *imprint* when the client reports one of five situations.

FIVE INDICATORS OF IMPRINTED SEXUAL BEHAVIORS

In my experience, there are five principal indicators of imprinted sexual behabior:

- 1. unwanted sexual reactions/turn-ons;
- 2. self-punishing behaviors;
- 3. negative self-esteem reactions;

- 4. unwanted and unexplained isolation behaviors; or
- 5. all of the above.

In my experience, the first of these effects is the most important. The other three factors appear to result from the first. Therefore, we will look in greater detail at that first factor and how to deal with it.

UNWANTED SEXUAL REACTIONS/TURN-ONS

This category includes all *unexpected and unplanned* sexual thoughts, fantasies and overt behaviors that have never occurred before nor been part of the individual's lifestyle. In fact, when this phenomenon first occurs, it is so *unanticipated* that a type of *shock* results that most individuals are unable to deal with. A type of reaction-formation follows and everyone, including the involved person is able to see the abrupt, contradictory or inverse behavior patterns that result.

An example, at this point, may prove helpful.

- TODD, *age 19, is a violent rapist, sentenced for treatment to a correctional institution for a maximum period of 20 years. Behavior and adjustment in the institution are excellent from the first day of his arrival. In fact, the staff all immediately liked "Todd" and saw him as a cooperative, mature, and well behaved "gentleman." These descriptions made "Todd" quite an unusual inmate for the average correctional population.*

    In therapy, however, while he attended all of his scheduled groups, "Todd" never took the floor (was the one presenting a problem) and, when asked for feedback for the presentation or problems of other group members, was reticent and would only offer a few neutral words or comments.

    It was, therefore, surprising one day when "Todd" requested an "emergency" individual therapy session with me, as his primary therapist. I saw him that evening as my last case of the day (to provide all the time necessary for his "emergency"). After hemming and hawing a great deal in obvious discomfort, "Todd" finally related what his emergency consisted of. He was having unwanted sexual reactions and turn-ons to other men in his dormitory unit and was requesting transfer to a room assignment with my help and intervention. He could no longer tolerate his compulsively watching the other men undressing or showering and subsequently becoming stimulated by it. "Todd" considered himself heterosexual and could not understand what was happening to him. He even wondered if he was "losing his mind."

    Initially, when the subject was broached, "Todd" vehemently denied ever having been sexually molested. His reaction was so intense that it triggered doubt, suspicion and several questions in my mind, so I continued in this line of probing. "Todd" made it quite clear that he was "not a queer or a fag" and did not want to discuss the matter any further. I ended the interview with the offer to see him again when he was ready to tell me the truth and really begin therapy. Needless to say, I did not recommend the transfer out of the dormitory to a room assignment.

    In about two weeks, "Todd" again requested an "emergency" individual session. He immediately tried to make a "deal" (a typical sex offender attempt at manipulation) by offering "If you promise to recommend a room assignment for me, I'll tell you what you want to know." My reply was "No deal! When you really want to do some therapy, let me know but with no strings attached!" "Todd" sat back for a moment or two, obviously angry and frustrated, then stood up and began to leave the office. I said nothing and continued shuffling papers on my desk. He opened the door, hesitated, closed the door, and sat back down. Within a minute or two, tears began flowing from his eyes and, with his head down, he murmured "Okay, you win!" At that moment, with that decision, "Todd's" therapy began. He related the following story.

When "Todd" was 12 years old, both of his parents worked and he often spent a great deal of time with his older brother, who was continuously moving in and out of the house, especially when a disagreement with his parents occurred. He was also using drugs and had several slight brushes with the law. One day, the brother called him into the bedroom and told him it was about time for him to learn about "the birds and the bees." The brother then ordered him to undress. Wanting his brother's acceptance and approval, "Todd" did as he was told (ordered!). As he undressed, "Todd" was frightened but also excited. By the time "Todd" was undressed, he was fully erect but did not understand why. His brother reached over and began stroking him. In response, "Todd" reached out and stroked his brother, who by then had also undressed and had an erection.

The first few incidents between "Todd" and his brother involved mutual masturbation only. "Todd" enjoyed the newly found relationship with his big brother, who normally ignored or maltreated him, calling him "little squirt" and never allowing him to go with him on hunting trips, walks in the woods, or out with his older friends. Now, "Todd" was allowed to tag along with his older brother, drive his car (a real treat), smoke cigarettes, go hunting with his brother and shoot his shotgun, etc.; "Todd" was elated.

*After about a month or so, "Todd's" big brother again initiated a sex play situation in his bedroom but this time stated that he was bored with this "jerking-off-stuff" and that it was time to do something better. He had "Todd" bend over the bed, lubricated both himself and "Todd" and then penetrated "Todd" without telling him what he was going to do or why. "Todd" yelled with pain and his brother told him to "shut up and just take it like a man!" When he finally reached orgasm, the brother lay back on the bed exhausted and said to "Todd" **"You were better than any of the broads I've ever fucked. Man have you got a great pussy!"***

All that night, "Todd" lay in bed and thought about what had happened but mostly about what his brother had said. The only conclusion 12-year-old "Todd" could come to is that he must somehow be feminine and therefore he must have turned his brother on. His final conclusion was that everything that had happened, including the forced sodomy, was his ("Todd's") fault.

*From that day forward, "Todd's" life changed dramatically. He no longer associated with his former male friends at school but now preferred spending all of his spare time in the woods near his home with his dog and the other animals. Animals now were the only friends that he trusted. He correctly perceived his relationship with his brother to be exclusively sexual and finally reached the conclusion that he was the one being **used**.*

"Todd's" initial stance in therapy was that he hated the sodomy and that he was too frightened to refuse his brother. He stated that he would hide in the woods after school and would not come home if his brother were there unless his parents were also home. He insisted that he refused all offers to accompany his brother on trips, hunting, hiking or anything else. He and his brother became what "Todd" termed "silent enemies." Later in therapy, this story dramatically changed (see below).

This remained "Todd's" story for the next several months of individual therapy. No amount of probing could change his need to deny that he ever enjoyed the sodomy with his brother or that he wanted it to occur again. "Todd" had reached what appeared to be a therapeutic impasse.

More than six months later, when one of his closest friends had been released on parole, "Todd" again requested an emergency session and confessed that he had been *lying. Secretly,* he was masturbating to fantasies of his brother sodomizing him. "Todd" had also been inserting objects (brush handles, toilet paper rolls stuffed for firmness, and eventually, a homemade "dildo" resembling his brother's erect penis) into his anus. All of the objects became substitutes for his brother's penis. He eventually reached a point where, *without an object in his anus, he could not reach an orgasm.* "Todd" hated this *unwanted sexual behavior* but could not stop it from occurring.

This identical sexual behavior had also occurred when he was still living at home. Whenever he tried to deny his homosexuality with heterosexual behavior, he would reach a point where he could not achieve an orgasm with a girl *unless* he treated her in both a degrading and sadistic manner. When asked why, he did not know. This reaction was also an *unwanted sexual reaction and turn-on.*

"Todd" began looking for "loose" girls and became a sexual satyr. He could not have enough intercourse; sometimes being with two or three different girls in a single night. After each act, he would slap the girl around, call her derogatory names and insist that *she knew nothing about sex.* No one was good enough for "Todd."

He next related that within six months of his own *"rape,"* he had already committed his first forceful rape. Unfortunately, out of fear, the victim never reported the crime and "Todd" felt he had *"finally destroyed the woman he had become and thus regained his manhood."* Unfortunately for many future victims, this feeling did not last and his sexual assaulting became compulsive.

These same type of unwanted sexual reactions and turn-on scenarios have been heard from girls and women, high school boys, scoutmasters, ministers and priests as well as other individuals from all professions and walks of life. Let us look at another non-sex-offender example.

- MIKE *had been married for ten years and his wife had just had the beautiful son he had always hoped and prayed for. "Mike" was a lieutenant in the naval reserves and was in line for promotion to captain. He had had many happy and successful working and socializing experiences with men, without problems. He was well-liked and highly sociable. Being community minded, he also was a sea scout leader and had been on several camping trips with a group of sea scouts. Shortly following his wife's return from the hospital with their new baby son, "Mike's" wife asked him to help her give the baby a bath and he willingly and excitedly agreed. While he held, washed and played with his infant son, he caught himself compulsively staring at the baby's penis and soon felt himself becoming aroused. He then, without thought or planning, fantasized touching and fondling his son's penis and wanting to "make his son feel good," in that manner. For "Mike" this was certainly an* **unwanted sexual reaction.** *He panicked, yelled for his wife and made the excuse that he feared hurting or dropping the baby. She took over and he left the room in a state of fear, tension and confusion. He never again helped in caring for his son.*

From that moment on, "Mike's" life changed dramatically. At work, he waited until all of the other officers had showered and were in bed before doing so himself and he copped-out of the upcoming hunting trip with several of his friends that he had been looking forward to for several months. He desperately tried to get out of taking his scouts on a scheduled camp-out but could not, so with intense trepidation, he went (the only adult on the trip).

The first night, after all the scouts were asleep, he stayed awake until two or three A.M., torturing himself with the memory of what had happened with his son. Glancing over at the sleeping boys, he noticed that one of the boys, EDDIE, had kicked off his blankets and went over to cover him. When he arrived at the bunk, he was startled to see that "Eddie" was exposed and had a rigid erection in his sleep. Without hesitation, he knelt by the bed and began to masturbate "Eddie" with his only thought being to bring him to his **first orgasm and ejaculation** *to make him* **feel good!"** *He did just that and it appeared that "Eddie" had slept through the entire incident, so he covered him up and left the area, again to torture himself with recriminations.*

Although "Mike" had spent many hours with "Eddie" and 20 other sea scouts on several former camp-outs and overnight hikes, he had never before had the slightest sexual interest in any of the boys. Only after the incident with bathing his son, did this hebophilic behavior surface. A second most certainly **unwanted sexual reaction and turn-on.**

"Mike's" concerns and fears were well founded. When they all returned home from the camping trip, that same evening two policemen arrived at "Mike's" home with a warrant for his arrest. "Eddie" had been awake and reported what had happened to his parents as soon as he arrived home. Due to his excellent record in the community, "Mike" was permitted diversion, [NOTE 1] with the agreement of immediate treatment. "Mike" called me and made an emergency appointment and that is when I first met him.

Finally, let's take a look at a case involving a woman that fits the negative imprinting criteria.

• MARY, *age 31, was still unmarried although she was a very attractive, intelligent woman with several degrees. At the time of her referral, she was functioning as a supervisor in a mental health agency that counseled and treated a great many adolescent clients. "Mary's" primary complaint was that she was* **anorgasmic.** *She had recently met and started dating a younger man,* TOM, *age 26, who was getting impatient with her excuses for not "going all the way" and she feared losing him. One evening, after an hour or more of heavy petting, "Tom," finally, after her last refusal to have intercourse, gave her an ultimatum, commenting that "maybe something is wrong with you." He took her home and promised to call. The call never came.*

*In the next week or so, "Mary" noticed several changes in both her personality and her behavior: she became less assertive and had difficulty making decisions; she isolated from most of her friends and avoided all of her former social activities; and she began to feel more and more attracted to her female supervisees, while she avoided prolonged contact with all of her male supervisees. In the third or fourth week, she began feeling **erotic** toward one of the females she supervised and panicked. That is when she made her first appointment, deciding not to tell me the real reason for coming to a sex therapist for treatment.*

SIX COMMON FACTORS

In each of the three cases illustrated above, there were several common factors.

1. A Trigger

Simply defined, a *trigger* is any event or occurrence that, before it occurred, would have been seen or considered to be normal but due to its association to the repressed sexual abuse produces an instantaneous *negative* physical, emotional or behavioral reaction. In the three cases listed above the triggers were:

- *"Todd's" living in a dormitory and showering with other men; "Mike's" finally having the son he wanted and dreamed of; and "Mary's" romance and falling in love with "Tom."*

It should be noted that the trigger could be a traumatic event as well, especially if it duplicated the original imprinting cause. (An example of this would be "LAUREN" and her penis-phobia that will be discussed in Chapter 6.) Traumatic triggers will be more fully discussed in later chapters.

2. The Unwanted Sexual Behavior or Reaction

A fantasy, thought or behavior (always with a physical component) that is totally out of the ordinary for the individual and, to his/her conscious memory, has never occurred before. For example:

- *"Todd's" staring at men's genitals and becoming sexually excited; "Mike's" wanting to touch his son's penis and later, and even more unwanted, his sexual molestation of one of his scouts; and "Mary's" becoming interested in one of her fellow female workers in an erotic way.*

3. A Confusion Reaction

Immediately following the first incident of the unwanted behavior, *a sense of bewilderment and confusion* occurs. This is primarily due to the fact that the unwanted thought, fantasy or behavior makes no sense and does not fit or belong in the individual's lifestyle.

- *"Todd's" bewilderment and confusion when he became aware that he was staring at the other men's genitals and felt himself becoming erect since he had consciously*

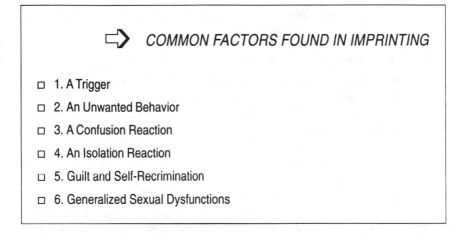

> ⇨ **COMMON FACTORS FOUND IN IMPRINTING**
>
> ☐ 1. A Trigger
>
> ☐ 2. An Unwanted Behavior
>
> ☐ 3. A Confusion Reaction
>
> ☐ 4. An Isolation Reaction
>
> ☐ 5. Guilt and Self-Recrimination
>
> ☐ 6. Generalized Sexual Dysfunctions

always considered himself to be heterosexual; "Mike's" confusion over the desire and fantasy of touching his son's penis and giving him pleasure through fondling it since he also believed that he was heterosexual and had a particular distaste and anger at all child molesters; and "Mary's" confusion over feeling erotic toward her women supervisees that she had known for years without ever experiencing a homosexual reaction or feeling before.

4. An Isolation Reaction

In all cases observed to date, an isolation reaction was seen and is considered to involve an *avoidance or escape behavior* whose motivation appears to be an attempt to prevent a second or more disastrous occurrence. All of the clients treated, paranoidally predicted that the next incident would intensify in depth or severity of the unwanted behavior. This appears to involve *a fear of acting out the impulse, fantasy, desire,* etc. The reaction is immediate and dramatic. While they continue to work daily and normally, in most instances, if not all, their social contacts and behaviors are dramatically altered or eliminated from their lifestyle completely.

5. Guilt and Self-Recrimination

In all cases seen over the past 30 years, *guilt* was the major reaction to such unwanted thoughts, fantasies or behaviors. The guilt resulted in self-damaging behavior as well as in an increased negative self-image (a negative self-image already existed prior to the incident and resulted from their own early seduction/molestation). Also, many of these individuals experience feelings of abnormality, perversion and imminent insanity ("I felt as if I had gone crazy!"). Destruction of self-esteem to a dangerous extent resulted in most cases. More than one of these cases experienced severe depression and had actively contemplated suicide. Several had actually gone so far as to have made a suicide attempt before seeking professional help.

6. Generalized Sexual Dysfunctions

Additionally, in each of the cases seen, there had been abrupt changes in sexual functioning. This was usually the reported reason for seeking sex therapy. These changes ranged from:

- *Inversion* of the former sexual identity, to
- *paraphilic* behaviors and finally to
- *desire-phase* problems accompanied by abstinence. Even masturbation now posed a threat.

Relating this factor to our three cases above:

- *"Todd" became overtly homosexually oriented although he was primarily a hetero-sexual rapist, "Mike" sexually molested the sea scout on the camping trip, and "Mary" lost all interest in sex and almost became sex-phobic.*

AN HYPOTHESIS FOR THE TWO IMPRINTING PHENOMENA

After experiencing several hundred cases of this type, I have developed a theoretical hypothesis to try to explain the *imprinting* phenomenon that would help create a treatment model. In each case where the *positive imprinting* phenomenon was observed, therapy uncovered an early, long-term (versus single occurrence) sexual seduction. This, in itself, did not explain the positive imprinting since, were this a traumatic and negative-affect experience, a different reaction would have been expected.

The imprint appears dependent on a long-term *positive-affect situation* — one where the sexual seduction occurred in a manner perceived by the survivor as positive due to the many benefits attached including affection, love (paraphilic), support, both emotional and material (clothes, trips, movies, physical contact, a port-in-the-storm to escape to when necessary, a parental substitute and a myriad of other benefits that the child wanted or needed). After a period of time, a relationship developed that was also *perceived* by the survivor as positive and beneficial *until* exposure or abrupt separation occurred.

Quite often, when the sexual molestation begins in early or late childhood, where the survivor's developmental stage is characterized by a need for acceptance and approval from adults, the *secret* relationship and behavior is accepted and not reported. In most cases this is due to either the request or demand of the offender, or results from a fear of losing the relationship and all of its benefits, or both.

In cases where the molestation was discovered, especially if the seduction occurred in late childhood or early adolescence, that trauma, in itself, often resulted in a partial or total *repression* of the event or a *delusional distortion* where the child now changes his/her perception and becomes the forced and threatened *victim,* even though, in reality, he/she had previously cooperated and even wanted and enjoyed the relationship. This reaction is often precipitated by one or more adults (either parents or investigating police or juvenile authorities) *negatively reacting* to the now-known abuse. The child then changes the reality and/or circumstances of the relationship and adds threat, fear, pressure, etc., that, in reality did not exist. This does not excuse the adult involved nor does it imply that any guilt should be placed on the survivor.

Caveat: The above explanation of this phenomenon only *explains* the behavior, it never *justifies* it.

When a repression results, years may pass, even an entire developmental stage, where no conscious memory of the relationship exists (the content-memories have been repressed) and the child develops along accepted, normal pathways.

Let us now see how this theoretical framework would fit into two of the three example cases discussed above.

In "Todd's" case, the early seduction and rape by his older brother at age 12 began his sexual molestation history. "Todd" was a sensitive, quiet, well behaved boy until his molestation. His parents both worked, sometimes two jobs, to keep the family going. The attention "Todd" received from his big brother was everything he had always wanted. Being allowed to drive the car, smoke, drink and shoot a shotgun were fantastic "perks" for the 12 year old. While the sex games began pleasantly enough with mutual masturbation, the painful sodomy followed and became their most usual sexual activity. After a few months, it was "Todd" who initiated the sex and wanted, then eventually needed, the sodomy. This admission came much later in therapy, since denial was dominant for many, many months. Once his older brother became tired of "Todd" and rejected him, "Todd" began seeking girls that he could easily *get over on, use* and *abuse,* just as his big brother had *used* and *abused* him. When involved sexually with girls, "Todd" often preferred sodomy to intercourse and always used fantasies of being with his brother *but in a role reversal.* He had always wanted to sodomize his big brother but was never permitted to and was never strong enough (perceived by "Todd" as "man enough") to force the issue.

However, regardless of the number of intercourse experiences he had, the homosexual imprint was too strong and "Todd" could not stop thinking about or fantasizing about being sodomized by his brother and being *his girl.* His rapes then became a desperate attempt to deny both his femininity and also his homosexual needs and desires, which he could not accept due to his desperate need for a "macho" image, like his big brother had.

In "Mike's" case, the scenario differed only in the cast. The seducer was a roomer that his mother had taken in to help pay the bills after his father died. The roomer slept nude in the same room with "Mike" and one night slid into "Mike's" bed and suggested that "Mike" also sleep nude. "Mike" willingly agreed. Within a short time, the roomer reached over, fondled, and then masturbated him. "Mike" was either nine or ten at the time and knew little or nothing about sex. This, therefore, was his *first sexual experience and he enjoyed it* (thus it imprinted). The relationship and the sexual behavior with the roomer lasted until he was 13. "Mike" liked his new friend and substitute father-figure. They went camping, fishing, to amusement parks, shopping centers, etc. The roomer supplied whatever "Mike" wanted that his mother and his absentee father did not. When the roomer moved out, "Mike" missed him and felt abandoned and rejected. Within a few months, he began associating more with his peer group. He was subsequently initiated into the wonders of the opposite sex, lost his virginity, and remained heterosexual in interest, fantasy and behavior until the birth of his long awaited son.

Even after the incident while bathing his son, "Mike" did not remember the roomer. It took six months of therapy before the early memories finally began to emerge, slowly at first and then like a raging waterfall. What was amazing was the depth and the detail that finally emerged. Once the barrier was broken, words, phrases, feelings, even tastes and smells emerged. The most important memory was that when "Mike" asked the roomer why he was masturbating him the roomer answered *"to make you feel good"* which was later expanded to include " . . . *because I love you."*

Negative Imprinting Resulting from Negative Sexual Trauma

While the above discussion focused on positive imprinting, *negative imprinting* may also occur. In these cases, some facet of painful, negatively-perceived sexual behavior occurs over a lengthy period of time and is eventually repressed. Years later, often in adulthood, these survivors experience unwanted negative reactions to normal sexual stimuli. Feelings of abnormality result and even thoughts of being "insane" occur. Suicidal thoughts and attempts are common in this group and need to be elicited and handled on a priority basis.

The major difference between *negative sexual imprinting* and *positive sexual imprinting* is that negative sexual imprinting is *not* necessarily permanent and can be resolved and changed to a large extent through therapeutic intervention. The main treatment technique difference is that of *desensitizing* the client to the trigger stimuli that produces the negative or phobic reaction. "Mary," discussed earlier, is an example of negative sexual imprinting. The difference in her case and those of "Todd" and "Mike" should be clear from the case discussion that follows.

"Mary," now 31, was seduced by an aunt when she began menstruating. The aunt performed clitoral stimulation to the point of pain on a regular basis until a horrifying day when her mother was observed watching them naked in bed. All of these factors slowly emerged in the course of her therapy. The last one — being caught by her mother — resulted in a plethora of curses, slurs, putdowns and name calling that ended in "Mary" being blamed for what the aunt (the mother's sister) had initiated.

Sex for "Mary" was labeled as sinful, dirty, evil, the invention of Satan, etc., and "Mary" was forbidden to ever touch herself *"there"* again. As time passed, "Mary" also repressed this incident but not the admonitions about sex. Although still not remembered (her memories returned periodically in small segments) there must have also been a warning about men and sex with men. "Mary" initially was still unable to respond sexually to a man or even to masturbate. Sexual thoughts, themselves, caused a great deal of guilt and she avoided them at all costs. Nothing in her therapy or in her exposed repressions accounted for this aversion nor for her anorgasmia. Therapy concentrated on desensitizing her to sexual thoughts, fantasies, and eventually to masturbation. To date, many of these barriers no longer exist and "Mary" has begun masturbating but still not to orgasm. She enjoys her body and wants to continue to destroy the old prohibitions that have prevented her from becoming a "complete woman" (her phrase). Once the remaining barriers are broken, desensitization to the male body and sexual anatomy will follow. Prognosis for change in this case is positive and the long-term goal will be to completely extinguish "Mary's" phobic aversion to sex. Were this a positive imprint, this goal would be impossible.

From the above cases, not only can the dynamics of *imprinting,* positive and negative, be clearly seen but also the differences when trauma results. The devastating effects each type of imprinting can produce when they remain unrecognized and untreated should be obvious.

THERAPEUTIC CONSIDERATIONS AND CAVEATS

In cases where either positive or negative imprinting is suspected, the logical first therapeutic goal is to discover the early event(s) that *imprinted* and, years later, *triggered* the unwanted fantasies, thoughts or behaviors. I have usually found this to be an early sexual seduction/molestation that lasted a long period of time and that was perceived, by the child, as either *positive and pleasant* or *negative and frightening.* This sexual seduction/molestation, when undiscovered and when an abrupt termination of the relationship with the abuser occurred, followed by feelings of betrayal, being used, etc., then often became totally repressed for quite a number of years, often into adulthood.

Once the event(s) is *totally* brought into consciousness through therapeutic intervention and all of the emotions, labeling, and recriminations have been ventilated, the therapist can then proceed exactly as he/she would with a recent survivor of any sexual seduction. The operative word here is *totally.* Often, only fragments and partial memories return to consciousness leaving the most sensitive and often the most traumatic elements of the trauma repressed. The therapist must make sure that all of the *nitty-gritty-details* of the trauma are exposed and that the accompanying emotions are thoroughly ventilated.

In cases of this type I prefer to use what I refer to as a *picture metaphor*. The survivor is instructed to retell the event in such minute detail that the therapist can actually picture the incident as if he/she were viewing a hidden videotape of the molestation. Behaviors, words, locations, step-by-step descriptions of all that occurred even to tastes and smells are important. For example, if the boy or girl states that the offender fondled his/her private parts, the therapist might intervene and ask how the offender was able to do this with their clothing on. The more details that the survivor is able to remember the more beneficial the ventilation.

The *feelings* about the molester must also be thoroughly explored and, whether positive, ambivalent or negative, be accepted as normal and permissible. This is especially true where incest or a long-term seductive relationship filled a deep void or desperate need in the child's life.

When *ambivalent* feelings are uncovered, they usually include one of the dichotomies: love-hate, joy-sadness, respect-disrespect, happiness-sadness, and many other sets of opposites that depend on the survivor and the circumstances of the abuse.

How Long Can A Sex Act Last?

One often overlooked cause of *ambivalence* needs to be explored in some detail. In cases of seductive sexual child molestation and incest, considering the survivor's perceptions, ask yourself the following question: How long can a sex act last? For example, when a boy is sexually molested on a weekend camping trip, lasting approximately from Friday afternoon after school until Sunday afternoon, about 48 hours, how many of the 48 hours are spent in sexual behavior? Even if there were three separate molestations on the trip, each lasting a full hour (which is very rare), there are still 45 hours left for other pleasant, exciting and positive activities.

The same for a girl's afternoon's molestation when visiting a separated father. Even if he molests his daughter for a full hour's time, there are still many hours where the father and daughter may go shopping, play games or watch T.V., have fun at a park or amusement area, etc. Additionally, the expressions of love, belonging, acceptance, importance, etc., are always there and are part of the seductive pedophile's/hebophile's *performance,* (his *modus operandi*). To ask the child to *forget* all of the positive elements or to understand that these behaviors were all part of the manipulation to seduce him/her is too difficult to accept and therefore an unfair request. They need something positive to assuage their deep feelings of guilt and shame, especially once the event becomes known by a parent, a teacher or law enforcement officials. If not, they feel and assume that they are perceived by everyone as *prostitutes,* selling themselves for the emotional and material gain. This aftereffect could then become as traumatic and, at times, even more traumatic than the molestation.

Caveat: Again, the reader is reminded that this factor in no way mitigates or justifies the behavior of the abuser but rather takes into account the perceptions of the abuse by the survivor.

THE ROLE OF VALUES

Often, religion, parental values, societal values and personal belief systems are at play in these cases and need to be thoroughly explored and ventilated. In positive imprinting types, while wanting and even enjoying the relationship with the abuser, after each occurrence, self-recrimination and guilt flood into their consciousness as do the words and teachings that they have been exposed to. In negative imprinting, the effects of these early teachings are even more damaging. The need for positive versus negative religious, moral and ethical instruction should be more than obvious in this regard.

Positive-Imprinting Effects in Homosexual Abuse

Involvement in a sex education course becomes a paramount consideration in all cases of imprinting, both positive and negative. In cases where *sexual inversion* is concerned, the client often labels himself/herself as queer, abnormal, sick, etc. In reality, these confused individuals are usually *bisexual* and need to understand that accepting this fact (that I believe is unalterable due to the "imprinting") does not mean that they ever have to act out on those feelings, thoughts, fantasies, attractions, etc. Thus "Todd," while he may catch himself sexually attracted to or stimulated by men, can remain heterosexual *behaviorally.* He never needs to become involved in an overt homosexual act, although homosexual fantasies and masturbation to these fantasies may occur. Individuals with "positive imprinting" problems containing inversion elements often feel and believe that once they have experienced sexual stimulation and orgasm from a same-sex person and especially if they *reciprocated* that they *must remain homosexually oriented.* It is an important role of therapy to deal with and clarify this all-important confusing and disturbing issue. The concept of *sexual preference* versus sexual identity will help with this confusion and give hope to the survivor.

Once "Todd" accepted the fact that having homosexual fantasies did not *obligate* him to act out those fantasies and that whatever sexual behaviors he chose would be his *preference,* rather than a predetermined, unchangeable reality, he was able to return to the dormitory, have similar fantasies and reactions, as in the original unwanted behavior, and not panic or resort to flight. He was able to accustom himself to these reactions and is now less threatened and concerned about them. His former social life has been reactivated to prior levels and beyond. He has become more sensitive to other men's needs and can even be socially-physical (hugging, horseplaying, wrestling, etc.) with them without a problem. His heterosexual lifestyle is still his main *preference* although his masturbation fantasies alternate between men and women, depending on his moods and his needs at the moment. The major change is that the *violence* that compulsively accompanied his former heterosexual behaviors no longer exists in his new fantasies.

"Mike," since he committed a sexual offense, remains in therapy on a monthly basis at the order of the court. He will continue at this level for at least another year or more. At that time, he can appeal to the court to terminate therapy. Sex with his wife is back to normal (they both went through a complete sex therapy course and needed it!). He can now change and bathe his son without problems, although his wife must be present to supervise by court order. Masturbation fantasies *at rare times* include memories of himself and the roomer but they are pleasant and erotic with no resulting panic or guilt. While presently not interested in a male-male encounter, he does not preclude the possibility in the future and has discussed this with his wife, who is willing to accept it *"as long as it does not involve love."*

Negative-Imprinting Effects in Homosexual Abuse

"Mary," however, even though she understands and accepts what happened to her and the "negative imprint" it left, is still in therapy. Progress has been made on a work level where she again is able to function well as a supervisor with both sexes. Her social life remains minimal with no man in her life at present. She has not decided whether she wants to work in that area or to *"leave things as they are since it is safe."* As with all survivors, the decision is hers and only time will tell what she will choose. She accepts her bisexual thoughts with little or no guilt but remains sexually inactive. She is learning to masturbate and become orgasmic and has had some success in that endeavor. This involved *letting-go* of her mother's imposed value not to touch herself *there*.

"IMPRINTING" IN SEX OFFENDERS

Where sex offenders are concerned, an even more interesting phenomenon has been observed that takes on *ritualistic* overtones. I have found the following pattern of ritual in both pedophiles and hebophiles. Choice of *victim type, sex and age,* choice of *setting* for the act, and choice of *specific sex act(s),* all appear to be determined by the *"positive-imprint"* made at the time of the offender's own victimization or seduction. An example will clarify.

- AL *was arrested for the sexual molestation of several six- and seven-year-old neighborhood boys. The offenses followed this pattern.*

   He would lure the child into his garage where there was nothing except a single chair near a workbench.

   *On the **first** occurrence with each child, he would sit him on his lap for a few seconds and then tell him to go home.*

   *On the **second** occurrence, he would sit him on his lap and rub his back.*

   *On the **third** occurrence, he would sit him on his lap, rub his back and extend the rubbing into his pants in order to rub his buttocks.*

*On the **fourth** occurrence, he would sit him on his lap, rub his back, extend the rubbing into his pants in order to rub his buttocks, and then reach around the front to fondle and masturbate him.*

This ritualistic behavior occurred with three boys before the fourth boy reported the incident to his parents with the result that "Al" was arrested and sent for treatment. Therapy over a six month period produced no pedophilic fantasies and no homosexual thoughts or occurrences. While he denied any conscious memory of being molested as a child, there was a total absence of any memories for the period around age six. Memories before and after this age were as expected. Finally, hypnosis was utilized and on the third hypnotic regression the following story unfolded.

"Al," age six, lived next door to a bachelor who had a toy shop in his garage. "Al" would hang around the open garage door, watching in fascination the tinkering and magic-like production of toys for the next Christmas season. Finally, the toy maker invited "Al" in and the following occurred during his next four visits.

*On the **first** visit, the toy maker sat "Al" on his lap.*

*On the **second** visit, the toy maker sat "Al" on his lap and rubbed "Al's" back.*

*On the **third** visit, the toy maker sat "Al" on his lap, rubbed his back, went into his pants and rubbed his buttocks.*

*On the **fourth** visit, the toy maker sat "Al" on his lap, rubbed his back, went into his pants, rubbed his buttocks and then moved to the front and fondled and masturbated him.*

This went on for over a year, unreported, and then, without explanation, the toy maker moved.

This *exact* repetition of the details and events of the original molestation that was later repressed, has been seen in literally hundreds of offenders over the last 31 years.

If asked why a specific age range (e.g., 7-9, 9-11, 12-14, 15-17) the most frequent response is *"They're best at that age!"* or an equivalent phrase with a similar meaning.

If asked why a specific choice of act (e.g., fondling versus oral or anal sex) the response is *"That's the one I like best!"* or *"That one feels best to me!"* or some equivalent response. I have actually, on many occasions, had arguments in groups of pedophiles/hebophiles as to what age, act, place, etc., is best.

The *positive-imprint effect* extends also to the place or setting of the seduction/molestation. If their own experience was in the woods or on a camping trip, this will usually be the setting they choose for seducing their victims; if it were in an attic or cellar, that will be their choice of setting; if in a garage (as with "Al") this will be the preferred setting.

In several hundred offenders queried (regardless of sex or age of victim), this phenomenon was observed and verified in over 90% of the cases. The remaining 10% had committed multiple seductions or molestations, all of different types, with different individuals and with a variety of sex acts. With these offenders, the "imprint effect" held only for age group and male/female choice.

$\Rightarrow$ *COMMON IMPRINT FACTORS IN OFFENDERS WHO*

WERE MOLESTED AS CHILDREN/ADOLESCENTS

BUT NEVER REPORTED

☐ 1. An early sexual seduction occurred that was not discovered or reported and that contained pleasurable elements.

☐ 2. The relationship ended abruptly, leaving emotional scarring that resulted in total repression of the event(s).

☐ 3. A trigger-event occurred and the original abuse behavior was reactivated but with a role-reversal.

☐ 4. Thoughts and fantasies containing the desire to re-enact the former scenario began and became first obsessive and then progressed into compulsive behavior over which the offender claimed little or no control.

☐ 5. Immediate behavioral changes occurred — flight, situational avoidance, guilt, and social isolation being the most frequently observed and reported.

COMMON IMPRINT-PATTERNS IN OFFENDERS WHO WERE MOLESTED BUT NEVER REPORTED

The following sequence appears to occur in sex offenders who were sexually abused as children and who *imprinted* but who never reported or received treatment.

- 1. An early sexual seduction occurred that was not discovered or reported and that contained pleasant elements (friendship, gifts, money, caring, trips, etc.).

- 2. The relationship ended abruptly either because the offender moved, the child moved, the child changed schools, etc., and this left an emotional scarring that lead to or resulted in a total *repression* of the events of the relationship until many years later.

- 3. A trigger-event occurred and the original abuse behavior was reactivated but with a *role reversal*. The former victim now became the adult victimizer with a same-age child as he was at the time of his own molestation. For "Mike" this was the birth of his son, while for "Todd" it was the sight of the naked men in the dormitory shower.

- 4. Thoughts and fantasies containing the desire to re-enact the former scenario began (sometimes instantly from the trigger event) and became first *obsessive* and then progressed into *compulsive* behavior over which the offender claimed little or no control, regardless of the severity of the consequences. Teachers, for example, knew they would never be allowed to teach again; husbands feared divorce; all feared exposure and prison but they did not stop. When finally caught and arrested, there was a sense of relief that is often openly expressed early in the treatment process.

- 5. Immediate behavioral changes occurred — flight, situational avoidance, guilt and social isolation being the most frequently observed and reported. "Todd" panicked in the dorm and demanded a private room where he could hide and not be exposed to other men; "Mike" ran out of his baby son's room and would never again participate in either changing the baby's diaper or bathing him. "Todd" sexually assaulted and abused women consistently and compulsively; "Mike" stopped having sex with his wife; "Mary" stopped dating men.

PREVENTION

Prevention appears dependent on reporting or some form of disclosure at the age that the seduction or molestation occurred.

I interviewed 100 adult male survivors, molested at an early age, who had reported the event and received either short-term therapy or were given adequate explanations to handle the associated fear, shame, guilt, negative subjective-judgments, etc.

The main difference in these men, when compared to sex offenders, was that *they did not put the blame and guilt on themselves but rather on the offender, where it belonged.* Their self-esteem remained basically intact. They did not change their sexual identity or orientation because of the molestation. On the whole, they were able to accept the *benefits* (whether the sexual pleasure, the gifts, the relationship, etc.) without feeling that they *caused* the molestation as other traumatized victims do, and as can be clearly seen in the statements *"I must have been seductive or too pretty or turned him/her on"* or *"My body was too nice or too sexual and caused him/her to do what he/she did"* or other such statements. Their lives remained basically unaltered and their development continued along normal lines.

From this group, I learned several important preventive factors that were part of their lives and not part of the usual sex offender's life.

Ten of these factors can be seen in the Illustration in Chapter 2.

CONCLUSIONS AND FUTURE CONSIDERATIONS

The effects of early "imprinting," positive and negative, resulting from seductive sexual molestation cannot be emphasized strongly enough. A large percentage of the sexually dysfunctional cases that end up in the offices of sex therapists around the world are often there due to this too often unknown, unrecognized, and undiagnosed factor.

Again, only specialized training by qualified professionals in the field can prepare practitioners on all levels to suspect, recognize, and correctly treat these difficult and resistant cases.

In this chapter, I have discussed my experiences with both *positive and negative imprinting* but only where sexually unwanted behavior is concerned. I have also worked with clients who have experienced unwanted guilt behaviors based on *negative sexual imprinting* from extremely restrictive, punitive, and punishing experiences in childhood and adolescence, especially those associated with incest.

The results of these two alternate forms of sexual abuse are just as disastrous. Treatment is identical: first identifying the imprint cause and then following identical treatment steps as with a survivor of sexual abuse at an early age and/or exposure.

While the treatment process can be painful and difficult, the majority of cases are adjustment oriented and end in success. The outcome depends mainly on the goals that the client sets. Specialized techniques are involved and a repeat *caveat* to our colleagues is not to attempt these cases without special training and supervised experience.

NOTE

1: Pre-trial *Diversion* is a process of the courts in any state whereby, instead of sending an individual who has committed a crime to prison, due to an excellent community record prior to the offense, the individual is permitted to remain on probation in the community and conditions to that promotion are addended by the court. In "Mike's" case, the conditions were therapy with a trained sex therapist and 100 hours of community service. Upon *successful* completion of the conditions of the probationary period, the individual may request that the charges and all other criminal records be expunged.

6

Behavioral Effects of Sexual Trauma

Unresolved but Conscious vs. Unidentified and Repressed

Too often, cases are either physician referred or self-referred for sexual dysfunctions that began abruptly and that have *no apparent cause.* The client usually has no explanation for the problem, is greatly disturbed by it, cannot understand what is happening to them, and most often denies any form of sexual molestation either in childhood, adolescence or adulthood.

In my experience, all of these cases of sexual dysfunction, without apparent etiology or cause, result from either an *unresolved* or *unidentified sexual trauma.* A practical rule of thumb that has worked for me for 30 years has been:

When a sudden sexual dysfunction occurs without logical or immediate cause and results in discomfort, confusion, guilt or embarrassment for the client, suspect either an unresolved or unidentified sexual trauma.

Since these two traumas are both different and distinct, they will be discussed separately.

UNRESOLVED BUT CONSCIOUS SEXUAL- ASSAULT TRAUMAS

This first group includes *sexual assaults,* during childhood or adolescence, that were never discovered or reported, either due to the relationship of the abuser or because of serious physical threat, fear of the reactions of family and friends, or fear of the possible consequences of reporting (expulsion from school, loss of employment, etc.). The survivor *consciously remembers* every detail of the sexual assault but is unable to resolve or let go of the emotional effects that resulted from the trauma or the *subjective judgments* that he/she had made regarding his/her *perceived* part in the abuse or his/her *perceived* degree of responsibility for it.

This *not-reporting* factor is quite often interpreted by the survivor as *complicity* in the abuse and increases both the degree and effects of the resulting *guilt.* An example will clarify.

- LAUREN, *a 24-year-old, recently married young woman, was referred by her gynecologist for severe **vaginismus**. Her condition was so serious that the doctor could not perform a digital examination with even a single finger. When all possible physical* *causes were eliminated, the physician referred the case to me. In our first contact, "Lauren" presented me with the following referral problem.*

After a one-year engagement, during which time there was no premarital sex ("Lauren" used her Catholic religion as a reason not to have intercourse with her fiance, although they kissed and petted), "Lauren" and BILL *were married. Immediately after the reception, they drove to Niagara Falls and checked into their hotel around midnight. After a champagne toast, provided by the hotel, they prepared for bed. "Lauren" went into the bathroom, locked the door and emerged 20 minutes or so later in a negligee. She sat at a dressing table and began combing her hair. "Bill" then went into the bathroom, showered and came out* **naked.** *As soon as "Lauren" saw him in the mirror she shouted "Cover yourself!" "Bill" at first thought it was a joke but when he saw that "Lauren" was truly upset, he hopped into bed and covered himself with a sheet. Fifteen or more minutes later, "Lauren" approached the bed and stood by "Bill" stating "You can do what you have to do but don't expect me to enjoy it!"*

By now, "Bill" was confused, angry and unsure of what was expected of him. When "Lauren" entered the bed, he rolled over to kiss her and she stiffened, closed her eyes and looked as if she feared being killed.

At this point, "Bill" had enough. He got up and told "Lauren" to "Get dressed, I'm taking you home!" Without any further conversation, they dressed, drove back to New Jersey and arrived at "Lauren's" home around 4 A.M. As soon as she was inside, "Bill" drove off in an angry burst of speed and that was the last time (over a month ago) that "Lauren" had seen him.

I decided a direct approach was the best way to shock "Lauren" into disclosing and asked her to tell me about her childhood sexual molestation. She looked terrified and responded "But I promised not to tell so that he wouldn't hurt me anymore!" After quite a while of crying and wringing her hands, "Lauren" finally calmed down. I reassured her that she was safe in the office and that no one would find out that she told me of the molestation without her explicit permission. She then revealed the following.

From the age of 10 to 14, she lived alone with her father after her mother had run away with another man. On her 11th birthday, her father told "Lauren" that he was bringing a **special present** *to her bedroom and ordered her to get dressed for bed and wait up for him. He then began his usual evening drinking pattern.*

An hour or so later, he entered her room stark naked with a jutting erection and a leer on his face. He pulled off her blankets and climbed into bed, sitting on her chest. He then ordered her to perform fellatio on him or to get the worst beating of her life. He slapped her face with his erection, over and over again. "Lauren" finally tried to obey, choked several times as he thrust into her throat but finally was able to do as he commanded. He then ejaculated and she gagged and spit out his semen. This angered him intensely. He beat her unmercifully and told her that she would perform fellatio over again and again until she learned to swallow and not **"spit me out!"**

This behavior continued for the next several years on a three-to-four times a week basis and eventually he tried unsuccessfully to vaginally penetrate her. "Lauren" also remembered that his genitals "smelled terribly, like rotting meat or cheese" (her father was uncircumcised and not particular about his hygiene). She would never forget that smell. She also described his penis as "ugly, immense and dangerous-looking, like a weapon and that's the way he used it!"

Once the story was out, "Lauren" cried and cried and had difficulty maintaining eye contact due to her perceived guilt and shame (subjective-judgment). She hated herself for being so frightened that she couldn't report her father's abuse and for the guilt and disgust she felt for what she was forced to do. The memories were always there and she had difficulty looking at men in bathing suits or tight shorts since it immediately *triggered* the memories of her abuse. She still feared another man attacking her.

Seeing "Bill" naked and looking at his penis, brought back all of the terror, shame, guilt and disgust she had felt with her father. While intellectually, "Lauren" knew and accepted the fact that "Bill" loved her and would not abuse her like her father did, it in no way diminished her *penis phobia* or her emotional reactions to seeing "Bill" walking toward her naked. "Lauren's" treatment will be discussed in Chapter 12.

UNRESOLVED, CONSCIOUS SEDUCTIVE SEXUAL MOLESTATION

While the effects of the first category, *sexual assault,* are more obvious, widely written on, and discussed, the insidious effects of the second category, *unresolved, conscious seductive sexual molestation,* are less obvious and less written on or discussed.

Seductive sexual molestation includes those cases where, while no physical force or threat was used, *bribery* in the form of gifts, trips, emotional support and affection, etc., are used to first, establish a *dependency relationship* on the abuser and secondly, to extract a *payment,* in the form of sexual behavior, with the implied threat of loss of all of the above benefits.

This second category includes survivors who were involved in seductive sexual molestations, during childhood or adolescence, that were never discovered or reported due to the relationship with and the feelings about the abuser. These feelings often include an ambivalent mixture of love and hate, that includes fear of loss of the "benefits" of being close to and accepted by the abuser or the threats of the abuser (pictures, tapes, videotapes of the sexual behavior that the abuser tells the survivor will be seen by parents, friends, etc., if the abuser is apprehended).

Two examples of survivors of consciously remembered seductive sexual molestation that I have treated will clarify this most important group.

• *First, let us consider the case of* TIM. *"Tim," when 10 or 11 years old, was molested by his brother who masturbated him several times, over a period of about one month. "Tim" was a shy, inhibited, frightened little boy who felt rejected by his father, friends, and the entire world. He desperately needed love, attention and acceptance from someone — anyone — and also craved the physical contact that he saw other children receiving. Thus, his brother's molestation was both well received and "the most exciting and pleasant experience" he could remember in his sad and lonely life. During the third or fourth masturbatory experience, his brother wanted to "paint"*

"Tim's" penis red with lipstick but *"Tim" refused. From that instant on, his brother would not speak to him nor would he masturbate him ever again. "Tim" did everything possible to reestablish the relationship with no success.*

Some 35 years later, as a clergyman, "Tim" began having young boys in his charge, masturbate him and also **paint his penis with a red lipstick.** He consciously knew that he was trying to **undo** his error, as a child, in stopping his brother and thus losing the only relationship he had and cherished. However, even with this conscious knowledge (insight), he could not stop his compulsion until apprehended after molesting approximately 20 children.

- A second, completely different case, is that of NIKOS. "Nikos" is a 23-year-old, **obscene phone caller** who makes random calls to adult females, asking if he could have intercourse with them, using blunt and crude expressions such as "I want to fuck you! Can I ?"

"Nikos" was molested from age 11 to 16 by his **mother** who, after a nasty divorce, moved out of state with "Nikos" and replaced her husband with her son, but only where sex was concerned. She began by masturbating him, which he "thoroughly enjoyed." She then progressed to fellating him and to teaching him to suck on her nipples and also to perform cunnilingus on her. However, even though the sex progressed, she would **never let him penetrate her** which is what he wanted to do the most.

Although "Nikos" appeared to develop along normal adolescent lines and dated girls his own age, **it was never enough.** His first intercourse at age 15 occurred while he was still having sex with his mother and he rated it "second-best" to what he and his mother were doing sexually. He became **obsessed** with sexual intercourse and lost several girlfriends due to his constant intercourse demands as well as his constantly berating their sexual performances.

Seven years later, he ran away from living with his mother and returned to living with his father in the eastern United States. He was still looking for a mother-figure who would allow him to have intercourse with her since he felt his mother's rejection was based on his "not being good enough or manly enough for her." Also, he was constantly concerned about his **penis size** (a very frequent sex offender concern) since his mother had commented on the size of his penis, compared to his father's, in a disparaging way.

Thus, the phone calling began and continued until he accidentally contacted an important police captain's wife whose phone was "tapped" due to recent threats against her husband. "Nikos" call was traced and he was caught while still talking to the woman. He was given probation with intensive therapy as a condition.

Early in his treatment, "Nikos" admitted to anger, bordering on rage, towards his mother. He also admitted to compulsive masturbation with fantasies of having intercourse with her **in a controlling, rough manner, with degrading and critical verbalizations about her body and her performance,** a definite form of sexual assault.

"Nikos'" conscious knowledge of the causes of his deviation (insight) in no way diminished the intensity or frequency of the deviant behavior.

UNIDENTIFIED, REPRESSED SEXUAL TRAUMA

In contrast to cases where the *cause* of the unwanted or deviant sexual behavior is consciously known are the cases where there is absolutely no conscious memory or suspicion of a sexual trauma but the presenting problem is sexual in nature. In cases of this type, I always suspect a repressed sexual trauma. An example will clarify.

- SCOTT, *a 38-year-old male, has a **sneaker fetish and obsession.** He compulsively goes to shopping centers, supermarkets, parking lots, etc., and finds teenagers or adults, male or female, whom he perceives as looking "not too bright or too swift" and "cons" them into letting him untie their sneakers and bend the backs down. He then tells them to walk on the sneakers that way to protect them and to increase the wear. He does this by convincing them that he is a shoe salesman and that he is concerned with helping them to get the most life out of their product. This whole process gets "Scott" semierect and definitely sexually stimulated ("I start dripping!"). Later at home, he masturbates to the incident.*

  "Scott's" only conscious motivation for this unique and unusual behavior is that he enjoys "getting-over" on individuals of this type. While he is aware that there must be a sexual component, he cannot remember any sexual molestation at any time in his life, although he suspects that he was molested by his father as a young boy.

  *Even though "Scott" is able to convince girlfriends to go through this **ritual** as foreplay to their sexual encounters, it does little to decrease the compulsion. His only reason for coming to therapy, at all, is that he had been arrested several times for simple assault and the judge was now threatening to throw him in jail if he did not receive treatment to end his deviant behavior.*

"Scott" has a Wechsler Adult Intelligence Scale (W.A.I.S.) I.Q. of 145, works in the computer field doing highly technical work and is successful in all other aspects of his life. He recently married and the marriage appeared to be going well, with his wife performing his rituals for him and wearing sneakers to bed during all of their sexual activities. However, after less than a year, his wife could no longer tolerate his deviant behavior and divorced him. "Scott" is now in another live-in relationship with a woman his own age who knows all about his problems and "wants to help in any way that she can" while admitting that she has some fears of "Scott." His compulsion continues and *is increasing in frequency.*

In over a year of former therapy, nothing worked including behavior modification techniques, cognitive restructuring, etc. Hypnosis did uncover a period of his early childhood around age seven where something traumatic did occur but exactly what is still hidden. Under hypnosis, "Scott" is in another state, where he is outside his father's house, wearing his favorite sneakers. He is staring at the house with apprehension about entering. The memory stops there and no amount of probing adds to it. There are also fragments of his being *nude in a room with only sneakers on* but this memory also stops there.

Part of "Scott's" *resistance* is due to the fact that he doesn't want to give up the behavior, consciously stating that he sees nothing wrong with what he's doing. His rationalization remains *"What's the big deal; no one is getting hurt!"* "Scott" is conscious of his resistance and its causes but is still not sufficiently motivated to change.

Before therapy, which necessarily involves *change* can occur, there are several pre-conditions, on the part of the client, that must be met. Change has three essential requirements.

- 1. The DESIRE to change,
- 2. The BELIEF that change is possible for me,
- 3. The BELIEF that I DESERVE to change.

"Scott" did not meet even the first requirement for change and I suspect that, in reality, he really never met the other two conditions as well. More on "Scott" later.

A similar yet very different case follows.

- DENNIS, *whom we met in Chapter 4, is a 29-year-old male-virgin who is seriously inadequate and has a severely defective self-image which effects all of his interpersonal relationships. He sees himself as a "nerd" or "dweeb" (his terms) and these are both realistic and appropriate descriptions.*

    "Dennis" is obsessed with seeking out and watching young boys, age seven, with no shirts on, roughhousing. He finds the boys everywhere he goes — in his own neighborhood, in schoolyards, on subways, buses, etc. "Dennis" continues to watch the young boys until he feels himself becoming sexually stimulated. He then goes home and masturbates to a fantasy involving one of the boys (usually the most weak and inadequate looking). In the fantasy one of the boy's older and stronger companions is punching him in the stomach. "Dennis" insists that while his masturbation is sexual that there are no sexual fantasies about the little boy and that he never sees the boy naked, only with his shirt off. This denial appears to be conscious and not an unconscious, repressive or censoring phenomenon.

    Interestingly, prior to therapy, "Dennis" never masturbated manually and still resists doing so. Instead, he simulates intercourse on a towel using some form of lubricant. The compulsion is so strong that, if lubricant is not available, he does without and irritates his penis to the point of actually rubbing some of the skin off. Although he denies it, this behavior appears to indicate that there is a self-punishing, masochistic element to his masturbatory behavior.

Resistance, from day one in therapy, was incredible and I suggested several times that he discontinue therapy until he was ready to really make some changes and do some work. One reason for this decision was that, while "Dennis" agreed to all of the homework assignments that were suggested at the end of each session, he would never complete or even attempt any of them. "Dennis" refused to stop coming for therapy and promised the therapist he would "try harder."

"Dennis" insists that he *must* have been molested as a child and suspects his own father, although he has no memories of it. In fact, he has no memories around the critical ages of 5 to 9. He also will not ask his parents or his older brother about that time of his life since he doesn't want them to "know that I am seeing a "shrink" since they'll think I'm crazy."

After one year of frustrating therapy with few gains, the fantasies (as predicted) progressively changed and are now overtly sexual. The beginning of the fantasy is the same except that in the new fantasy, the boy whom he just watched playing in the street, is now standing *naked across his room and "Dennis" wants to play with the boy's genitals*. While this fantasy frightens him to a serious degree, he is still blocking and resisting all therapeutic efforts. Part of the reason for this resistance appear to be that he fears that if he gives up his deviant behavior, he will have nothing. He refuses any suggestion of masturbating to normal adult fantasies, either heterosexual or homosexual. When asked why he refuses, he simply states "I don't want to!"

As with "Scott," "Dennis" has an excellent, technical job where he does quite well. However, unlike "Scott," "Dennis" has no real friends, no relationships, and no adult sex life.

COMMENTARY

There are several factors that must be considered in the two cases of "Scott" and "Dennis."

- 1. Neither individual has learned to *distance* from the *child-within,* further discussed in Chapter 13. Both resist doing so.
- 2. Neither individual seems to really want to give up or let-go of their deviant behavior. They are primarily in therapy out of fear of arrest and incarceration.
- 3. Both individuals accept and believe that they were molested as children but resist all efforts at remembering the event.
- 4. Both individuals have limited social lives but are highly successful in their employment where they overcompensate for the failures in the rest of their lives.
- 5. Both individuals are extremely frightened, passive dependent, and inadequate types (*"wimps"*) and have been stuck in the same rut for many, many years.
- 6. Both individuals are guilt ridden due to their present deviant behavior and also for being who and what they are. There also appears to be *residual guilt* from some early childhood sexual trauma that cannot be remembered. The problem is that they refuse to resolve or let-go of these self-destructive judgments and feelings.

Treatment techniques for both types of cases will be discussed later in this work under "Specialized Treatment Techniques" beginning with Chapter 10.

7

Pre-Treatment Considerations

Before discussing specific treatment techniques that work with survivors, it is necessary to look at several *predisposing factors* to any treatment consideration.

READINESS

One of the most frequently seen *errors* made by individuals attempting to treat survivors is an *intrusiveness* into the shock and privacy of the survivor *before he/she is ready*. The first meeting that the survivor has with the potential counselor or therapist is crucial and if errors are made at this time, *there may not be another chance*. The time needed for this session varies from survivor to survivor and cannot be predicted in advance.

Because of this factor, I always suggest that, if at all possible, the first meeting with a survivor should be scheduled for the *last* appointment of the day/evening. In this way, if extra time is needed, it is available and the therapist will remain more comfortable and less anxious about clients in the waiting room.

A primary consideration when *readiness* does occur and the survivor is prepared to discuss all of the "nitty-gritty" details of the abuse, is that there can be *no time limit*. It is important, therefore, to instruct the survivor that he/she should, *if possible* give the therapist a week's warning that the next session will be the one in which he/she chooses to deal with the abuse-event. This is necessary in order to allow the therapist to reserve at least two patient time periods for that all-important session or to assure, as stated above, that the survivor is scheduled for the last patient time period of the day. However, in some cases, this decision to disclose the details of the abuse can occur spontaneously and the therapist must be flexible enough to alter his patient schedule when this occurs.

The decision to share any details of his/her sexual abuse or to disclose the full story must always be the survivor's. When the survivor is responding to pressures from authorities, family and even professionals, the benefits will not be the same and it is doubtful that all of the *nitty-gritty-details* will actually be exposed, especially the most traumatizing ones.

This problem can be avoided with simple questioning as to why the survivor has come to the therapist in the first place or why he/she has chosen this particular time to divulge all the elements of his/her abuse. The following answers bode problems for any therapist.

- "The police told me I should go for therapy."
- "My family told me that I had to go for therapy or that I would never be normal again."
- "My employer insisted that I go for therapy before returning to work."

In all of the above instances, motivating the survivor to want treatment for themselves must be a primary goal. Giving the survivor permission *not* to fully disclose at that point if he/she is not ready is essential.

I compare this process to *peeling an onion*. Disclosure occurs in layers: the surface and easy-to-tell details come first and then slowly more and more details are added. It may take many sessions and many retellings of the abuse-event before the core of the onion — the facts or details that are more subjectively traumatic for the survivor — can be reached. Patience, on the part of the therapist, during this *peeling process* is critical to the success or failure of the therapy.

CONTROL CONSIDERATIONS

Once readiness is considered and respected, the next factor in order of importance is that of *control*. Since control was the major element of the abuse from the offender's need-perspective, one of the therapist's initial functions in therapy is to *return all control to the survivor.* This can be achieved in a number of simple but effective ways. I suggest the following considerations or pre-conditions to treating survivors.

TEN CAVEATS AND PRINCIPLES

1. Greet the prospective client at the door to the office and, where appropriate, give him/her the choice of where the first session will take place.

In my own private practice, where I primarily treat survivors, I greet the client at the door, indicate where my office is, and communicate that that is *eventually* where we will talk. I then ask him/her what he/she would prefer to do on our first visit: either go directly to the office or do something else, such as go for a walk around the complex, or sit out on the deck (weather permitting). Young children, especially, respond positively to this technique since formal settings are perceived as authoritative and, therefore, frightening. They may *associate authority to their molestation* if the molester was a person in authority over them (teachers, priests, ministers, big-brothers, babysitters, scoutmasters, etc.). Only when the survivor is ready and willing do we go to the office.

2. When finally in the office, allow the survivor to choose the seating arrangement.

This is especially important with children, who often prefer to sit on pillows on the floor or to simply walk around and not sit at all. The counselor or therapist should also be sure that there is never any furniture, such as a desk, separating the survivor from him/her. Sitting across from a survivor, with a desk or table in between, produces a *distancing factor* when openness and physical closeness are the desired ambiance. Distancing can also be perceived as a *protection and safety* factor, insulating the counselor or therapist from any *danger* from the survivor.

3. Next, allow the survivor to chose the topic of conversation for the first session.

A simple question such as "What would you like to talk about today?" or any simple introductory opening that offers the topic of the session to the survivor works well for me. Suggesting that the survivor might like to include any questions that he/she may have about the course of treatment and the specific techniques that will be utilized is considered appropriate in the first and second sessions. These arrangements can then become an *informal contract* between the survivor and the therapist that can be referred to whenever necessary by either party.

4. The appearance of the counselor or therapist, including clothing, may affect the positive rapport needed on this first contact.

The overly formal counselor or therapist in his/her three-piece suit may (and often does) create an even further *distancing factor* between himself/herself and the survivor, especially children. Informal clothing and appearance have

---

⇨ *TEN TREATMENT CAVEATS AND PRINCIPLES*

☐ 1. Greet the Survivor at the Door, Especially on the First Contact

☐ 2. Allow the Survivor to Choose the Seating Arrangements in the Therapy Room

☐ 3. Allow the Survivor to Choose the Topic of the Session

☐ 4. The Appearance of the Therapist May Affect Rapport

☐ 5. Don't Force the Survivor to Reveal the Details of the Abuse in the First Session. Follow Readiness Principles

☐ 6. There Can Be No Time Limit for the First Contact or for the Session in which the Abuse is Revealed

☐ 7. The Parent(s), Partner, or Significant Other in the Survivor's Life Must be Peripherally Involved

☐ 8. Physical Contact is Essential to the Recovery Process

☐ 9. The Therapist Must be Careful Not to Promise Help that He/She Cannot Provide

☐ 10. The Therapist's Knowledge of and Comfort with Sexuality on all Levels is Essential to Positive Treatment

always worked much better for me and saved many weeks of unnecessary work in establishing trust and rapport with a survivor (and a great deal of silence!).

5. One of the most serious mistakes that can be made at this juncture is to open the session with a statement like "Tell me what happened."

Rarely is the survivor ready to discuss the abuse on the first contact and *forcing* the issue may lose the survivor forever. In our experience, survivors need a great deal of *courage* to even come to therapy and even more courage to reveal the intimate details of their molestation. If the therapist blunders in the first session, the survivor's fears and defenses may prevent another attempt.

6. There should be no time limit for the first contact.

There is no way to predict what will happen once the survivor has made up his/her mind to seek help. A *Niagara-Falls* reaction may occur where some word or phrase or just the built-up pressure itself may produce an emotional deluge. This emotional release could then produce memories (even some repressed ones), details that had never been told to anyone since the incident itself, feelings from childhood or from past events (such as another abuse that went unreported), guilt feelings that had never before been shared, etc. If any of these areas are stifled by time constraints, they may be rerepressed or never again mentioned. The survivor could easily interpret the cutoff to mean that the issue or subject under discussion was considered unimportant or unnecessary for treatment by the therapist or that the therapist simply did not care.

In my own practice, I schedule all first appointments for survivors as the *last case of the day* so there will be no pressing schedule to follow. Some of these initial sessions have lasted for as long as two hours or more. If there had been another survivor waiting, the pressure on the therapist would affect concentration, observation and, in my opinion, the rights of the survivor.

It also quite probable that the survivor would have picked up the body language of the therapist (clock watching, thumping fingers, fidgeting, etc.,) and interpreted it to mean some form of *rejection* or *displeasure*.

7. The partner, parent or significant other in the survivor's life must be peripherally involved in the treatment as well as remaining in close contact with the therapist.

Nothing that the therapist does in one hour can be meaningful if everything else in the survivor's life contradicts it. Also there is a need for an *objective source* of current information about the survivor's behavior, including progress or regression as therapy continues. Lastly, especially with children and married survivors, the parents and/or partners must know what to expect and what behaviors on their part would be either beneficial or harmful. During the early phases of treatment, these significant others need to agree and be willing to *submit to the lead of the survivor* if therapy is to succeed. This is especially true in a marriage or other relationship where sex is involved.

A word of caution is necessary regarding the therapist's involvement with significant others. It must be made perfectly clear to the survivor that he/she alone is the client. Therefore, the therapist may not divulge any facts or behaviors of the survivor to *anyone* without first obtaining specific permission to do so from the survivor. (I always obtain this permission in writing.) This is especially true where children and adolescents are concerned when the therapist has private contact with a parent, especially a mother. Where married individuals are concerned, it is always the marital partner that is of concern. These private contacts should not begin until a high level of trust has been established between the survivor and the therapist.

Where details of the sexual abuse(s) are concerned, I have always made it a practice, with few exceptions, that it is the responsibility of the survivor to relate these details to significant others, albeit in my presence if that makes them feel safer and more comfortable.

8. Physical contact is essential in the recovery process of the survivor, when the survivor wants and will permit it. Lack of such contact and intimacy on the part of family members, partners, parents, etc., further convinces the survivor that he/she is bad, dirty, disgusting, contaminated, etc., (and therefore untouchable). Self-esteem and self-image remain negatively confirmed and therapy progress is delayed.

The therapist also should include *appropriate* physical contact in the sessions, if permitted by the survivor. A hand on the shoulder, touching the survivor's hand during an emotional episode and even a hug at the end of the session can all be positive factors in the survivor's recovery, *if they are real.* Survivor's are extremely sensitive to artificial or feigned smiles, statements and touches and react negatively with further distrust and distancing when they occur.

9. The therapist, as an authority figure, must be extremely careful not to promise help that he/she cannot provide!

Statements such as "I'll never let this happen to you again!" when the child is still living at home, or "I'll see to it that you are protected!" or "I'll see to it that he/she is punished or sent to jail!" are dangerous and unrealistic. Once the promise fails, the trust the child began to have in the therapist and ultimately in treatment itself disappears, *possibly forever.*

10. Last and most important as a pre-condition to treating survivors is the therapist's knowledge of and comfort with sexuality, on all levels. This includes responding to sexually-explicit street-language. Here, an example is mandatory.

- ANDY, *a 12-year-old boy, was referred to a local counseling center by a local Youth Services Agency. "Andy" had been sexually molested by a truck driver who gave him a ride while he was hitchhiking home from ice skating at a lake.*

    "Andy" was assigned to a female social worker in her early fifties, since she had an open slot in her caseload. No consideration was given to "Andy's" stated-preference for a male counselor by the supervisor.

    Fewer than five minutes into their first interview, the counselor asked "Andy" to tell her what happened to him. The counselor was sitting at her desk but had swiveled around to face him. "Andy" first asked if it was all right to tell her what the truck driver had done and she replied "Of course, you can tell me anything." "Andy" then trustingly stated "He made me suck his dick!"

    The social worker immediately swiveled back to face her desk and began to furiously take notes with her head as close to the desk as possible. "Andy" got up and left the office, tears of anger streaming down his cheeks, screaming "You lied to me!"

"Andy" refused to return to the center. Problems began in school and "Andy" was referred to me for his truancy, poor adjustment, failures in tests, and refusals to do his homework. Following the caveats above, our first session was a long walk to the local shopping center where we had lunch at a "Friendly's." "Andy" talked about his dislike for school, his avoidance of both his fellow students and the teachers, and his wish that he could move to a new city. He was given supportive feedback and encouraged to continue in treatment.

The next session, I cautiously asked for some demographic information. In addition to answering my questions, "Andy" volunteered that prior to his molestation, he was a good student, had many friends (both students and teachers), and was planning to go to college someday to become a veterinarian. Since he had made the connection to the molestation, the door was slightly opened and I cautiously asked if he would ever considering working on that issue, since it was my specialty. His immediate answer was a loud "NO!" After a moment, he calmed down and said he would think about it. I accepted that response and pushed no further.

During our fourth visit, "Andy" brought up what happened at the counseling center with the female social-worker and how it had made him feel dirty, bad, disgusting, and how the counselor's behavior had convinced him that she did not like him, was angry at him and that she did not want to deal with his molestation problem. He also admitted that it made him extremely angry and that he felt victimized ("screwed") again by another adult. I then asked him to give me a chance and he agreed, testing me from that day on with the most lurid and shocking fantasies and sexual statements he could conceive. When he was convinced that I had passed the test, he then admitted that he had made most of it up and his real therapy began.

VALIDITY OF THE SURVIVOR'S STATEMENTS

One of the major legal, moral, and ethical issues that affects the therapist working with survivors concerns the *credibility* or validity of the survivor's story. The majority of unmasked offenders will deny the charges and say that the victim is lying (especially in cases of incest and long-term child molestation) or that he/she has identified the wrong individual (more often in sexual assault cases).

Often the therapist will be asked to evaluate the *truthfulness* of the survivor's claims and, here again, specialized training and experience are absolutely necessary.

With young children, anatomically correct dolls have been used for quite a while but, once again, the untrained or unethical therapist can *misuse* this technique in many ways. The following *misuses* were observed during my supervision of several therapists.

- 1. Choosing the doll for the child and stating *"This is the way the man looked, isn't it?"*

- 2. Undressing the adult male doll and pointing to the genitals and saying "This is what he made you touch, isn't it?"

- 3. Using police or arrest reports as facts, saying to the child "Show me how he did . . . to you with these two dolls!"

- 4. Stating "The quicker you show me what he did, the quicker we will be finished."

And on and on and on.

There are several very simple methods to use with young children that, from my experience, help to validate or invalidate the accusation.

1. Listen to the words of the child.

Children have their own names for anatomical parts and acts. Prior to the interview with the child, ask one of the parents (usually the mother) to fill out a form with the child's terms for his/her body parts, bodily functions, etc.

If a young child consistently uses medically-correct anatomical terms, I become very suspicious of a *rehearsal* phenomenon and ask the child to retell the story, using his/her own terms. An example will clarify.

- MICHELE, *a seven-year-old girl related to me that her uncle had "exposed his penis to me several times." When asked to tell me what happened, in detail, using her own terms, she stated "Well, I was in my bedroom,* UNCLE MARTIN *came in and sat on my bed and then he took this "little snake" out of his pants that got bigger and bigger. He wanted me to touch the "snake" but I was too scared and started to cry. Then he left me alone and I told Mommy when she came home."*

2. Consistency in telling the minute details of the story during more than one interview.

While children do exaggerate and add or delete facts during story retelling, this is a normal developmental phenomenon. However, the main *substance* of the story should remain intact if the incident really occurred. An example will clarify.

- *During the first interview, nine-year-old* TOMMY *told me that his father "had done bad things to him in the shed in their backyard." When asked for more details he stated "Well, he took my shorts off and played with my dingee." However, two weeks later, "Tommy," when asked to tell me the story again, stated "Well, Daddy took me into the shed in the backyard to put on my bathing suit and tickled me between my legs." A week later, crying, "Tommy" related that his mother had told him what to say the first time and told him that, if he didn't, she would leave and never come back. The parents were in the middle of a nasty divorce and the mother felt using "Tommy," when he told her about Daddy's tickling, would speed up the process.*

Questioning inconsistencies and listening carefully to each response will usually expose both lies and rehearsals. *If I can change the substance of the story, I then become doubtful of the truth of the accusation.* With minimal further gentle questioning and probing, I usually obtain the truth of what happened.

It is very important to make the child feel *comfortable* with you, as the investigator, counselor or therapist and to assure the child that *he/she will not be scolded or punished* for telling the truth.

3. In older teenagers and adults, the process is more difficult and the reverse, — perfect consistency, — appears to indicate lies. When the story is told many times without the slightest change in the smallest detail, I suspect rehearsal and possibly untruth.

An example will help to clarify.

- *During the investigation of a teacher who had been accused of molesting several boys in his home, I interviewed two boys from his class that he denied ever touching. Both were problem students that he had had to discipline several times. Their stories were* *told with a great deal of emotion but with **absolute consistency** down to even the **smallest detail**. The first thing I did was separate the two and then inject seeming inconsistencies in the story of one by simply stating "But "Ron" told me it happened on Tuesdays, not Wednesdays." The weaker of the two immediately changed his story to agree with "Ron's" and from there on it was a simple task to prove they were lying. I suggested a description of the photography darkroom, where the molestations allegedly occurred, that was grossly different from the real one and both boys agreed that that was the room in which the molestation occurred.*

Caveat: To attempt to ascertain credibility in a *single interview, regardless of the length of time spent,* is dangerous and usually will produce inaccurate results. *Time* is the best ally of truth in cases of this type. A truly traumatized survivor will not forget the details of what happened, including visual, tactile, olfactory and other sensual events, possibly for the rest of her/his life.

Clinicians must be prepared to make mistakes in this area of dealing with survivors and, in some cases, will never be sure of exactly what occurred between the abuser and the survivor. This is especially true where the survivor is suffering a great deal of *guilt* due to either enjoying the sexual acts or having initiated the sexual behavior on at least one occasion. This type of guilt is particularly true in boys since boys are easier to bring to a first orgasm than are girls.

What appears to happen in these cases (and I've seen literally hundreds of them) is that in order to *deny complicity or equal guilt* with the molester, the child or adolescent survivor *adds or exaggerates* the threats and dangers that were present in the actual occurrences. An example of a true case will explain.

- JOSH, *whom we already met in Chapter 4, was sexually molested from age 10 to age 12 by his* UNCLE CARL, *his mother's brother, who lived with the family over a period of three years. One day by accident (or on purpose?) his mother caught them in the uncle's bed in a "sixty-nine" (mutual oral sex) position. She became hysterical and ordered her brother out of the home, calling him every type of pervert and deviate that she could think of and expressing the acts she would like to perform on him (ranging from castration to death). Her next act (she had still said nothing to "Josh") was to call the police.*

  *When "Josh" was questioned, he was **stupidly** asked by one of the investigating officers why he had let the molestations go on for three years without saying anything to his mother. "Josh" immediately came up with the following story.*

  "After the first time, "Uncle Carl" took me up to the top of the hill in back of our house and we both sat down in the grass. "Uncle Carl" then told me that if I ever told anyone about 'our games' that he would tie up my father and mother to their beds and do the same to my little sister. Then he would pour gasoline all over them and over the furniture and set the house on fire and make me sit up here and watch it burn and have to listen to them screaming while they burned up."

  In reality, the threat "Uncle Carl" made was that he would show his mother and father and all of "Josh's" friends the Polaroid pictures he had taken (with a timer) of them having sex while "Josh" was smiling, laughing and looked like he was having a good time. "Josh's" guilt and shame (for having enjoyed the oral sex that his uncle performed on him and asking for it on several occasions) was unbearable and he feared that his mother, especially, would feel the same way about him that she did about "Uncle Carl."

Once "Josh" believed that he would not be punished or rejected by his mother and family, he admitted that he had made up the story.

THE THERAPIST'S COMFORT WITH SEXUALITY

Professionals or paraprofessionals with sexual hangups, prejudices, phobias, moral mandates, etc., *should, in my opinion, never be involved with treating survivors.* At the minimum, attendance at a full three-day Sex-Attitude-Restructuring (S.A.R.) training seminar should be a mandatory training prerequisite for all therapists planning to specialize in or work with survivors of sexual abuse to preclude this from occurring.

A typical S.A.R. that I might conduct would be composed of the following elements.

- 1. Participants are exposed to simultaneous multiscreen viewings of sexually explicit behaviors for approximately twenty-minute sessions. The first screenings are usually fairly nonthreatening and consist of artistic slides of sexual content, nudity, masturbation, sexual playfulness and the expected "lovemaking."

- 2. At the end of each 20 minute screening session, the large group breaks up into smaller *discussion groups* of approximately five to six participants and a trained facilitator. The purpose of the small discussion groups is:
  - a. to provide a "break" or a "rest" from the intensity of the viewing sessions,
  - b. to allow comments, criticisms, emotional reactions and personal sharings to occur in a *nonjudgmental* setting where each member's opinion is respected and accepted.
  - c. At the end of the small group discussion, preparation is made for the next screening segment. The facilitator, at this point, may recommend that a particular individual sit next to him/her or recommend that he/she discontinue attending the S.A.R. if it is apparent that he/she is having a problem dealing with the sexually explicit materials.

- 3. Everyone then returns to the next screening. Each subsequent screening will contain more and more emotionally laden sexual material and even unusual or bizarre sexual behaviors (animal sex, rape and gang rape scenes, flashers, etc.,) as the three-day S.A.R. progresses.

- 4. Provision for individual counseling during the lunch break or during the evenings of the first and second day are made and participants are encouraged to request a time slot at these sessions.

- 5. Suggested reading lists are distributed and appropriate homework assignments are suggested, throughout the three days.

- 6. Each participant is asked to prepare a short written critique and evaluation of each day's sessions with suggestions for areas of interest that he/she would like covered in the remaining days.

- 7. Where time permits, appropriate lectures by specialists in the field of sex therapy with audience participation and feedback are included.

- 8. Provision is made in the small groups for role plays of minority sexual groups including homosexuals, lesbians, PWA's (persons with aids), sexually active adolescents, parents, and any other role plays suggested by the small groups.

Caveat: While the above is the format that I use in conducting S.A.R.s for potential therapists who intend working with survivors or sex offenders, there are a multitude of different formats and each individual conducting an S.A.R. usually adapts the S.A.R. to the needs of his/her audience. An S.A.R., at minimum, will uncover an individual's *sexually sensitive areas* and allow any and all potentially damaging reactions to a specific sexual area or behavior to occur in a *safe and supervised* environment. An S.A.R. will also allow the therapist to determine his or her capacity to *tolerate* working in this field and the potential effects such involvement could have.

Survivors, morally and ethically, should never become guinea pigs to train new therapists or professionals in practice who are looking to expand their caseloads into an area where they are untrained.

8

Treatment Issues: Overview

INTERVIEWING TECHNIQUES AND WARNINGS

One of the areas where untrained professionals make their initial most serious errors is in the technique of interviewing. Since the first contact often determines the future relationship of the survivor and the therapist, this area is of paramount concern and must be thoroughly discussed before any other treatment concepts can be presented. I have listed those factors that I consider to be the most important interviewing issues in a table that follows. Each of these principles will be discussed in detail in this chapter and examples given where applicable.

SOME PRINCIPLES OF CLINICAL INTERVIEWING

Readiness

As clearly emphasized in the previous chapter, *readiness,* on both the part of the survivor and the therapist, must be considered prior to any interviewing attempt concerning the details of the abuse. In my experience, the survivor will let the therapist know when he/she is ready to get into the "nitty-gritty-details" of the abuse, either by directly stating so or by leading statements and body-language, indicating that the survivor wants the therapist to ask. Once this readiness is observed, the therapist needs to be prepared for a very heavy and emotional session.

Confidentiality Issues

Before any serious or factual discussion of the abuse can take place, the *issue of confidentiality* must be thoroughly addressed. In New Jersey, where I practice, child abuse revelations, of any type, are exempt from normal confidentiality rules and *must be reported.* This law must be explained to the survivor *before* any facts are shared or revealed by the survivor to prevent any conflicts from arising or to prevent any further trauma being inflicted upon the survivor. As discussed before, there are also *control issues* involved in this discussion.

For adults, the fact that prior crime, *exclusive of child sexual or physical abuse*, is covered by confidentiality, if it does not pose an *imminent threat* to the community, must also be explained. The survivor must be allowed to ask questions regarding this issue and must be given time to consider all of the ramifications before proceeding any further.

My own preference is to cover the issue of confidentiality in the first session, before any serious material is discussed or accidentally revealed. The survivor then has at least a week to consider his/her options and to make a realistic and appropriate decision.

Following this session on confidentiality, if facts are proffered that clearly indicate a reportable occurrence, then it should be obvious to the therapist or counselor that the survivor *wants* the incident reported to the appropriate authorities and is either unwilling or unable to do so himself/herself. In New Jersey, this reporting would be made to the Division of Youth and Family Services — D.Y.F.S.

Where really young children are concerned, (my youngest was three years old) this issue must be discussed with the primary parent (the one bringing the child to therapy who has legal custody and who is most involved in the primary care of the child). This is especially essential when an *incestuous* situation is suspected from the referral factors.

All the Nitty-Gritty Details

It is necessary to obtain *all the nitty-gritty details* of the incident preferably the first time that the survivor is willing to talk about the actual abuse, although this rarely occurs. In sessions discussing details of the abuse, the therapist/counselor should not allow generalities or vague and suggestive statements, without further probing.

It is quite common for children, adolescents and even adults to try to get away with revealing as little as possible since in order to tell the therapist all of the terrible details, they must hear it again themselves and therefore *relive* it, to some degree. They often use statements such as:

- "He made me have sex with him."

- "He made me do dirty or bad things."

- "He made me touch him."

- "He, you know, did it to me."

These and similar statements are often used as opening gambits. In the "peeling an onion" metaphor, this is the outer skin only and possibly all that the survivor is capable of sharing at that time. Through encouragement and support, the therapist must elicit the remainder of the abuse story in a gentle and reassuring manner, over a period of time. Each retelling of the abuse can be seen as "peeling the onion" one layer deeper. Each time the story or incident is retold, more and more details will emerge until finally the *core* of the problem is reached. Exposing this core is the ultimate goal of "all the nitty-gritty details."

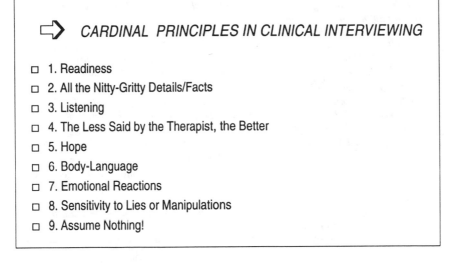

CARDINAL PRINCIPLES IN CLINICAL INTERVIEWING

☐ 1. Readiness

☐ 2. All the Nitty-Gritty Details/Facts

☐ 3. Listening

☐ 4. The Less Said by the Therapist, the Better

☐ 5. Hope

☐ 6. Body-Language

☐ 7. Emotional Reactions

☐ 8. Sensitivity to Lies or Manipulations

☐ 9. Assume Nothing!

Caveat: The *core* may not be what appears obvious to the authorities or even to the therapist at the outset of therapy. For example, in sexual assault cases, the sexual assault itself (the act) may not have been the most traumatic part of the abuse. At times, the words of the offender or some other act that the offender made the victim perform and that made the survivor feel disgusted, degraded, even more embarrassed or guilt ridden, or even the fact of experiencing a pleasurable orgasm, may be more guilt producing and more traumatic than the unwanted, forced act of intercourse (in females) or sodomy (in both males and females), or oral sex or masturbation in each.

To accept *minimums* can be dangerous and prolong the therapy as well as delay any significant recovery. An example, where this *almost* occurred in my own practice, may help to clarify.

• MARISA, *a practicing clinical psychologist, was brutally and viciously sexually assaulted while attending a professional conference. Her original story to the police, her husband and to me was as follows.*

After a long day of workshops and lectures followed by dinner with friends, "Marisa" returned to her hotel room. While preparing for bed, there was a knock on the door. Opening the door with the security chain attached, "Marisa" observed a handsome, smiling young man standing there. Since she did not know who the individual was, she asked him what he wanted and he gave her a convincing, long, and convoluted story about being a psychology student in a local university who knew several of the psychologists attending the conference. Discussing a problem with one of these attendees, the psychologist, a friend of "Marisa's," recommended that he talk to her.

The young man had a proper conference identification badge on the lapel of his jacket and did accurately identify one of her friends and colleagues by name and specialty. Abandoning her usual good sense, she gave in to his request and allowed the young man into her room.

As soon as he entered, he locked the door. His whole demeanor changed from a friendly and innocent looking young student to an angry, threatening and vicious person. He shoved "Marisa" on the bed, called her a litany of filthy names and, when she got up and resisted, punched her in the jaw and into unconsciousness.

When "Marisa" regained consciousness, she was naked and tied "spread-eagle" to the bed. The attacker was sitting on her chest, naked, and slapping her face with his erect penis. He then forced her to fellate him, continuing his verbal onslaught and threats of impending physical damage and death. Next he raped her and, unsatisfied that he was producing sufficient pain and humiliation, he then sodomized her as forcibly and as viciously as he could.

The following morning, "Marisa" was found by a hotel maid, still naked and tied to the bed with adhesive tape over her mouth. The maid ran screaming down the hotel corridor, leaving the door open for curious people from adjoining rooms to stare incredulously at her. Finally, a female staff member arrived and had the sense to cover her up and to remove the adhesive tape from her mouth. "Marisa" became instantaneously hysterical and remained so until the police and first aid squad arrived.

After being treated at the emergency room of a nearby hospital, "Marisa" left the conference and went home. She related the same story to her husband and family that she had given to the police and eventually to me.

Almost a year later, still having nightmares and unable to travel, even with her husband and children, or to consider even entering a hotel or motel, "Marisa" called and asked if I would see her.

The immediate impression I received on her first visit was that of a survivor who was still in serious shock and turmoil. Her *personal guilt* was incredible and she stated that she could not stop blaming herself for releasing the security chain and allowing the attacker into her hotel room. She insisted that this was the *only* cause of her intense guilt. The problem, for me, was that this reason for the guilt did not explain why she refused to kiss her husband or children or be kissed by them. Oral sex was no problem or hangup for "Marisa," so why was this particular symptom present and why was there no respite from the severe degree of guilt she was experiencing?

Deciding on a direct confrontive technique, I flatly insisted that "Marisa" was *hiding something* that was the true cause of the guilt and accompanying strange behavior. While at first resisting and denying that there was anything else, "Marisa" finally broke down and after a hysterical, drenching crying session of over 20 minutes related the following additional information.

After painfully and viciously sodomizing her and reaching his climax, the attacker once again sat on her chest and gave her the following choice: "Either lick off the filth and blood that you left on my penis or I'll slit your throat!" He brandished a large, shiny, switchblade knife in front of her eyes, while he forced his bloody and fecally-soiled penis into her mouth. "Marisa" believed his threats and reluctantly did as she was told to save her life.

It took "Marisa" over 30 minutes to get these facts out between hysterical sobbing and hiding her face in her hands as well as gagging throughout. When she recovered sufficiently, she then angrily stated "I should have let him kill me rather than doing that filthy, disgusting, sick act."

Now the core of the trauma was exposed and treatment could begin. Surprisingly, "Marisa" did most of her own therapy and within a short six-month period, she was *ready* to take the next big step — traveling to another professional conference, with me. At the hotel, I arranged to have the connecting room to hers since I felt it was essential that she stay alone for the one night of the conference.

As fate would have it, minutes after "Marisa" returned to her room for the night, there was a knock on her door and a conference attendee whom she recognized asked to speak to her for a few minutes. "Marisa" politely refused and arranged to see the individual the following morning at breakfast. This gave her the opportunity to "undo" her previous behavior and to regain her sense of self-confidence and security in her own judgment process.

Within a few more months, all of the symptoms began to disappear and the guilt greatly subsided, although there were residual elements that would continue to surface for several years.

An example of a male with a similar *hiding* problem will further help clarify the concept of "all the nitty-gritty details."

- CHUCK, *an athletic and handsome young executive, age 26, arrived at his first interview with a complaint of sexual impotency and loss of all sexual desire. He was only married for two years and until his recent promotion had no sexual problems. In fact, both he and his wife insisted that their sex life was exciting, varied and fulfilling. (Confirmed in an interview with his wife.) At first, "Chuck" tried to blame physical exhaustion and the stress of his new promotion at work for the problem. As the therapist, I did not accept this explanation since he had just had a complete physical examination and was diagnosed to be in excellent health. In fact, it was his own physician who had referred him to me for sex therapy, believing the cause of his impotence to be psychological or emotional.*

  After some minimal resistance, "Chuck" related the following incident as the only sex-linked occurrence he could remember around the time the problem began. With his new promotion, "Chuck" had also received a membership to a private health club that the company used for its executives. In the first week of his new job, he was invited to play racquetball with the other executives and gladly agreed. When he arrived, the game was already in progress. He quickly changed into his gym clothes, joined the others and had a wonderful time, impressing his new associates with his sports' ability.

  After the game, one of the vice-presidents suggested that the group shower, change, and then go to one of the local restaurants for some beers and something to eat. "Chuck" was invited and gladly accepted, feeling, for the first time, that he was accepted as "one of the boys." However, when the others headed for the locker room to shower, "Chuck" was delayed since he had to have an identification photo taken for his new membership card. When he finally arrived in the locker room, the rest of the men were in the showers, an open area with no curtains or separations.

*As "Chuck" undressed, he became aware that he was not only staring at the other
naked men and **at their genitals** but that he was also becoming sexually stimulated.
He immediately put his street clothes on over his gym clothing and left the locker
room, feigning illness.*

   *From that evening on, his behavior totally changed, both at home and at work.
Formerly quite affectionate and a "touchy-feely" type, he now avoided all physical
contact with his wife. At work, he avoided coffee breaks and always had an alibi for
not joining the others after work for a few beers. Eventually, his alibis wore off and
he agreed to have sex with his wife. That was when he first failed to get an erection.
He was embarrassed and confused by his impotence and refused to discuss it with
her. Sleep was disturbed by nightmares that he "couldn't remember." Finally, he
went to see his family physician and was referred to me.*

For weeks, following the admission of the locker room incident, "Chuck"
denied knowing any reason that he should have behaved this way and vehemently denied (too strongly) that he had ever had a homosexual experience or
that he had ever been molested as a child. When I slowly pushed him harder
in this area, he began missing appointments and it looked like he was going to
quit therapy.

Surprisingly, after about a month, he called for an *"emergency"* session. He
said that he couldn't take it any more and was now willing to do whatever was
necessary to alleviate his problems.

   *In great distress and with a great deal of emotion, "Chuck" related that, between
the ages of 12-14, he was sexually molested by a roomer in his mother's home. He
said that he never told his mother since they desperately needed the money and he
didn't want to cause a problem (rationalizations). Very reluctantly, he related the
details of the abuse by the roomer. He and the roomer shared the same bedroom but
had their own beds. The roomer practiced Yoga nightly, in the nude, and encouraged
"Chuck" to join him. He did. From this initiation, the roomer would lie on "Chuck's"
bed to discuss Yoga with him (both of them still nude). After a month or more, the
roomer offered to massage "Chuck," starting with his back and concentrating on
his buttocks and perineal areas; then would have him turn over and beginning with
his chest would end up at his penis.*

   *On the second night of massage, the roomer masturbated "Chuck" to orgasm
(his first). From there the progression was predictable. It was now "Chuck's" turn
to massage the roomer and masturbate him. Mutual fellatio followed within a few
days. Throughout relating the details of his molestation, "Chuck" insisted that he
tolerated the situation only for his mother's sake.*

It took several weeks of *highly confrontational* therapy to finally elicit the
facts that *"Chuck" had enjoyed the sex and that when the roomer left, that he
missed it. He also admitted that he had continuously masturbated to memories
of these incidents with the roomer from age 14 into his marriage.* These last
two admissions could easily have been considered to be the *"core"* of the
abuse, however, there was a nagging thought in my mind that there could be
even more.

Without this last admission, allowing "Chuck" to have been a resistant
victim, forced into sex by the roomer would have led to the wrong therapeutic

approach and never resolved the real problems i.e., his *terrible guilt* about enjoying the sex with the roomer and his continually masturbating to the memories leading to his self doubts about his masculinity and his sexual normality.

A third *late admission* surfaced several months later. "Chuck" admitted that during the locker room incident, one of his nude fellow workers in the showers at the gym *resembled the roomer to a remarkable degree* and while staring at him in the showers, "Chuck" had fantasized about having sex with him.

This was the last and true *"core."* Not only did he feel *guilty* over his present fantasies but the *guilt* from his past behavior was magnified by the current, related sexual reaction in the locker room. Without pushing and being confrontational with "Chuck," the critical issues in the case would never have surfaced or been available for the therapist to treat.

Lastly, in "Chuck's" distorted thinking, he felt that because he fantasized sex with men, *he would eventually have to have sex with a man.* "Chuck" had never heard of *bisexuality* or *sexual preference*. "Chuck" did not realize that, although he would probably again experience attraction to specific male types (who resembled the roomer), that whom he had sex with would always be his choice and not determined by his past behavior or experiences (molestation).

Following this re-education, "Chuck" was able to progress swiftly and in less than a month was once again able to have sex with his wife. "Chuck's" behavioral sexual preference was heterosexual monogamy. He had made the decision that his *homosexual side* could and would be satisfied with masturbation *for the time being,* leaving future possibilities to a change in this decision open. The case was concluded at what I label a *"PRN"* status (call in when necessary), with the door always open if "Chuck" ever wanted to go further in therapy regarding the early molestation period or if any new sexual problems occurred. To date (some seven years), "Chuck" has been doing fine and calls in, at least once a year, usually around the holidays, to give me an update on himself and the family.

To clarify the need for full disclosure with new or resistant survivors, I have often used the metaphor of a *medical visit* to the physician's office for an embarrassing problem, such as the possibility of a sexually transmitted disease.

If the patient, due to fear of judgment, punishment or rejection, leaves out *specific and graphic details*, the doctor may make a wrong diagnosis and then prescribe the wrong medication and treatment. The patient will then be worse off than if he/she never went to the physician in the first place. Even small children are able to understand the significance of the metaphor as long as it is stated in vocabulary specific to their developmental age.

DEFINITION OF THE THERAPIST'S ROLE

It is also important for the therapist to *define his/her role* as a "therapist" to the survivor. This definition should include several factors:

- Assuring the survivor that the therapist will not be judgmental or punitive.
- Explaining the *neutral position* of the therapist.

In this area, care must be taken to clarify that the therapist is not a father or mother, is not a representative of the law or other authority, is not a friend, in the usual sense of the word, but is supportive and on the side of the survivor, and, most importantly, that the therapist is there to help.

Listening

In supervising many new therapists over the years, another of my most frequent criticisms has been that *they have never learned to listen.* Lecturing, preaching, interrupting, rapid-fire questioning, taking notes during the session, answering telephones and other forms of distraction replace the art of listening to what the survivor has to say, needs to deal with, or must reveal to the therapist.

During sometimes lengthy *pauses*, a lack of the necessary patience to wait until the survivor is *ready* to speak or to continue often disrupts his/her concentration and train of thought. Even more frequently, the therapist's interruption gives the survivor a convenient excuse to *forget* what he/she was talking about. As stated in prior sections, the survivor will use any excuse or alibi to avoid a sensitive, embarrassing or guilt provoking topic and, *too often*, the therapist provides the way out.

I have experienced *pauses* of as long as three to five minutes, a seeming lifetime of silence in a therapy session. Usually, the wait is well worth it. Often, what occurred during the *pause* was that the survivor was fighting with himself/herself over revealing something difficult or embarrassing, betraying a confidence, or identifying an abuser. A helpful rule of thumb to remember is:

- *The pause may, and usually does, identify a crucial area and/or subject for the therapist, if he/she is attentive and willing to listen!*

The Less Said By The Therapist The Better

As a result of the need for proper listening skills, I have developed the concept of *Cue Words*, in order to accomplish good listening skills and yet keep the session moving. I suggest the use of a few carefully chosen cue words rather than the lengthy lectures or comments that therapists so often use. Some of the ones I use most often are:

- *"Because?"* For statements or feelings expressed without reasons.
- *"And?"* There must be more to the thought/statement.
- "'Pzzzzzt!" A polite "I don't believe you."
- "Picture?" I don't understand. Make me see a picture of what you're talking about.
- "Tilt!" You're off the subject. Get back to it.

- "Bellybutton!" This term is used where statements or behavioral changes that the therapist finds hard to believe are concerned. It means don't tell me, *show* it to me by examples in your daily life.

Many survivors, to prove *change* to the therapist, will make statements such as:

- I've learned to love myself.
- I'm not the same person anymore.
- I don't need therapy anymore.
- I'm not a "wimp" anymore."
- I'm assertive now and can handle anyone.

When the survivor knows that the therapist will use *bellybutton* and ask for concrete proof of his/her statements by some behavioral example that can be verified by witnesses, the attempted deceptions and lies are minimized. Utilizing *cue words* is a skill that requires experience and practice before the therapist can become proficient in their use.

Hope

It is important, at the very first opportunity, for the therapist to communicate to the survivor that:

- survivors are not sick, perverted, dirty, abnormal, etc.
- their future depends on working through their feelings, especially their anger and/or rage reactions.
- the survivor did not cause the problem, the offender/abuser did.
- the offender never has the right to do what he wants, regardless of the relationship, the reasons, the circumstances, his/her position of authority, etc.
- survivors need a return to reality not judgment, punishment, distortion, etc., and finally that
- survivors should be proud not ashamed — they made it, they survived!

Where this last factor is concerned, some explanation is necessary to assure that the survivor does not misinterpret this statement to mean that the therapist is implying that the survivor should be proud of having been sexually assaulted.

Terms, Adjectives, Body Language and Emotional Reactions

The survivor's *choice of words* can tell the therapist a great deal about:

- 1. how he/she feels about what happened,
- 2. how much guilt exists,
- 3. how judgmental the survivor is being about himself/herself, and
- 4. how much rapport, trust and confidence the survivor has.

The above four factors will be exposed in word choices as well as in spontaneous emotional reactions.

When, for example, a little girl states that *"he took an ugly little worm out of his pants,"* it is far more significant than if she used the term *"penis"* and much more credible. For a preadolescent or early adolescent boy to use slang sex terms, such as *"cock" and "fuck"* rather than precise anatomical or medical terms indicates much more trust and rapport with the therapist and also increases credibility.

Adding an *adjective* to a term may clearly indicate the degree of guilt, anger, or pain that the survivor is communicating. For example *"It was dirty, filthy, disgusting, and sickening"* is far more emotional and revealing than *"It was terrible."*

Keeping track of the survivor's terms and adjectives also enables the therapist to measure desensitization and progress over a period of time and indicates when the next level of therapy can be initiated. For example, the survivor's spontaneous statement *"You know, therapy is not as bad and scary as I first thought it was. I really don't mind coming and talking about having sex with Mr. J____ (his teacher)"* clearly informs the therapist that he/she can now probe deeper and deal with more potentially disturbing areas such as the survivor's present fantasies and needs.

All of these factors are the therapist's best diagnostic tools. Once the therapist has mastered the skill of listening, then, learning to concentrate and to pay attention to *anything and everything* the survivor says or does is paramount in importance.

Regarding *body language*, a change of position, change of facial expression, a sudden downward glance or avoidance of prior eye contact, all *signal* the attentive therapist that a sensitive, painful or embarrassing area has been broached or that the survivor is lying. Depending on the situation, the therapist may choose silence with some form of physical support, such as simply nodding his/her head or moving or leaning closer. The therapist may also choose some form of verbal support, from the simplest *"Uh-huh"* to *"Take your time"* or *"Are you O.K.?"* or *"Do you want to continue?"* The therapist, at this point, must know the survivor and know what is most appropriate for the particular situation. Where suspected lying is concerned, confrontation by the therapist *at the time of the lie* is an appropriate action.

Caveat: Under no circumstances should the therapist use the too frequently stated *"I understand"* or *"I know how you feel"* where survivors are concerned, unless he/she has been a victim of sexual abuse and is willing to disclose that fact. Rapport can be lost with this one patronizing statement. Rather than perceiving it as support, the survivor will most likely perceive it as artificial or patronizing and then become angry, and rightfully so.

During supervision, I have observed this reaction on videotape, countless times, when a new or inexperienced therapist makes this critical mistake and then cannot understand the survivor's reaction of anger and hostility.

Regarding *emotional reactions,* any emotional response during therapy will have some significance. What the therapist must be on guard for and closely observe are the emotional reactions that are unexpected, the *spontaneous and uncontrolled emotional reactions* that even the survivor did not or could not anticipate.

When such a reaction occurs, the therapist must make the decision to interrupt the material being shared at the moment and explore the reasons for the emotional reaction or outburst or, on the other hand, to allow the survivor to continue with the account or disclosure and deal with the emotional reaction when the survivor has finished.

This decision depends on the difficulty the survivor may be having in the telling of a particular event, reaction, behavior, etc., and the possible *loss* that an interruption could cause. In either case, only training and experience will allow the therapist to make the correct decision.

Survivors Are Extremely Sensitive To Lies Or Manipulations

While supervising a new therapist who had been added to the treatment staff of an outpatient clinic, I observed the following incident on videotape.

- CHRISTOPHER, *a young male psychologist, just out of graduate school with his masters degree and freshly out of a clinical internship in a state mental hospital, was conducting his first interview with a 15-year-old male who had been molested. Early in the first interview, the boy stated "It was terrible, awful, the worse thing that ever happened to me! I still feel dirty and contaminated!"*

   Without the least hesitation or time to think, the young psychologist replied "I know, I know! I understand just how you feel."

   *Immediately, the young boy became enraged, stood up and yelled down at the stunned psychologist "Oh, yeah! **When did you get fucked in the ass?**" The psychologist stammered something so quietly it was not picked up on the videotape and the boy left the room, slamming the door.*

A more appropriate response that the young psychologist might have chosen could have been: *"It certainly must have been a terrible experience for you. I really don't know what you must have gone through but I'd like to, if you are willing to share it with me."*

Not only is support present in this response but also a chance to gain trust with openness and honesty. It may also encourage the survivor to continue with the story, going further into detail in order to help the therapist to understand.

Where *choice of terms, adjectives and emotions* (discussed above) are concerned, the therapist will be most effective and miss the least amount of important material if the following principle is followed.

Assume Nothing!

In training new therapists, I always suggest that where any form of sexual abuse is concerned, regardless of the age of the survivor, that he/she use the analogy that he/she had just arrived from *another planet and knows nothing about the sexual behaviors of human beings*. The therapist then stresses to the survivor that he/she needs every word, phrase and term clearly defined and explained in order to see a clear picture of exactly what had occurred. Using the therapist's own background knowledge or personal experiences can cause confusion and lose valuable material while it is fresh in the survivor's memory. This is especially true in the session where the facts of the abuse are first divulged.

A tragic example can best demonstrate this all important point.

- TONY, *a good-looking, well-developed 16-year-old male, was sent to the old New Jersey State Diagnostic Center (now defunct) on a charge of juvenile delinquency involving impregnating his 14-year-old sister,* JILL. *Since both "Tony" and his sister admitted the charges, the case seemed cut and dry and the only diagnostic or therapeutic work left was to decide on a course of future action. The choices were either to return "Tony" to his home under strict supervision, or to send "Tony" to a reformatory for punishment (since there was little treatment available in those days.)*

  However, my gut reaction was that there was something wrong in this case. "Tony" just seemed too naive, open, and innocent for this particular charge and there was definitely something unusual about the whole family. The social worker on the case was asked to do a really in-depth workup on the family while I decided to do some brief therapy with "Tony" on an emergency crisis basis.

  Following the principles outlined above, I asked "Tony" to make believe that I was from another planet and knew nothing about the sexual or reproductive behavior of humans. Smiling, he agreed and thought this would be an interesting "game." I then instructed him to take me through the impregnation of his sister, step by step, leaving nothing to my imagination and the following story emerged.

  Due to money problems in the family, "Tony" and his sister were only allowed one bath per week. Since he was older, "Tony" went first. To save money, he was not to drain the water but leave it for his sister to bathe in. Being a normal adolescent, he became stimulated while washing his genitals and proceeded to masturbate to ejaculation. "Jill" then bathed, not knowing what "Tony" had done. A month or so later, "Jill" announced that she was pregnant. When "Tony" was questioned by his parents, he admitted to masturbating in the bathtub and they told him that that was how his sister became pregnant and that he was the father.

  When I recovered from my shock at hearing his story, I asked "Tony" about his intercourse experiences and he admitted that the whole family "played those fun games" on a regular basis: "Tony" with his mother, and "Jill" with her father. The younger children were allowed to watch and were taught to pleasure themselves and each other through masturbation. When asked about babies, "Tony" stated that they were a "gift of God." Neither "Tony" or "Jill" connected pregnancy to the family's "fun games" in any way.

I then spoke to "Jill," who was also at the Diagnostic Center. She readily admitted playing the "fun games," not only at home but also with several of the boys on the football team at school. She also discussed playing the "fun games" with her father but added that she and "Tony" were forbidden to have intercourse with each other, "since it was unnatural."

The social worker on the case was informed and reluctantly (due to her own personal embarrassment) discussed the "fun games" with "Tony" and "Jill's" parents who surprisingly readily admitted that this was their only pleasure since they couldn't afford T.V. or any other form of entertainment. They added that *"it was the best way to show their kids that they loved them."* Needless to say, the parents were referred for evaluation and found to be of borderline intelligence and socially retarded. They had kept their family in almost total isolation.

The real *trauma* in this case occurred at the arrest. The exposure to public ridicule by peers and neighbors and the deriding and callous attitude of the juvenile officers in the case did incredible damage to both "Tony" and "Jill." Needless to say, the family had to be relocated. A total program of re-education and resocialization training was undertaken. Both "Tony" and "Jill" were provided with specialized sex education and therapy. "Jill" had her baby and, due to the unusual circumstances of the case, the parents were allowed to adopt the child as their own. Supervision was provided by the then Bureau of Children's Services on a fairly intensive level.

Through psychological testing, "Tony" was found to be of above average to superior intelligence and, with a great deal of tutoring, improved in his school work sufficiently to go to a local community college.

Without the principle of *Assume Nothing* as a guide and without listening to *gut reactions*, the true facts of this case would never have emerged. "Tony" and "Jill" would have ended up in reformatories and the rest of the young children would have continued to be unwittingly sexually abused.

It is important to state here that I have dealt with several hundred cases *where the surface facts in no way reflected the true facts of the case.*

CONCLUSIONS

Since interviewing usually precedes treatment and begins in the first contact with the survivor, it is essential to develop the necessary skills to accomplish this task in a positive and professional manner, before attempting treatment with any survivor of sexual abuse. Interviewing cannot occur effectively without taking into mind the feelings and sensitivities of the survivor.

As in all areas of survivor treatment, the needs and best interests of the *survivor* must take precedence over any needs and interests of the therapist.

As I will reiterate over and over again throughout this work, the *survivor* has already been victimized and therapists, in their attempts to help him/her *cannot* use them as *"guinea pigs"* to advance their professional repertoire or to aid them in becoming financially successful.

9

Ten Initial Steps in Survivor Treatment

In Chapters 1 to 6, the makeup, personality and other dynamics of the survivor were discussed. Chapters 7 and 8 discussed pre-treatment considerations and an overview of treatment issues. Emphasis on the need for treatment now becomes paramount in our discussion of this complex subject. Sexual molestation does not simply go away nor will it cure itself. Trained, professional intervention is necessary for a minimum of a short, limited amount of time in the recovery process of some survivors and for a great deal of time in the recovery process of other survivors.

From my 31 years of various experiences with survivors, I have found that ten important and progressive steps are necessary in the survivor treatment process. These steps are listed in chart form in this chapter.

Each of these ten steps in survivor treatment will be discussed with practical examples of each and also with practical suggestions as to how each might be implemented.

RETURN CONTROL/RESPONSIBILITY TO THE SURVIVOR

As discussed in Chapter 7, since *control* was a primary factor throughout the abuse or attack and usually lasted during the entire relationship in long-term abuse, it is imperative to return this control to the survivor from the very first contact. Of all the pervasive feelings that survivors experience and eventually relate, the most frequent and damaging one is that they no longer feel they have control over their lives or even over their daily functioning.

Control in sexual abuse can take many forms.

- In *sexual assault*, the control originated during and following the assault.
- In *incest* it may have existed throughout the survivor's entire lifetime.
- In *long-term child/adolescent seductive sexual molestation*, the control factor is not usually recognized at the beginning of the relationship.

The delusion that the survivor is in control is proffered with the abuser's statements such as "It's your decision! — We'll do whatever you want to do, when you're ready!" etc. It is usually only when the survivor begins to refuse the demands of the molester that the control surfaces, either through some form of coercion, physical threat, blackmail (pictures or videotapes of the survivor apparently enjoying an overt sexual behavior with the molester are their favorites) or any overt threat of loss (scoutmaster's assistant can be fired, teacher's pet can be replaced, etc.).

Control and Decision Making

Since control issues frequently involve decision making, the therapist must take great care not to fall into the trap of answering control-oriented requests such as *"Tell me what to do,"* or *"How shall I handle this or that situation,"* or even *"Do you want to see me next week?"*

Survivors attempt these ploys for two major reasons:

- they are so used to being told what to do that they fear making a decision on their own, and

- they don't want the *responsibility* of making any decision about their lives. If they do and fail at anything, their already large amount of guilt will be incremented. If the therapist makes a decision for the survivor and it fails, it is then his/her fault, not the fault of the survivor. When faced with a standstill and possible damage to the therapeutic process, the therapist *may* offer a reasonable number of suggestions or alternatives *as long as the final decision is that of the survivor.*

One of the most frequent situations where this dilemma occurs is when the survivor relates a secret or traumatic part of the abuse that he/she has never told anyone before. The question of whether to share this material with a parent, spouse, significant other, friend, etc., is always one, in my experience, where the survivor wants the therapist to make the decision. *To do so would be a serious error.* In situations of this type, what appears most helpful is to explore:

- the *comfort level* of the survivor with the newly divulged information,

- the *expected reactions* of the proposed receiver of the information, and

- the *comfort level* of the survivor regarding the expected reactions of the receiver.

The therapist may then aide the survivor in evaluating the *emotional price* of divulging the new information, and provide a time frame for the survivor to consider all of the above factors.

Caveat: The decision does not have to be made in the same session in which the question was asked.

The positive rewards for the survivor of making his/her first major decision make the stress and frustration that will be experienced in the above process well worth it. *Patience and firmness* on the part of the therapist are critical during decision-making sessions, especially regarding revealing facts about the abuse. These facts will usually not only include acts that were perpetrated on the survivor by the molester but, equally importantly, will include *reactive emotions* experienced by the survivor towards the abuser as well as towards others perceived as indirectly to blame.

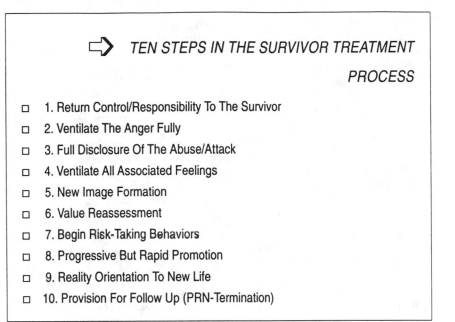

⇨ *TEN STEPS IN THE SURVIVOR TREATMENT*

PROCESS

☐   1. Return Control/Responsibility To The Survivor

☐   2. Ventilate The Anger Fully

☐   3. Full Disclosure Of The Abuse/Attack

☐   4. Ventilate All Associated Feelings

☐   5. New Image Formation

☐   6. Value Reassessment

☐   7. Begin Risk-Taking Behaviors

☐   8. Progressive But Rapid Promotion

☐   9. Reality Orientation To New Life

☐   10. Provision For Follow Up (PRN-Termination)

VENTILATE THE ANGER FULLY

One of the most difficult decision-making sessions that I ever experienced involved JERRY, a 31-year-old male who had been sodomized (raped) painfully and forcibly by his father from age 11-14.

While the facts of the case were known to the mother, "Jerry's" anger and rage towards her for permitting this to go on, year after year (in his perception), had never been expressed. The reason that the need to deal with this issue with his mother was so urgent was that "Jerry" was compulsively fantasizing and masturbating to raping older women who reminded him of his mother. Also, he was treating her quite miserably — screaming and yelling at her, threatening her, demeaning her in any way he could and, in general, making her life (and his) unbearable since he still lived at home.

Normally, "Jerry" was a quiet and passive-type individual who was highly intelligent and preferred to discuss everything on an *intellectual level*. While he could *verbalize* his anger, there was no more emotion in his expressions of anger than if he were discussing the weather or relating a complicated computer problem he had dealt with at work. He insisted that he *felt* the emotion but just *"couldn't get it out!"* His "emotional tanks" were overflowing and close to exploding. Ventilating these feelings, especially the rage he felt towards his mother, became a primary and paramount goal of therapy.

Regular monitoring of "Jerry's" behavior was also critical. Even when he began ventilating the anger, his behavior towards his mother and his masturbation fantasies did not essentially change. It was only when every minute anger element was fully released with the degree of emotions attached to the anger that changes began.

FULL DISCLOSURE OF THE ABUSE/ATTACK

One of the treatment methods I most frequently employ in cases like "Jerry's" is a type of *Guided Imagery* (fully discussed in Chapter 10). Guided imagery is a type of mild self-hypnosis that is less threatening to survivors than formal hypnosis and one in which the survivor maintains total control of the situation. Stories, called *embedded metaphors*, are used to evoke memories or to produce emotional responses in an indirect, rather than direct manner.

- *When all else had failed to get "Jerry" to fully ventilate his anger and rage, guided imagery was explained to him and suggested as a possible means of getting to the deeper feelings. "Jerry" liked the idea and agreed.*

  In his next scheduled session, I played some soft, relaxing, instrumental music in the background, had him sit back and become as relaxed as possible (with some direct progressive relaxation suggestions) and then proceeded to relate the events of his sexual molestation **but** *as if it were happening to another child that was a close and special friend of his. I changed many of the facts of the case but kept the essential elements in the metaphor: the wicked king as the molester and the evil queen (the child's stepmother) as the passive but knowing accomplice. As the story progressed, slowly and with colorful details, "Jerry" began to cry softly. Tears rolled down his cheeks as he clenched his fists and began slowly pounding the arms of his chair. When I felt the time was right, I had the survivor in the story go to his friend for help and support and asked "Jerry" to pick up the story from there.*

  What happened next was incredible. His face changed and the tears stopped and were replaced by a look of **pure hatred** *with accompanying verbal outrage and condemnation of both the king and the queen. Slowly, the rage intensified and "Jerry" began walking around the office, his voice growing louder and louder as he screamed obscenities against both parental figures in the story and suggested to his victimized friend methods of torture, revenge and horror that should be inflicted on the pair. After a half hour or so, "Jerry" was exhausted, sat back in the chair, and wept deeply and at length. I gently touched his arm and he looked up at me and smiled through his tears.*

  Later, after he had composed himself, "Jerry" recounted how he **had always been taught by both his parents that to show emotions was a sign of weakness and encouraged attack and harm from others.** *Also, he remembered that his father strongly felt and conditioned him to believe that* **"only little girls, fags and sissies ever cried."**

Treatment progress was rapid after that session and could be verified by the total change in his masturbation fantasies. His new fantasies no longer involved rape fantasies but now involved a girl he had been dating for some time and felt he could love and possibly marry. The new fantasies were also warm, sensitive and loving.

In one way or another, the survivor's feelings, whether sorrow, hurt, fear or anger/rage *must be thoroughly ventilated* if any real and permanent changes are to occur.

Naturally, there are as many varied forms of Guided Imagery as there are therapists using the technique. The above format is only one of the many that I employ, depending entirely on the survivor I am treating at the time and the circumstances and needs of the case.

VENTILATE ALL ASSOCIATED FEELINGS

In addition to the primary feelings and emotions, the therapist must make sure that all other *associated or attached feelings* and emotions are also ventilated. These could include:

- love and attraction simultaneously with anger and hate (ambivalence),

- feelings of self-hate and disgust,

- feelings of fear of recurrence,

- feelings that he/she may genetically pass the trait to his/her offspring,

- feelings of sexual attraction for the molester, etc.

Caveat: As stated in prior discussions, only the *lack of behavioral change*, especially of any unwanted behaviors or fantasies, points to the presence of an unrevealed or still unshared factor surrounding either the survivor or the abuse. The survivor's own evaluation of his/her progress and where he/she stands at any given point in therapy are very valid indicators that change has either occurred or not occurred. However, *confirmation* from an outside source remains a necessity since survivors may report positive changes *only* to please the therapist or to prove that they are really working and progressing.

AMBIVALENCE

One of the most problematic factors in dealing with survivors is the presence of *ambivalent feelings* towards the abuser. In both incest and seductive pedophilia/hebophilia, I have encountered survivors who both hated and loved their abuser *at the same time.* They were experiencing ambivalence. This very important factor often causes problems in therapy, especially when the therapist does not elicit it and also makes negative, condemning statements about the abuser. A good ruler to use, regarding ambivalence is: *the longer the relationship lasted, the more chance that ambivalence will exist, have to be brought to the surface, and then accepted as natural and nothing to be ashamed of.*

A value that parents fail to teach or espouse is that we can *always love someone yet, at times, hate something he/she does.* We have all used that value many times in our lives and yet do not think to teach it to our children or to survivors. An example is important at this point.

• *One of the incestuous fathers I was treating,* JESS, *(affectionately known by his peers and by some of the staff as* GRANDPA*) finally, after four years, was able to get his daughter,* JANINE *(his victim) to agree to come and see him for a visit. She was in therapy and her therapist agreed that the visit and the possible confrontation could be beneficial. In the session preceding the visit, "Jess" told me, that regardless of what his daughter did, he would not react or leave the office. He had accurately predicted that there would be some negative emotions forthcoming.*

    *I met "Janine," her mother, and her therapist and escorted all of them to my office. After I assured them that the abusive father would not harm them or become assaultive (he had been quite physically as well as sexually abusive at home), I sent for him. He walked in and stood by the door. After minimal social chit-chat ("How are you?" "I'm happy to see you," etc.,) I asked "Janine" if she had anything she wanted to either ask or say to her father. She got up from her chair, walked over to him and **slapped him as hard as she could** while screaming at him about all the anger and negative effects that the abuse had generated in her. "Janine's" tirade went on for more than ten minutes (an eternity for all involved) and then she calmly wept, put her arms around him and said **"Daddy, I'd like to kill you right here and now but I still love you!"***

    This statement was more painful and cutting to her father than anything else that had happened to him since his exposure and arrest. It would take many, many group and individual sessions before "Jess" could talk about the visit without weeping and becoming so emotional that he could not speak.

    "Janine's" therapist informed me privately that ambivalence was the area that was causing the most conflict and confusion for the young teenage girl since "all of her family and friends were telling her she should hate him and never forgive him for what he had done to her."

Here we can clearly see yet another classical example of how well-meaning individuals (especially family and close friends) can cause more harm and damage to a survivor who has already been badly traumatized. I encouraged the therapist to tell "Janine" that she had a right to still love her father while hating what he had done to her and to ignore what other people said. She eventually realized that she had as much right to her opinions and feelings as her family and friends had to theirs. "Janine" was able to return to see her father once or twice a year and finally grew able to tolerate being alone with him under video supervision.

Note: I would never allow this meeting to take place without video supervision for the protection of both the survivor and the offender. However, no microphones should be used for this meeting to be truly effective.

Incest Survivors Need One Session Alone with the Abusive Parent

I consider at least one such session between incestuous fathers or mothers and their victims (whether daughters or sons) to be *essential* since there are questions that the survivor must ask and statements that she/he must make that are no one else's business. The key question of most of the survivors of incest will always be *"Why me?"* since statistically, most incest occurs in a multi-child home. Even when the other children are also being incestuously abused, the abuser usually makes sure that they do not discuss their experiences with each other. Not surprisingly, the abuser's most frequent response to that question is *"Because I loved you the most!"* It may surprise some to know that this statement is more often the truth and not a rationalization due to yet another example of the *distorted love equals sex value of the abuser.*

NEW IMAGE FORMATION

Once all the facts, feelings and anger have been dealt with, therapy can begin to *focus on change.* The first goal to set is the formation of a *new image.* This new image will *always* differ from both the pre-abuse self-image and the post-abuse self-image.

An early learned principle when working with survivors is that *they will never again be the same.* This does not mean that they will necessarily be worse or less than they were before the abuse. It can mean that they may become *stronger, more assertive, more confident,* etc., depending on their reaction to the abuse and the success of the treatment they receive.

Here we see yet another urgent reason for adequate and proper training for anyone dealing with or intending to deal with this highly sensitive and easily damaged group.

In keeping with our returning control and responsibility rule (see section on *Control* earlier), exactly what the new personality and image of the survivor will be must remain her/his *sole choice*, not the choice of parents, significant others or even the therapist. This is one of the areas where *even suggestion* can be harmful due to the extreme vulnerability and suggestibility of the survivor at this stage of treatment. The therapist must take great care not to fall into any of the traps that the survivor will lay out while still encouraging and aiding her/him. The most frequent trap is asking the therapist to decide who he/she should become. Positive support and encouragement to have the decision made by the survivor is the best therapeutic choice in this situation.

In guiding the survivor in taking this first new-image-step, the therapist must be extremely alert as to the methods that the survivor uses in making this most important decision. Considering the survivor's self-doubts, vulnerabilities and often distorted perception and thinking, there are several serious dangers that need to be avoided. These dangers are listed for the reader in this chapter in table form.

It is important to remember that as long as we deal with survivors, there will always be new experiences, new reactions, and new choices since each survivor is unique and individual.

VALUE REASSESSMENT

Coupled with and inseparable from new image formation is *the development of a new set of values to live by.*

An Overview of Value Formation

Before any discussion of value change can be considered, we must first understand how values develop. Dealing with both offenders and survivors of all ages made it necessary to formulate a descriptive, easily understood value formation progression. I have developed a five stage value development schematic that has worked successfully for me for the last 30 years:

FIVE STAGES OF VALUE FORMATION

Stage 1 — The Prisoner Stage (From Birth to 2 Years)

- All values are learned from parents and other adults in the child's home.
- Absolute obedience is necessary for acceptance and love.
- No comparisons are made at this stage.

⇨ *NEW IMAGE DANGERS*

☐ 1. Trying to become what parents, friends or the therapist want them to be.

☐ 2. Imitating an idol that exists in their life that they not only admire but whom they perceive would not have allowed the abuse to occur.

☐ 3. Trying to become the exact opposite of who they were at the time of the original abuse. The problem here is that in doing this they also deny any and all personality traits that are positive and part of their original, pre-abuse personality.

☐ 4. Becoming so frightened and confused that they stay the way they are since they are comfortable with that personality.

☐ 5. Believing that they don't deserve to change and become happy because of what they had done (especially the possible times they wanted or initiated the sex); the guilt factor.

☐ 6. Not believing that change is possible for them: "I've always been like this and I always will be!" This is part of the damage done by the abuser. In later years, it becomes the cliche: "Once a ..., always a ...." and many, many, many more!

Stage 2 — The Neighborhood Stage (From 2 to 5 Years)

- Friends, neighbors, relatives and others outside the home introduce new values.
- Comparisons by the developing child begin, and result in confusion and the first negative perceptions of parents and self.
- The first blame and guilt for failures also occurs during this stage.
- *Inadequacy* as a characteristic most likely begins in this stage.

Stage 3 — The Societal Stage (From 5 years to Puberty)

- School, religion and the law introduce additional values.
- Teachers, ministers, priests, scoutmasters, policemen, and other authority figures become new parent symbols and comparison intensifies.
- Value confusion is strong, especially when a behavior is acceptable at home and is not acceptable in school or vice versa.
- The need to please adults appears strongest in this stage and the child is therefore more vulnerable to seduction by the child molester, especially when the home is not fulfilling his or her needs.
- Parent-substitute interaction during this stage is critical to the mature and stable development of the child. Each needs to know what values the other is teaching and which values they are in disagreement with.

Stage 4 — The Peer Stage (From the Onset of Puberty)

An abrupt psychological change occurs from the beginning of this stage until its completion, with the needs for acceptance and approval *shifting from adults to peers*. The initial result of this shift depends on the first three stages and how smoothly they were experienced.

Parents are most upset and disturbed about their children during this stage since they do not understand what is happening. Their formerly wonderful, obedient and loving child may now turn into a *monster* who is defiant, disobedient, argumentative and a constant source of irritation or even embarrassment.

In his/her quest for independence and personal identity, the child must now *break away* from the parents protection and direction and develop his/her own values, behaviors, decisions and even his/her own appearance (dress, hairstyles, etc.). The delusion that the awakening adolescent experiences is that these new decisions are his/her own, when in reality they are strongly influenced and dictated by peer standards and pressures. The fear of *being different* is magnified in this stage to its greatest proportions.

Parents who, for status' sake, force their adolescent to attend high school in shirt, tie and jacket can expect problems of all sorts as a result, including defiance, torn or damaged clothing and hostility (bordering on rage). For both the sex offender and the survivor, *this stage is the most upsetting and leaves a*

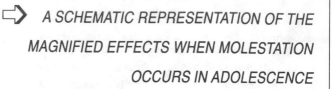

A SCHEMATIC REPRESENTATION OF THE MAGNIFIED EFFECTS WHEN MOLESTATION OCCURS IN ADOLESCENCE

BOYS

- If molested during stage 4 have a totally different reaction and experience. The need to be strong, macho and heterosexual dominates the male adolescent value system.

- A strong homophobic aura exists in male peer groups during this stage. In fact, it is my personal belief that this is the stage where true and intractable homophobia develops and remains with many males throughout their lives.

- Boys molested by older men during this stage cannot seek out support and comfort from their peers or from the majority of their male authority figure contacts, such as teachers, coaches, gym instructors, etc., or, most importantly, their fathers.

GIRLS

- If molested during stage 4 receive support, empathy and protection from both male and female peers as well as authority figures that they are involved with daily (e.g., their teachers).

- While the molestation is still traumatic, they do not feel rejected by their peers nor are they labeled or blamed for the occurrence, as frequently as boys are.

- They tend to report more readily and are much more motivated to become involved in therapy and then to get on with their lives. Naturally, there are exceptions to these reactions, especially when a girl is chronologically an adolescent but emotionally still a much younger child.

lasting set of effects that must be dealt with in therapy. The following problems may occur:

- Fears, self-doubts, confusion, shifts of loyalty, body-image problems and constant *testing* of both themselves and others.
- Communication abruptly stops and needs to be fostered regularly.
- Definitions of adult are fluid. Subtle help in deciding on a mature definition is needed but feared and/or rejected.
- Sexuality explodes and becomes a major focus. Indecisiveness and confusion about all aspects of sex dominate this stage.
- A war between old values (Stages 1, 2 and 3) and peer pressure occurs, and adds to the confusion.
- Guilt of all types flourishes and imprints.

- AIDS-phobia makes sexuality even more disturbing and confusing.
- Boy/girl expectations and demands separate more widely here than in any other stage.

Should sexual molestation occur during this stage, the effects will be *magnified* and become more *long lasting* than in any other stage. In addition, there is a major difference in peer reaction to an exposed molestation. These effects are displayed schematically in the accompanying diagram.

Two different types of examples of why boys *cannot* seek support from male authority figures follow:

- *While speaking to a high school senior class assembly on the effects of sexual molestation and the serious need for treatment when it occurs, I invited anyone who wanted to speak to me personally to remain after the assembly. (This had been pre-arranged with the school principal.) Six girls and five boys remained, forming two small groups on opposite sides of the auditorium.*

  In speaking to the girls first, I discovered that all but one were being incestuously molested at home. The sixth girl was molested by a male babysitter and never forgot the experience. All six were affected by the presentation and were now sobbing and allowing emotional reactions to pour out. There was little trouble in getting them all referred to therapists (this was pre-arranged with specialists in this area). The girls were willing to discuss their feelings with each other as a group and I networked them, since they all lived in the same general neighborhood.

  The five boys were a totally different story. Although seen individually and confidentially, I learned that they were all involved with the same teacher. The time span of the molestations ranged from a minimum of one year to three years. None of the boys would consider reporting the problem or becoming involved in therapy. Their unanimous opinion was that if the story were ever revealed they would have to leave school, leave home and run away to a different state. They anticipated total rejection, putdown and labeling as "fags" or "queers" should their friends (peers) or other teachers find out. The problem of the teacher was resolved with the school authorities without my revealing the facts or the identities of the boys. However, none of the boys (to the best of my knowledge) was ever treated for the molestations.

  Coincidentally, I was conducting a training seminar for all of the teachers, administrators and school board members of a different school district where a similar teacher-student sex scandal of several years duration had recently erupted. A male teacher had been arrested for his molestation of more than ten boys over a three year period. My function was to clarify and desensitize the situation. Still bothered and affected by the five boys in the first school, I decided to use a dramatic opening. I asked for a gym instructor or coach in the audience to stand up and help me with the presentation. A burly, muscle-bound football coach stood and said "Glad to be of service, Doc."

  I knew I had the right person. I then instructed my "assistant" to be prepared to answer a question as quickly as possible without thinking or hesitation. He agreed. The question was: "What would you do if you discovered that one of the boys on your basketball team has been sexually involved with one of the other male teachers in the school?" I then snapped my fingers and the coach instantly replied "Kick the fuckin' fag off of the team and make sure that all of the rest of my boys knew about these two perverts!"

Needless to say, the five boys' predictions had been more than correct. A silence fell on the entire auditorium and I then thanked the coach for explaining why the molestations in his school had been going on unreported for several years.

Until we change these destructive values and reactions in adults, including parents and anyone entrusted with molding the minds and values of our children, sex offenders will have little trouble finding as many victims as their perverse desires require/demand. As will be discussed in Chapter 12, Monmouth County, New Jersey's program *"It Happens to Boys Too ..."* is a simple and effective method of attempting to correct this inequity between the way girl and boy victims (survivors) are treated by both peers and adults in authority that they deal with. Boys need to be told that it is *acceptable and proper* to report their molestations without being labeled, rejected and ostracized. Without programs of this type, the *merry-go-round of sexual abuse* will continue perpetually.

Stage 5 — The "I" Stage

All other stages and values are reexamined and decisions for adult life are made in this stage. Most adults either never reach this stage or continue throughout life to fluctuate between Stage 4 and Stage 5, depending on their emotional maturity, reaction(s) to trauma, need for approval and degree of ego strength.

Adolescents need to be made aware of this goal early in their development and must be encouraged to make decisions that will result in happiness. They must be urged not to settle for mere acceptance by peers, but aim for self-acceptance.

SEX = LOVE (LUV!)

Another insidious value, learned early in the life of both the sex offender, who was molested as a child/adolescent, and the child victim is that of *"sex = love."* How often has the challenge *"If you loved me, you'd ..."* been used by teenagers as well as adults to get a sex partner to do their will? Equally damaging is the molester's (both pedophile and hebophile) explanation of his/her sexual behavior as *showing love* to the victim.

In the United States more than in any other country, the damaging and destructive phrase *"making love"* has been used — due to embarrassment or puritanical needs — to justify or explain sexual behavior. Parents caught in the act of sex teach children from the earliest age that what they are doing is "making love," not having sex. *Love* then becomes *sex* and vice versa, and physical disability, old age, etc., must mean that love no longer exists. Learned in the home, this becomes an easy tool for the molester to teach his victims all about adult lovemaking and to avoid the use of the dirty word "sex" at all costs. Even upon involvement in therapy, whether in a correctional setting or private practice, this *euphemism* acts as a defense mechanism against accepting the responsibility for the damage done to the victim. Hardened, repetitive compulsive rapists have stated in the beginning of therapy that they were only trying to show love to their victim (whether she wanted it from him or not!), or that they were hoping that if they satisfied her that she would then "love me."

VALUE CHANGE TECHNIQUES

No discussion of value change can be undertaken without first giving consideration to the important works of Professors Jane Loevinger and Lawrence Kohlberg. The reader is encouraged to take the time to research their all-important theories.

Changing a distorted, damaging or guilt-provoking value has been a seemingly impossible task both with the offenders and the survivors, as well. Traditional or behavioral modification methods have not worked for me in this area and have produced levels of frustration that, for many survivors, resulted in their quitting therapy. One of the most common guilt-provoking values found in these individuals is that of *masturbation guilt.* Regardless of the intellectual exercises that the survivor goes through, when he/she next masturbates, the guilt returns and is perceived as even stronger. Part of the reason for this is that in almost every survivor I have worked with who was involved in a long-term seductive type of molestation, including incest, there was at least one occasion during which he/she enjoyed the sexual behavior and also at least one occasion in which he/she may have initiated the sex. Masturbation could bring the memories of these instances back into consciousness and remove any denial of his/her part in the abuse, increasing the already large amount of guilt.

For years I struggled with this dilemma with no success until I developed the following explanation and homework assignment, as illustrated in the schematic. If one identifies the *unwanted behavior* and its underlying or associated *value(s),* but then jumps to the *change/confirm* step, failure results most of the time and the above mentioned frustration ensues. Adding the *source of the value* step and carefully analyzing this area before attempting to change the value produces a positive result. When tested (for example by masturbating that evening) the guilt is gone, the frustration does not occur and the individual feels encouraged to attempt to change other, more difficult and entrenched values.

One phenomenon I have observed in this process is that in the *source of the value* step there are *embedded attached values* in addition to the obvious one that is being worked on. An example, at this point, will help.

- JOHN, *when 11 years old, was caught masturbating in the bathtub by his mother. With a stern and shocked look, mother admonished "John," telling him that "he will run out of sperm and never have babies if he continues this dirty and disgusting practice." Although guilt-ridden and embarrassed for a short time, John continued with his masturbation but now experienced terrible guilt following each orgasm. Of course, he was careful to never again get caught by his mother. In working in therapy to change this value, "John" intellectually realized that he would not run out of sperm and that what he was doing was natural and not dirty. However, try as he might to change or eliminate the value, he suffered severe guilt after each masturbatory event. When "John" first used the above value change method, there was still no change in the guilt reaction. He was encouraged to search for an embedded attached value that might also have been learned from his mother (the source). When he came to the realization that his mother's love was dependent on his conforming to her values (total obedience) and that rejecting one of her values would result in his being rejected by her, he was able to see the total picture of conditioning that had occurred from his earliest memory. That evening "John's" masturbation was the best and most pleasurable he had experienced and he fell asleep content with no guilt reaction. "John" was also able to apply this same source method to rid himself of many other negative, limiting and guilt-producing values, and his progress in therapy accelerated.*

It appears quite clear that beneath each surface value that cannot be changed through normal therapeutic methods there is an important person in the child's life who taught him that *"love = obedience."*

Bringing memories that contain this value to consciousness must be an essential part of the value change process and must be initiated early in the overall treatment process with both the offender and the survivor. These insidious values are imprinted at an early age and will remain there, affecting behavior and self-image to the point of sexual dysfunctions if not resolved. The damage is multiplied in cases where *pleasure results in guilt* and the persistent tug of war produces a level of mental anguish that easily leads to alcohol, drugs, and other forms of escape from the pain.

There are many other distorted and destructive values that need to be identified when working with survivors.

"Sex = love" and *"obedience = love"* are two defective values that most frequently affect the adult behavior of this group. The remaining list of destructive values includes:

- Love = slavery,
- Acceptance = conformity,
- Sex = pain,
- Pleasure = evil,
- Love = punishment,
- Free will = delusion,
- Deviancy = genetic,
- Silence = loyalty,
- Love = loyalty.

The list is endless. However, the value change technique is the same for any distorted, justifying or deviant value that is identified.

The types of values that are of most concern to the therapist working with survivors include the following.

- Values about moral and religious concepts, especially good and evil, sin and punishment,

---

⇨ *VALUE CHANGE WORKSHEET USING*

MASTURBATORY GUILT AS A WORKING EXAMPLE

THE UNWANTED BEHAVIOR
➤ Guilt following each masturbatory episode.

THE ASSOCIATED VALUE
➤ Masturbation is dirty, sinful, abnormal, unhealthy.

THE SOURCE OF THAT VALUE AND ANY OTHER ASSOCIATED VALUES
➤ I was caught masturbating by mother and punished; mother also stated that masturbation would lead to insanity and sterility. An associated mother-taught value was that "obedience = love."

THE CHOSEN NEW VALUE
➤ Masturbation is normal and I don't have to give blind obedience to all of my mother's values to receive her love or to prove that I love her.

- values about sex and sexual preference (where applicable),
- values about life and the future,
- values about relationships, marriage and children (if applicable),
- values about educational and employment goals,
- social values and any and all other values that pertain to the survivor's present and future life.

All of these values must be uncovered, discussed and reformatted, utilizing experimentation (trial and error methods) and success/failure concepts.

In my experience, the easiest method of accomplishing this task has always been to suggest to the survivor a simple bottom line goal of *happiness* thus allowing happiness to become his/her new ruler. Very few survivors that I have worked with were ever truly happy, *even before the sexual abuse.* This appears to fit the profile of a large percentage of abused children and may be one of the factors that the abuser looks for in his/her search for a potential victim. The offender's often obvious purpose is to dangle his version of *happiness* on a string before the potential victim's eyes.

At this stage of therapy, a new and complete, personal and unique definition of happiness must be established by trial and error on the part of the survivor. The therapist's role in this process is to make sure that neither "seeming happiness" nor "immediate gratification" are mistaken for long-lasting, true and inviable happiness. A difficult task at best.

This happiness goal is impossible to achieve until the survivor changes *the way that he/she feels about himself/herself.* As long as there is guilt and self-recrimination and an utter dislike for his/her "friend-in-the-mirror" (refer to Chapter 13) there can be no happiness.

Once forgiveness and acceptance of himself/herself has begun, other behavioral changes will occur automatically, including self-esteem and self-concept enhancement.

SUBJECTIVE-JUDGMENT MEMORIES

A major resistance to any personal value change is the presence of unresolved *subjective-judgment memories.* A simple definition of this phenomenon would be:

> A subjective-judgment memory involves a value judgment about a past behavior that is based on parental or authority "rulers" and not the "rulers" of the child or adult. These "judgments" usually are negative and guilt-producing on an irrational level and the survivor is unable to resolve them, regardless of the methods he/she employs.

In cases where all reported problems have been dealt with in therapy and either self-punitive behaviors continue or there is a significant lack of any meaningful progress, the therapist should look for the subjective judgment memory phenomenon. A simple rule of thumb that appears to detect the phenomenon is:

- *Whenever a survivor is unable to forgive himself or let go of the guilt regarding a past behavior but has no problems, in the present, accepting the same behavior in a friend or peer, a subjective-judgment memory exists.*

Two examples will clarify.

- TODD *(introduced in Chapter 5) could easily discuss the gruesome details of his rapes both in his group and also with his friends with little or no problem. He could even share his sexual molestation by his older brother over a lengthy period of time with them with little discomfort or embarrassment. However, he adamantly refused to discuss with anyone except his therapist his obsession with other men's bodies in the dormitory and his masturbation fantasies of being sodomized by them or his using dildos to achieve orgasm.*

  When asked to bring these matters to his group, "Todd" threatened to quit therapy and complete a lengthy sentence. To "Todd" being homosexual was unforgivable, horrible and disgusting. He feared total rejection by anyone who found out. When asked by the therapist how he felt about other group members who had admitted to the same feelings and urges or even admitted to overt homosexual behaviors, his comment was "So what! They were only kids and lonely," or " They have a right to be anything they want to be and its nobody's business!"

  In other words, "Todd" saw no problem with other offenders doing what he had done but could not forgive himself for the same behavior. Had he done so, he might not have become a sexually assaultive person. The double standard is obvious.

Shortly after "Todd's" disclosure of this secret to his therapist, the therapist brought the general subject of homosexual behavior into a group discussion that "Todd" attended. Several of the offenders there admitted to homosexual experiences both when they were younger boys and also in the present. These disclosures had no effect on "Todd" who sat there silently and did not join the discussion.

• *Similarly,* MARK *admitted to his therapist that he had been peeping on his mother when she was changing clothes or coming out of the shower and then masturbating to incestuous fantasies about her. While openly admitting all of his other problems to his group, including his violent and shameful sexual assault (rape) of an elderly woman who was a deaf mute, he would never disclose his peeping-behavior secret to his peers or his group members. He was also unable to stop inflicting punishment on himself, which everyone felt was for his rape offense but which in reality was for his incestuous masturbation as a young boy. "Mark" simultaneously was understanding and nonjudgmental about two of his group members who had had actual long-term incestuous relationships with their mothers.*

Both instances involved a subjective judgment memory. For "Todd" it was his homosexual obsessions about the men in his dormitory and his subsequent masturbatory experiences to these fantasies, and for "Mark" it was his incestuously-motivated masturbation.

All subjective-judgment memories *must* be uncovered and resolved before any further therapeutic progress can be expected.

BEGIN RISK-TAKING BEHAVIORS

Concurrently with the value reassessment step in the survivor's therapy is the initiation of *risk-taking* behaviors. This step is sometimes more successful when included in the "New Image Formation Step."

Note: From this juncture on, progress will be rapid, confusing, and stormy and the therapist must always be alert to any possible accompanying problems.

The majority of traumatized survivors tend to isolate and avoid many of their former social, educational and interpersonal activities. They are not sure how others feel about them and often, *due to distorted guilt feelings,* project negative judgments on everyone around them. These guilt reactions are usually generated:

• By the abuser in his need to place all blame on the victim:
  • "If you weren't walking alone at night, this wouldn't have happened!" or
  • "If you weren't so cute and seductive, I wouldn't have done this!" or
  • "If you didn't open your door for me, I couldn't have raped you!" etc.

• By police, investigators and, even today, at times, by untrained or insensitive crisis workers asking questions like:
  • "What were you doing on that street all alone at night?" or
  • "Did you try to fight him off?" or
  • "Why didn't you tell your teachers or someone else what your father was doing to you?" or especially
  • "Why did you wait all this time?"

• By upset and embarrassed parents, relatives and friends:

- "Why didn't you come to me for help?" or
- "Why did it take you so long to tell someone?" or
- "Did you enjoy what was happening?" or
- "How am I ever going to face the relatives, neighbors, etc.?"

Effective therapy, at this stage, should have exposed all of these judgmental errors and dealt with them prior to the risk-taking step being initiated. The task now is to alter the behavior (the isolation, guilt and embarrassment) and to realistically help the survivor to face the fact that some of the above prejudiced and judgmental individuals will never change and that's okay. A new value must also be included. *Negative comments and judgments say nothing about the survivor but a great deal about the other person.*

Once this area has been *thoroughly* resolved, former positive behaviors that stopped after the trauma must *slowly* be reinstituted into the survivor's daily schedule. The most important old behaviors to be reactivated will be the activities that the survivor associated with the sexual assault/abuse. For example:

- walking in the park where the attack occurred,
- returning to a meeting at the troop where the boy scout was molested,
- shopping in the same place where the abuse occurred, etc.

Caveat: As with all other changes, the therapist must make sure that the *easiest and most likely to succeed* behaviors are attempted first in order to assure success.

In my experience, when risk-taking behaviors are first attempted, *group* behaviors are easier and much safer than *individual* behaviors. For example, going to a shopping mall with the family or a group of friends is preferable to a visit to an old friend on a one-to-one private basis. Since "nothing succeeds like success," the survivor should be encouraged to add old, risk behaviors slowly and in an *easy to more difficult priority order*. Repetition of a successful behavior is also important in order to establish an increasing comfort level until repeating the re-established behavior becomes easy, automatic, and fear free.

As time progresses, the tendency to *anticipate* a recurrence will subside. Also, the tendency to *generalize* the resultant fears will decrease. For example:

- *"Not all men who look at me are planning to assault me" replaces*
- "If I go there again, another rapist will hurt me."
- *"The park can be a safe, fun place for me to go with a friend" replaces*
- "If I go to the park, even with a friend, something terrible will happen to me again."

PROGRESSIVE BUT RAPID PROMOTION

Therapy promotion should begin during this phase of returning to old and formerly satisfying behaviors. Resistance to promotion, on the part of the survivor, will usually exist in the beginning of this phase and there may be times when the therapist has to subtly force the issue. The therapist's vacations,

---

⇨ *SUBJECTIVE JUDGMENT MEMORIES*

☐ Subjective judgment memory: A value judgment about a past behavior based on parental or authority values [rulers] that are not the values of the present child/adult

☐ Perfectionism develops — failure is assured

☐ Self punishing behavior results and affects motivation

☐ Severe guilt persists and affects all aspects of life

☐ The same behavior in others is considered acceptable

---

trips, and conferences offer ample opportunities for this type of forced promotion and will not be seen as rejection by the survivor. Upon resumption of treatment, the therapist should make an issue of the survivor's ability to cope on his/her own during the absence, even if it was only for one week. Promotion can then again be suggested using the missed session(s) as proof of the survivor's readiness for it. Should the survivor become overly concerned regarding the therapist's impending absence, a colleague's phone number can be offered should any emergency arise. In my experience, although subjectively perceived crises have occurred on one or two occasions, not one of my survivors has made use of the emergency number. It really becomes a form of "security blanket."

The *dependency on the therapist* that develops during treatment with survivors cannot be avoided but must be consistently monitored and worked on. This dependency is often a cause of the resistance to promotion in the beginning of this phase. However, as the survivor becomes more comfortable and confident with returning to old behaviors and old friends, the resistance usually becomes less and less. Naturally, *time tables* cannot be set since each survivor is different as is his/her degree of trauma.

If the resistance to promotion appears insurmountable, the therapist should definitely suspect that there are still facts or elements connected with the abuse that have not been exposed or discussed or that a degree of transference has occurred that neither party has been conscious of. *Confrontation with the survivor in either case is then both appropriate and necessary.*

For those therapists who *fear* taking this promotion/separation step in the treatment process, it must be remembered that nothing is written in stone or unchangeable. Even when promotion occurs along normal lines (weekly to biweekly to monthly to quarterly to PRN) there are no hard rules that the progression cannot be reversed for a short period of time, especially during some emotional occurrence (e.g., the first sexual event for a rape survivor, going away to camp for a child survivor, etc.).

Unfortunately, in my supervision of many therapists, one of my greatest fears has been that the insecure or unethical practitioner in private practice may continue weekly contacts for *too long* a time, due to his/her own insecurity about paying bills, having enough funds for a cruise or for skiing in the Alps, etc. As distasteful as it is to believe that there are therapists of this type, they do exist and need to be weeded out from any referral list for survivor treatment.

REALITY ORIENTATION TO A NEW LIFE

In this step of the survivor's treatment, the *concept of distancing* must be introduced and practiced. Distancing involves a *letting-go* of the past with all its fears, guilts, horrors, etc. It also involves *letting-go* of the old-self in preference to a new-self as discussed in New Image Formation. It is a difficult process for anyone and even more difficult for the survivor.

Over the years, I have had to invent a procedure for dealing with this problem and, as a result, *"Now Therapy"* came into existence (see Chapter 13). Basically, NOW is a self-confrontation, distancing technique whose major rule is that during the procedure only events, thoughts and personality traits that exist from awakening that morning to the time of the self-confrontation can be included in the session. *Nothing from the past, distant or close, can be mentioned, discussed or dealt with.* Once learned, the survivor becomes comfortable with distinguishing between the *"old me"* and *"the new or present me"* and can comfortably laugh, criticize and even admonish the "old me" while accepting, encouraging, and caring about "this me."

Once the distancing is accomplished, the reality of today must be faced. This new reality might include:

- "I am and always will be a survivor."

- "What I (the 'old me') did in the past will never go away and forgetting it will be harmful to me rather than helpful."

- "I now have to make changes in my life since I'm no longer the 'old me.' Once I make changes, I then need to let family, friends and others know what these changes are."

- "Trusting will always be a difficult but not impossible task for me and, if I go slowly and *test* people I want to trust, it will happen."

- "I will be *used* again but only with my permission. True friends do use each other and that's acceptable and appropriate."

Caveat: A redefinition of "being used" and "using others" must be carefully formulated and monitored.

- "New situations may frighten me for a long time but that's okay. Eventually, it will get easier and better."

Many, many other new realities will also need to be individualized according to the needs of the particular survivor.

PROVISION FOR FOLLOW UP (PRN)

I learned a long time ago that *terminating* therapy with the survivor was a crucial error. Survivors are never truly "cured" (a word that I wish could be eliminated from treatment concepts) so there will be times when, after a long period of separation, a survivor will need to return to treatment for a brief period, possibly a single session.

To make this lucidly clear, when the times comes, I explain the concept of *PRN* ("pro-re-nata" or "call in when necessary") and that it is my final promotion step for all of my survivors.

Termination implies not only the *end* of treatment but also implies that the survivor is now ready to handle all situations. This makes it difficult, if not impossible, for many survivors to phone in and ask for help when a recurrence of symptoms begins. The most frequent comment made when the survivor finally returns to see the therapist is *"I thought that since I finished treatment (was cured), I should be able to handle any situation by myself, so I was ashamed to call in; I felt like I was a failure!"*

PRN prevents this pressure and distortion from occurring. The therapist needs to carefully and honestly explain that a "cure" does not exist and that therapy is a lifelong process of growth. Also the therapist must inform the survivor that progress is never a *straight line upward* but that there are stages of growth, *leveling off* stages and even some *regressive stages,* although these regressions will never quite reach the lowest levels that formerly existed. This informing-process gives permission for the emancipated survivor to be *human,* when human means *imperfect.*

PRN also provides security for the survivor, whereas termination may produce panic and, at times, a regression to prove that he/she is not ready. As long as the survivor knows that he/she is not being thrown out or rejected and that he/she still may either call and speak to the therapist or even schedule an appointment, he/she normally retains the progress made to this point and continues to grow.

As stated in the above discussion, any new pressure-experience that the survivor faces could produce panic and a loss of the prior confidence. This often occurs when a *similar experience* to the original trauma occurs. An example may clarify.

- *Eight years after* JOAN, *an incest survivor, had successfully reached PRN status and returned to the majority of her former behaviors, she was "mugged" on the streets of New York. During a purse snatching incident, "Joan" was cut on the arm when the thief cut the straps of her handbag. In shock, she returned to her apartment, bandaged the arm (which later needed stitches) and mentally replayed the tape of an attack by her father when he used a knife and cut her on the same arm to force her to submit to his sexual demands. Fortunately a friend made an unexpected visit to "Joan's" apartment, found her with the door unlocked, sitting on the floor of the bathroom bleeding, and took her to a hospital. Knowing of her past trauma, he stayed the night and made her talk about her feelings. While this helped, she still refused to leave the apartment for almost a week and finally called me to talk. I was able to see her the same day and slowly connected the two incidents but emphasized the differences. At the end of the session, she reluctantly agreed to go out to dinner that night with her friend.*

"Joan" called me the next morning to say that she had "eventually relaxed a bit and had a fairly good time." The next day, with the friend picking her up and promising to take her home, "Joan" returned to work and explained what had happened to her supervisor and to her friends, who were supportive and helpful.

For "Joan," one session and several phone calls were all that were needed to put her back on track. Incidents like this could occur the rest of her life and as long as she knows she can return to her therapist, she will be more equipped to face them and deal appropriately with them.

From the above discussion, it should become clear that treatment for survivors is *a technique unto itself* and that the elements of the treatment process must be prioritized and follow a specific, logical sequence in order to undo the damage caused by the sexual abuser.

10

Specialized Treatment Techniques for Survivors: Unresolved and Unidentified Sexual Trauma

This chapter will deal specifically with specialized treatment techniques for two groups of survivors: survivors with unresolved sexual traumas and survivors with unidentified sexual traumas.

As promised in Chapter 6, this chapter will offer some specialized techniques that I have found to be both practical and successful for the above two problems. However, before we can discuss treatment methods and techniques for these two special categories, we once again have to review the means of *identifying* the problems themselves. Let us review the "practical rule of thumb" that was introduced in Chapter 6.

When a sudden sexual dysfunction occurs and causes discomfort, guilt or embarrassment for the survivor, the therapist should suspect either an unresolved or unidentified sexual trauma.

The major difference between the unresolved and unidentified sexual traumas depends on whether or not the sexual trauma is *consciously remembered but was never dealt with* or whether the sexual trauma was *repressed at the time of the abuse and is no longer in consciousness.* Survivors in the latter group deny that they were ever sexually abused and are technically *telling the truth* as they remember it, while survivors in the first group, who make the same denial, may be *lying* to avoid shame, guilt and embarrassment.

Treatment for both groups is, on the one hand, *similar* but also contains *specific differences.* We will first deal with the *differences* and then with the *similarities* in treating each group.

SPECIFIC TREATMENT TECHNIQUES FOR UNRESOLVED BUT CONSCIOUS SEXUAL TRAUMA

Two specific elements of the sex offender's pathology are: first, his/her need to place blame on the victim and secondly, to use any and all methods possible to prevent the victim from reporting the incident(s). In this manner, the sex offender attempts both to prevent exposure and its consequences and to assuage guilt and responsibility for the molestation by projecting on the victim(s). The dynamics of this guilt projection onto the survivor differ depending on whether we are dealing with seductive sexual molestation (pedophiles, hebophiles and some incestuous fathers/mothers) or whether we are dealing with sexually assaultive persons (forced/assaultive pedophilia, hebophilia or adult sexual abuse).

In Seductive Sexual Abuse/Molestation

Where the *seductive sexual molesters* are concerned, several situations that demonstrate these pathological elements come to mind.

- 1. In the *first* encounter:
  - The child (especially boys) may respond to the seductive sexual molestation with a pleasure response (erection, orgasm, giggling, smiles, laughter, positive statements such as *"That felt good!"* or *"Yes, I liked it!"* etc.). The sex offender encourages then reinforces the positive statements with an open invitation for further encounters.

- 2. In the *second* encounter:
  - The sex offender manipulates the victim into asking for the sexual activity and/or into initiating the first moves in the sexual behavior in order to make the entire activity the *victim's choice* and therefore the *victim's responsibility*. Reminders are provided during and after the act that the victim wanted the sex and enjoyed it (reinforcement).

- 3. In one or more of the encounters, even the first, *photographs,* either Polaroids or a videotape, are taken of the victim performing sexual acts on the offender or on another victim while smiling, looking at the camera or in some other way conveying the image that what is happening is voluntary and pleasurable.
  - The victim is then constantly reminded (usually after the sexual encounter is over and the victim is preparing to leave) that if the offender is ever apprehended, the police will find the photographs/videotapes and then show them to his/her parents, friends, teachers, etc. The effect is both brutal and effective, and is firmly implanted in the victim's memory and reinforced on each successive encounter. *Tape recordings,* can also be used in this manner. With today's technology, the sex offender is rapidly changing over from Polaroid pictures to videotape recordings of the entire sexual encounter, with the same post-encounter reinforcement, warning and implied threat.

- 4. Usually by the *second* encounter:
  - The sex offender feels that he has the victim *hooked.* Every possible opportunity is used to reinforce the perception that he, the sex offender, always knew that this (the sexual behavior) was what the victim *wanted* and that the victim's return for *more* of the same proves the argument. Each successive encounter deepens the responsibility that the sex offender places on the victim and the victim's *guilt* increases geometrically. The victim is no longer a victim but rather a *co-conspirator with the sex offender,* equally guilty and equally sick or perverted.

An example will clarify:

- TODD, *whom we met in Chapters 5 & 9, is a typical example of this type of **induced guilt and secrecy**. After "Todd's" brother manipulated him into sexual activity with his friendship and companionship as the bait, "Todd" was **imprinted** (see Chapter 5). He accepted the confused and defective value that the sex his brother had with him was his brother's way of showing him that he loved him (sex equals "luv"). As their mutual masturbation progressed to "Todd" being sodomized, his brother continued to comment on "Todd's" body being **better than any girl he had been with and giving him greater pleasure and greater orgasms than any girl ever could**. Now the hook was in and set. For "Todd" to now go to his parents, a friend or the authorities would* *mean admitting to and telling everyone else that he was a "girl" who enjoyed being sodomized by a male. Even when his brother rejected him or left town for months and even years at a time, "Todd" had to insert objects into his rectum to replace his brother's penis or he could not achieve orgasm. Had "Todd" been able to accept his homosexual side, he could have found another male partner or lover. His guilt prevented that from happening but did not extinguish his need for repeating the sexual behavior.*

In Assaultive Sexual Abuse

Where the sexually assaultive person is concerned, several similarities in their *modus operandi* occur but there are also differences. The main difference is that of physical threat and intimidation. This can be aimed at the survivor himself/herself or at someone that the survivor loves dearly (a parent, young child, brother or sister, pet, etc.). These threats are not limited to cases of stranger sexual assault but also occur frequently in incest. Several situations that demonstrate this pathological element come to mind.

Sexually assaultive persons abusing adult males or females often use the time of day, the manner in which the survivor is dressed, the place of the encounter, etc., to convince the survivor that he/she was looking for trouble and that it would be easy to convince the authorities as well as their families of this fact. A specific case will clarify.

- *Late one evening,* DIANA, *a housewife suddenly realized that there was no milk or cream for the morning breakfast. Although it was close to 1 A.M. and she was already in a nightgown and negligee, "Diana" threw a topcoat on and drove to a convenience store that was open all night. No one was in the store so she parked in front of the door, opened the car door, leaving the motor running, and dashed into the store with the correct monies in hand. The whole occurrence lasted less than three minutes. When she returned to the car and slammed the door, a man jumped up from the rear seat and put a knife to her neck. He directed her to drive to the rear of the shopping mall where he violently sexually assaulted her in the back seat of the car. Before leaving, he said "I only came here to find someone to expose myself to but seeing you dressed that way and leaving the car door open for me gave me the courage I needed to graduate to rape. If you report this, I'll tell everyone that we had a date set up and that you came on to me."*

  "Diana," after sitting in the car in shock for some twenty minutes, drove home, showered and told no one what had happened. Self-recrimination followed and she blamed herself for the whole affair. It was only after many years and two broken marriages that she was able to ask for help.

Incestuous parents use family-related threats that they know the survivor will be susceptible to. A specific example will clarify.

- *An incestuous father molested all of his eight children, both girls and boys. No one ever told the mother or anyone else since he showed them a six-inch knife threatening to kill their mother or one of the younger children (than the one he was molesting at the time). He had instilled a value into the family that each child was totally responsible for the safety and welfare of the next youngest child to them. The value*

*worked and no one ever told until some 40 years later when the whole family was in
distress and turmoil and one of the girls, under hypnosis, remembered the molestations.*

FIVE SPECIFIC TECHNIQUES

The treatment steps for cases of this type that I have found to be most
effective are presented in priority order.

1. Ventilate All of the Nitty-Gritty Facts and Details

Any and all facts that occurred during and after the sexual abuse must be
ventilated over and over again until there is nothing new added to the retelling.
In most cases, the *first* telling of the story will be somewhat vague and void of
too many specific details, especially those facts that were most traumatic. As
trust (rapport) and self-comfort (desensitizing) develop, more and more details
will be "remembered" and more and more sensitive material will be elicited.
The therapist must continue this ventilating process until no new facts or details
emerge and the telling of the story is relatively calm and void of pauses
(censoring) or memory lags (blocking). The sequence of abuse memories often
follows the following progression:

- First come static pictures like snapshots in no particular order.
- Movement is added next and now the memories are like watching films or
  videotapes. Again no particular order is followed.
- Sounds come next including words, sobs, crying, screams, etc.
- Physical feelings come next and include pain, pleasure, nausea, temperature (hot
  and cold flashes), wetness, etc.
- Threats often are next and include threatening-object memories including knives,
  straps, baseball bats, whips, ropes, pillows (usually over their faces or heads), etc.
- Last come the emotional feelings including fear, terror, hate, anger, guilt, shame,
  disgust, etc.

Caveat: The emotional feelings are the most difficult to elicit yet are the
most important memory factors to uncover.

2. Elicit All of the Associated Feelings

In most cases, the feelings about the offender are the *last to emerge.* In the
first retelling, the usual emotions elicited are shame, fear, and embarrassment,
in the present. If any personal emotions emerge they are aimed at the survivor,
himself/herself, and revolve around stupidity, cowardice and self-recrimination for allowing the abuse to occur in the first place or to continue over a long
period of time. *Judgmental* emotions come next and are again aimed at the
survivor himself/herself. These include guilt, sinfulness, feeling dirty, bad,
evil, abnormal, etc.

It is essential for the therapist to find the means to elicit and ventilate all of
these feelings as well as those that are attached to the offender, *both positive
and negative.* Once the molestation or abuse is exposed, most survivors feel

that everyone expects them to feel negatively towards their abuser. They thus act as expected and often *exaggerate negative feelings* that they are supposed to possess. This especially applies to incest cases, although I have also found it frequently in the long-term seductive molestations.

In most long-term seductive sexual molestation, a great deal of positive feelings have also developed. Often the positive feelings outweigh the negative ones. These positive feelings need to be elicited, exposed and discussed.

3. Approval of the Survivor's Feelings, Both Positive and Negative.

Feelings about the sex offender and about others involved in the incident, including parents, police, friends, relatives, etc., need to be elicited. Once these feelings have been identified, then the survivor needs to know that he/she has a right to the feelings and that these feelings do not have to agree with the feelings communicated from significant others in his/her lives.

This step allows the therapist to help the survivor to clarify the survivor's feelings and definitions about "love." As they should have learned in early childhood, they can now learn to love the individual and to hate the individual's behavior. This is especially important in all cases of incest with a natural parent, especially when the other parent is imposing negative and judgmental attitudes towards the incestuous parent on the survivor. Too often, when incest has been uncovered in a family, the nonoffending parent experiences intense anger towards the offending parent and too often attempts to elicit the same or corresponding levels of anger from the incest survivor. Judgmental and con-demning words and phrases are the exclusive means of discussing the offend-ing parent and the survivor, especially a child, may feel obligated to have the same feelings and reactions as the nonoffending parent upon whom they now are totally dependent.

The frequently uncovered positive feelings that survivors of long-term seductive sexual abuse experience also need to be approved in this step. Again, a new value about "love" needs to be offered to the survivor in order to elicit these positive feelings.

4. Guilt Must Be Addressed

Once all of the facts and details surrounding the abuse have been elicited and discussed, and once the feelings associated with all of the factors in the abuse have been dealt with, then *guilt* must be addressed.

As stated several time before in this work, guilt is seen by this writer as the *most destructive force in the universe*. The guilt experienced by survivors often results in:

- depression,
- procrastination problems,
- alcohol and drug addiction,
- bulimia and anorexia,
- money problems (many end up in bankruptcy),

- failed marriages,
- failed careers,
- sexual dysfunctions of all types,
- prostitution,
- ritual repeating of the offense (especially in males),
- and suicide.

This list is by no means all-inclusive since each survivor *subjectively handles their guilt in their own peculiar ways.* The common factor, however, is that, if left unresolved, the result of guilt is always some form of *self-punitive behavior.*

At the risk of being repetitious, the bottom line of all treatment has to include the formation of a new self-image since *how the survivor feels about himself/herself will determine his or her future happiness or failure.* Nothing others can say or do will alter this self-image. Only the survivor himself/herself can alter the negative, deprecatory feelings he/she harbors towards himself/herself. In my experience, no real change can or will occur in the presence of unresolved guilt.

In working with *guilt problems,* my initial approach is to help the survivor to *accept the guilt for his/her past behavior(s)* and then to mentally *distance* from the "old self" — the child or adult who was involved in the sexual abuse — to the present self — "the survivor." Allowing or encouraging the survivor to deny or mitigate the guilt has never worked with any survivor that I have treated. While they may *appear* to have dealt with the guilt in order to comply with the minimizing techniques that some therapists employ, their behavior shortly proves that the guilt remains and to the same, if not a greater, degree. Also, placing 100% of the blame on the sex offender in these cases *does not work!* While it may be the belief or opinion of society and of those who love the survivor that the abuser was fully to blame and that the survivor was completely innocent, the reality is that most survivors feel some level of blame or responsibility for what happened to them. Whether it was the time or place, or being alone in a dangerous area, or any other facet of the total abuse experience, the survivor has a right to his/her feelings of responsibility for that portion of the occurrence. It is their own *subjective judgment* that must be elicited and accepted first and then dealt with *realistically and appropriately.*

Think of the last time that you were either complimented or not complimented for something you did and you internally disagreed with the compliment or lack thereof. How much did outside opinion change your original perception of what you did or did not deserve? Little if any, if you're being honest with yourself. In seductive sexual molestation and often in incest, the survivor has lived through the sexual abuse and experienced his/her own desires, pleasures, degree of willing participation, need for recurrence of the sexual behavior, and the guilt felt afterwards as well as the fear of exposure. In forced or assaultive sexual abuse, there is often a physical response (sexual stimulation or even orgasm) as well as the mental recriminations for being *vulnerable* and unable to defend or protect oneself or for being available to the sexually assaultive individual. All of these feelings and experiences cannot be dismissed or mitigated by the loving intentions of a parent or the well-meaning intentions of a therapist.

A great deal of time and frustration can be avoided by initially simply *accepting the survivor's self-judgment and guilt* and going on from there instead of trying to change what is a "fait accompli." It is essential in this step to be sure that *all* of the guilt is elicited, identified and discussed before going any further. Once this point is reached, *value reassessment* is used to defuse the degree or intensity of the guilt. I often suggest the value that *human equals imperfect* at this stage and help the survivor to reinterpret his/her behavior before, during, and after the abuse/assault from that perspective. Survivors, as well as the rest of us, are unable to identify a single *perfect* human being. The therapist may also chose to share some simple experience of his/her own that will clarify the point. This type of disclosure is dependent on the comfort level of the therapist.

5. Final Steps

The rest of the treatment for this group follows the steps outlined and discussed in Chapter 9, beginning at this point with a new image formation.

PRE-TREATMENT CONSIDERATIONS FOR UNIDENTIFIED (REPRESSED) SEXUAL TRAUMAS

Unidentified sexual traumas pose a much more difficult treatment problem. As stated previously, the only way that we know that the possibility of an unidentified or repressed sexual trauma may have occurred is by the presence of *unwanted sexual fantasies, obsessions or behaviors that are illogical, make no sense and are causing psychological and emotional pain* for the survivor. In traumas of this type there is usually no conscious memory or even a suspicion of sexual trauma.

In Chapter 6, we discussed two cases of this type: "Scott" and his sneaker fetish and "Dennis" and his obsession with young boys (5-7) with their shirts off. Also where "Dennis" is concerned, his resistance to change and insistence that he is "worthless, disgusting, and not worth caring about" — with no logical reasons for these negative self-judgments — cannot be explained.

In all of these cases, the common factor is the complete and baffling lack of any sense of the etiology of the presenting symptoms or sexual dysfunctions. In other types of sexual dysfunction cases, there is always some logical (subjective) reason for the behavior or some attempt at an explanation or defense. In these cases, there is absolutely none. The survivor often feels that he/she is losing their minds — "I feel like I am going crazy or losing it!" The total lack of any memory of sexual trauma or abuse becomes the major stumbling block to any analysis of the problem, practical sex therapy home-work, or suggestions for change.

The survivor has usually already spent a great deal of time and effort in simply trying to *stop* or *ignore* the thoughts, fantasies, urges or compulsions but to no avail. The usual reason for finally entering therapy is a desperate frustration level, depression, and often suicidal thoughts or attempts. Inability to concentrate, work or socialize are accompanying symptoms presented in the intake session. One devastating overall result of this type of situation is a severely negative self-image and an almost total lack of self-esteem.

NECESSARY CLUES BEFORE ACTUAL TREATMENT BEGINS

Before specific treatment can begin, several sessions must be spent *gathering clues* as to possible causations. Some of the facts that are important and necessary to determine in each case include:

1. The Age and Sex of the Sex Object (Potential Victim) in the Survivor's Preoccupations, Thoughts, or Fantasies.

This will indicate for the therapist both the sex of the significant other involved in the suspected sexual trauma/abuse as well as the probable age that the survivor was at the time of the suspected sexual trauma/abuse (+ or -2 years). I have incorporated a plus or minus two year rule in these cases due to imprecise memories in early childhood and also since in some cases there is still a need to *avoid* anything connected with the *repressed sexual trauma* including the exact age that it occurred.

- SCOTT, *for example, persistently returns to age 6 or 7 whenever he discusses a frightening time in his childhood. He also consciously remembers standing terrified outside of a house where his father lived in California at the same period of time. No further memories about this age or about California have been recalled. While discussing this age and incident, "Scott" becomes visibly emotionally upset and beings to sweat and shake while tears flow from his eyes. However, there are never any conscious reasons why this memory upsets him. The result is confusion, fear and extreme frustration.*

- DENNIS *is obsessed **only** with seven-year-old boys, playing with their shirts off. He will spend hours searching for young boys in his neighborhood or in the parks. Once he has found the right boy, he simply stares at him for a sufficient period of time for him to become sexually aroused. He then will return home and masturbate using a fantasy of the boy he has just seen being punched in the stomach by an older, bully-type boy. Once he has reached orgasm, overpowering guilt floods in and he becomes even more disgusted with himself. Frustration increases as well since he neither can stop the compulsive behavior nor understand its origin or purpose. His greatest fear is that someday he will actually molest one of these boys.*

2. The Specific Act, With All Its Nitty-Gritty Details That Recurs in the Thoughts, Fantasies, and/or Unwanted Behavior and that Produces the Sexual Arousal, Must Be Elicited.

Rarely, if ever, have I experienced a case where the *act* in the thoughts, fantasies and/or unwanted behavior was not the *exact and identical act* that occurred in the sexual trauma or molestation/abuse. In a significant number of cases, the *repetition* of the act and the behavior in general is seen, as an attempt to *"undo,"* by role reversal, the perceived damage and guilt that resulted from the original molestation/abuse. Also, in a significant percentage of these cases, there often is a craving and need to *recapture the positive factors that existed in the original relationship involved in the sexual molestation/abuse.* Here, again, the survivor uses role reversal.

Since neither scenario is obvious from the information consciously remembered, both have to be thoroughly explored. Even in cases where the present symptoms are unwanted and disturbing, the original relationship in the sexual abuse/molestation possibly could have been considered positive at the time, especially when we are dealing with child ages versus adult ages. What a child may have participated in with an adult to please that adult most likely will not be acceptable behavior to the present adult survivor or even to most adolescents.

3. The Affect Attached to the Present Symptoms: The Unwanted Thoughts, Fantasies or Behaviors.

As a general rule, the more *negative* the emotions are that accompany the present symptoms, the more probable it is that we are dealing with force or sexual assault. On the other hand, when minimal confusion, anxiety and a sense of curiosity rather than fear is seen, the more probable it is that we are dealing with a case of childhood/early adolescent seductive sexual molestation. The *fear cases* also strongly suggest that there was a serious threat attached to the warning never to tell anyone what had occurred — *the secret.*

One clear indicator of the above described scenario is when the present sexual thoughts, obsessions, fantasies or behavior are seen as dirty, bad, sinful, sick, etc., to an *exaggerated degree.* Some of these survivors have a great deal of difficulty even describing their symptoms and a fair amount of time must be spent in gaining rapport before they are able to trust the therapist sufficiently to relate what is truly bothering them. Rarely does this occur in the first several sessions. Forcing or using coercive tactics at this point not only will not work but could result in the risk of losing the survivor or increasing the strength and depth of the repression.

- *"Scott" can only become aroused if he feels that his behavior results in his "**getting over**" on the victim. Even in therapy today, when he describes one of the events in detail, "Scott" becomes visibly excited, smiling, laughing and he even reports becoming partially erect. His pleasure and euphoria are obvious and admitted to.*

- *"Dennis," on the other hand, resists discussing his behavior to the fullest extent. When he finally does, there is a great deal of hesitation, pauses, obvious pain, shame, and guilt involved. He cannot maintain eye contact, puts his head down, lowers his voice until it is almost inaudible, and ends up either crying or cursing himself with a lengthy list of deprecatory and judgmental remarks.*

  A major element in "Dennis'" arousal pattern is his conscious, obsessive thought that someone will "punch the little boy with his shirt off in the stomach." Maintaining this fantasy results in his becoming sexually aroused to the point of orgasm. For almost three years of therapy, no further memories, thoughts or explanations (reasons) for this obsessive masturbation fantasy have been elicited, regardless of the many techniques utilized.

SPECIFIC TREATMENT TECHNIQUES FOR UNIDENTIFIED SEXUAL TRAUMA

There are several specific goals that the therapist must consider for this group as can be seen in the accompanying illustration. While applicable to treatment for all types of sexual abuse, I have found the following sequence of techniques to be essential where a *repressed sexual trauma* is suspected.

1. Establish Trust and an Atmosphere of Safety

For many of the initial sessions with this type of survivor, the above condition has to be the primary goal. Discussing the survivor's present situation, his/her day-by-day behavior since the last session, and anything bothering him/her at the present time, permits the survivor to begin exposing "secrets" about himself/herself to the therapist on a gradual and increasingly more personal basis.

Focusing on the specific referral symptoms *too soon* can terrify the survivor sufficiently to lose him/her. Also, in the beginning, retelling the problem behavior over and over, week after week only adds to the depression and frustration of the survivor and results in little, if any, therapeutic gain.

2. Begin Self-Esteem and Self-Image Work Immediately

Most of the survivors in this group, as stated above, have an extremely negative self-image and totally negative, judgmental concept of who they are. This defective image needs to be changed before any real therapeutic results will occur. The *"I don't deserve to change or to improve"* syndrome is involved here. Self-confrontation techniques (described fully in Chapter 13) should be begun as soon as the survivor is ready and willing.

Changing the way the survivor sees himself/herself is usually a difficult task. Added to self-confrontation must be a realistic planning for and later appraisal of the survivor's day-by-day behaviors and functioning. One technique that I employ is to help the survivor find at least one positive behavior that occurred since he/she woke up the day of the therapy session. While any positive behavior will suffice, I find that these positive behaviors usually occur

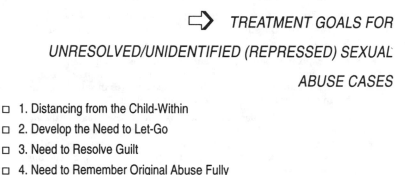

⇨ *TREATMENT GOALS FOR*

UNRESOLVED/UNIDENTIFIED (REPRESSED) SEXUAL

ABUSE CASES

☐ 1. Distancing from the Child-Within

☐ 2. Develop the Need to Let-Go

☐ 3. Need to Resolve Guilt

☐ 4. Need to Remember Original Abuse Fully

☐ 5. Need to Develop A New, Strong, Assertive Self

outside of the home, often in the workplace on an impersonal level. Two examples will clarify.

- *For "Scott," his trouble-shooting function in a major high tech communications company, provides this positive factor. He is bright, talented and a fantastic technician who earns a fabulous salary for someone his age. He agrees that when none of the other technicians can solve the problem, he is called in and can usually solve the problem in a short amount of time. He receives plaudits and bonuses from the company but places them in the back of his mind as unimportant, preferring to concentrate on his negative features.*

  In his heterosexual relationships with women his own age, he does extremely well on both the social as well as the sexual levels. He receives constant praise for his sexual performances and skills but, here again, minimizes the importance of the positive feedback. This negative focus and devaluing of positive accomplishments has to be dealt with before even approaching his repressed sexual problem.

- *For "Dennis" the first part, technical success in the workplace, also exists and is minimized and "forgotten as soon as it happens." The second part, the interpersonal relationship area, differs dramatically from "Scott's" experience. "Dennis" is a wimpy, nerd type (his description) individual who is classified by everyone he associates with almost immediately as being "weird."*

  His "friends" all either "tolerate" or "use" him and he uses every form of denial to defend them in order to consider them as real friends. Yet, he refuses to discuss anything personal with them or to ask them for help. However, using his "double ruler" (see Chapter 9 where Subjective Judgment Memories were discussed), he offers to listen, suggest and even counsel friends in trouble. When pressured to explain the discrepancy, he responds: "There is no one as perverted, disgusting or sick as I am and, if they (his friends) knew what I was really like, they would all drop me immediately!"

3. Guilt Resolution and Value Reassessment

The type of *"double standard"* or *"double ruler"* that "Dennis" employs, exists in the majority of survivors as well as in their molesters, the sex offenders. Several factors are involved:

- a. Simply exposing these values and logically assessing them does not cause immediate change. The survivor must first *want to change!* Verbalizing this "want" means little until the above delineated changes in self-image and self-esteem begin to occur and can be behaviorally verified.

- b. No change will take place until the survivor believes that he/she *deserves to change and be happy.* In order for this to occur, guilt must be identified and resolved. The guilt I am referring to here is both deep-rooted and practically lifelong. Most of these survivors even feel guilty about having been born (not an exaggeration). Every minimal transgression in their lives is remembered, noted, and continuously paid for, over and over by self-punishing and happiness-preventing behaviors and thoughts (self-judgments). Their logic is simple.

  - "I'm no good and never have been. All that I've done is cause trouble and pain for my parents and family, as well as my friends. It would have been better if I had never been born!"

- c. The damaging influence of negative religion must be considered. If the survivor was brought up in a negative, punitive, hell-and-damnation threatening religion, the problem is greatly magnified. Sin and damnation dominate this group's thoughts and they develop a *need for perfection* that becomes a defeating and self-fulfilling prophesy of their worthlessness and evil.

- d. Every goal they set is either *too high or too short.* The result is constant failure and the cycle begins:
  - Set a goal too high;
  - fail;
  - confirm all negative self-perceptions;
  - esteem lowers and then quit.

This pattern is seen constantly with this type of survivor. Until the guilt is resolved and values are reassessed and realistically changed no further therapy will occur.

4. Worst Scene Scenario Technique

Once some changes in self-esteem have begun and the most damaging values have been altered, even to a minimal degree, the therapy can be slightly accelerated.

At this juncture, I suggest, for the next week's homework, a self-confrontation session using the *worst scene scenario* as the subject matter of the session. The survivor is instructed to: imagine the worst possible sexual trauma, assault or molestation that could have occurred when he/she was (?) years old. Note that the age used is the age of the fantasized/obsessed victim or significant other. For "Scott" it would be girls or boys from children to teenagers; for "Dennis" it would be boys, age seven. *Caveat:* No other instructions for the assignment should be given!

The reason for the above caveat is that what the therapist should be looking for at this stage are *clues* coming from the unconscious mind of the survivor. When the survivor chooses an age, an act, a significant other, a setting, etc., they all should be considered *highly significant*. In my experience, when this assignment is seriously and honestly performed, the results always produce some significant clues as to *what, where and when* the survivor was actually traumatized. The choices that are available to the survivor are so numerous that it is only logical and reasonable to surmise that the choices he/she chooses must have significance.

When "Scott" was given this assignment, he filled in the rest of the missing memory of standing outside of his father's house in California. What he presented to this therapist in his next session was as follows.

* *"The little boy is standing outside of the house, scared and frightened for as long as he can. When it begins to get dark, he finally goes inside and there is no one on the bottom floor. His father calls him upstairs to his bedroom. When he opens the door, his father is sitting on the bed naked, calls the little boy over and undresses him, all except for his sneakers, which his father unties. He then has him hop around the room that way, naked with only his untied sneakers on. His father laughs and laughs and calls him a stupid, little ninny and then tells him that for being so stupid he has to be punished. The father pulls him to the bed and forces him to touch and then suck his erect penis. The boy gags and when the father ejaculates, vomits all over the father and the bed. For vomiting, he is beaten to within an inch of his life."*

At that point, "Scott" could no longer stand the pain, ran from the mirror (where he was doing the assignment) to his bed and cried hysterically for over a half hour.

After relating the story, "Scott" added that he always suspected that he had been molested by his father but could never tell me about his suspicion directly. He also *now* remembers his mother always calling his father a *pervert* but never was told why.

Once this assignment was over, there was a great deal of material about "Scott's" father that became the focus of the next several sessions, although *the conscious memory of being molested by his father has still not surfaced.* However, "Scott" does remember being severely beaten by his father when he lived with him in California and on one occasion being hospitalized as a result. The *worst scene scenario* assignment will be given to "Scott" again as the emotional reactions to this material are fully ventilated.

"Dennis," on the other hand, has been given this assignment on five separate occasions and on each has either *"forgotten the assignment," "didn't have the time to do it,"* or *"didn't want to do it."* Thus, it has been avoided and "Dennis" stays in limbo with no movement seen in almost three full years of treatment.

5. Guided Imagery (Mild Hypnosis) Technique

In this section, I will be dealing only with those aspects of guided imagery that I utilize in my own practice with survivors. For a more complete understanding of the use of hypnosis and guided imagery, the reader is referred to the following two excellent sources: *Ericksonian Approaches to Hypnosis and Psychotherapy,* edited by Jeffrey K. Zeig and published by Brunner/Mazel, 1982, and *Hypnosis and Sex Therapy,* by Daniel L. Araoz and published by Brunner/Mazel, 1982.

When I encounter a totally resistant survivor and all other methods fail or end up in frustration for both the survivor and myself, I turn to *guided imagery* techniques, which involve a form of mild hypnosis. At this stage of the treatment, the survivor is usually so desperate that he/she is both willing and anxious to try anything that may offer him/her help as well as some relief. Thus, resistance to guided imagery is usually minimal.

The permission of the survivor to utilize this technique is both necessary and demanded by ethical standards. My personal preference is for this permission to be obtained in writing with a witness' signature as a necessary adjunct.

Before beginning the actual guided imagery technique, the survivor must be taught progressive relaxation and be encouraged to practice these relaxation techniques at home, on a daily basis. I suggest bedtime as the best time of the day for this practice, since it often provides the bonus of a good night's sleep. Whether the therapist chooses to utilize Erickson's methods of relaxation or not, does not matter in the overall process. Any relaxation method will work equally well.

Once the survivor is able to achieve a true level of relaxation, the therapist uses a prepared story (embedded metaphor) that closely parallels the problem area(s) being dealt with. Care is taken that the metaphor is not so close to the survivor's problem reality that a panic reaction upsets the state of relaxation. Fairy tales and children's stories, utilizing cartoon and television characters, are modified to fit the survivor's problems/circumstances since they offer a vast array of possible choices.

An example at this point will clarify. With "Scott" and his unresolved sneaker fetish, the metaphor I used was as follow, with the sections in bold constructed as embedded references to the survivor's life situation:

- *"This is a story of a little boy named* JODY, *who lived in the woods with his **widowed mother**. I want you to picture "Jody" in a peaceful wooded area with the sun shining warmly through the leaves and the birds and other animals making pleasant and comforting sounds. When you have a clear picture of "Jody" in the woods, just lift your index finger to let me know."* [Here, I pause until the survivor has fantasized the image as instructed. This may take a few minutes or longer to accomplish the first time.]

    *"As "Jody" walks along a well-trodden path, singing and playing with the animals, he comes upon a small wooden cottage that he has never been to before **but that for some reason frightens him. He stands there, shaking, frozen in his tracks and not knowing what to do.** Just then the door opens and an old man with a beard appears in the doorway. The old man beckons to "Jody" and asks him to step into the cottage where he will give him some cookies and milk. "Jody," although frightened, is also very hungry since he hasn't eaten since breakfast and slowly and*

hesitantly walks toward the door." [Here, the second pause occurs and again the instruction is given to lift the index finger when the image is complete.]

"*Slowly, "Jody" enters the cottage but does not see the man. He is behind the door and as "Jody" enters, he slams it shut and locks it. He then tells "Jody" that before he can have his cookies and milk that they have to play the man's favorite game. The man pulls "Jody" over to his bed and undresses him completely. "Jody" begins to cry since the floor is so cold on his little bare feet and the man **lets him put on his unlaced shoes but not fully. He has to walk on the bent backs of the shoes** so that he cannot run away.* [Here the third pause occurs and the finger instruction is again given. If the survivor has been cooperative to this point, the therapist may suggest that the survivor finish the story from that point on. If not, the therapist supplies a vague molestation theme.]

The next step in the process depends on whether the therapist considers the survivor a *cooperative* or *resistant* individual.

For Cooperative Survivors

The therapist continues with the metaphor.

- "*Do you have the picture so far? Can you see "Jody standing there, frightened, with no clothes on and **stepping on the backs of his untied shoes**?*" (Here the fourth pause occurs while the therapist waits for the finger signal to occur. By this time, whenever a question is asked, there will be an automatic response with the raising of the index finger even though it may not have been suggested. The therapist then suggests that the survivor may like to finish the story. If the survivor chooses to complete the story, then whatever the survivor uses as a continuation of the story must be recorded since it will have major significance at some time in his/her therapy.)

For Non-Cooperative/Resistant Survivors

The therapist must become more directive in the guided imagery.

- "*Now the man does something to "Jody" that "Jody" does not understand and that feels strange or may hurt. "Jody" is too frightened to run or to try to stop the man since he fears that he will be hurt even more or possibly killed, so he has to let the man do whatever he wants. When the man is finished, he lets "Jody" dress, gives him the cookies and milk and then lets him leave with a warning that if he ever tells anyone what happened in the cottage something terrible will happen to him or to his mother. Now, try to feel the way that "Jody" felt as he ran down the path towards his home.*" [Here the therapist pauses again and carefully observes the survivor's breathing, eyes, hands, etc., for any visible signs of affect. If emotions begin to surface, the therapist suggests that the feelings are all right and that the survivor should just let them happen.]

For both scenarios, the therapist may finish the story with:

- "*As "Jody" is running home down the wooded path, he sees a bright light and then a friendly looking fairy-godfather (if the therapist is a female, then it should be a "fairy-godmother") appears directly in front of him. He is smiling and makes "Jody" feel safe and comfortable. The fairy-godfather tells "Jody" that he is there to help him to take away the hurt and to feel safe.*

"*The fairy-godfather tells "Jody" that he knows all about the man in the cottage and what happened there and that it is all right for "Jody" to talk about it to him.*

He will protect him from all harm and not let the man do anything to either him or his mother. "Jody" wants to tell someone what happened and decides to try to trust the fairy-godfather." The therapist then asks "What do you think "Jody" told the smiling, friendly, protective fairy-godfather?"

Again, whatever the survivor says needs to be recorded (after the session) for future use. With all of the possible responses that the survivor might choose, it is reasonable to assume that what he/she does choose is important and relevant to his/her life or to the problem/trauma.

The above metaphor is only one of many types of stories and scenarios that can be used in guided imagery to tap into the repressed materials and the fears that are keeping them deeply hidden in the unconscious.

It is extremely important to elicit the feelings, reactions and fantasies that may have occurred during the guided imagery technique either immediately after the session or at the beginning of the next therapy session. It is also very helpful to query the survivor as to any possible changes he/she would have made in the story or about any method that might have made the session either easier, deeper or more meaningful. Often, the survivor makes suggestions that either directly or indirectly *hint* at areas that are blocked or that are beginning to emerge into consciousness.

Asking for the survivor's advice also makes him/her feel like a partner or co-therapist on his own case and aids in the *distancing* necessary to breach the repressed trauma(s).

6. The Third Chair Technique

An alternate method to Guided Imagery is what I have termed the *third chair technique*. This method includes using *exactly* what happened to the survivor but having it happen to a close friend who has come to the survivor for comfort, help and advice and is sitting in a third (empty) chair in the office. An alternate to a close friend might be that it happened to another survivor that the therapist is treating who is of similar age and has a similar problem. In the latter scenario, the present survivor becomes a co-therapist, helping a peer. This method works equally well with resistant young children, adolescents and adults. It also exposes the survivor's problem of utilizing a double-ruler, if one exists. An example will clarify.

- *"Dennis," whom we have met several times and who compulsively masturbates to seven-year-old boys with their shirts off being punched in the stomach by a bully, is so resistant that the embedded-metaphor in the guided imagery technique did not work. He never reached a sufficiently relaxed state to even begin a mild, hypnotic session and answered "I don't know!" to all of the question sections of the technique. I then decided to try the third-chair technique.*

  I told "Dennis" to imagine that a seven-year-old boy that I was treating was sitting in the third chair. He had been playing in front of his house **with his shirt off and his little belly sticking out over his belt** *and then this* **older boy who was a bully came over to him and began punching him in the belly to make him do something he did not want to do.** *I then asked "Dennis" to become his friend and to try to calm* *him down and help him to feel better about himself and help him to talk about what the older boy made him do. "Dennis" proved to be an excellent co-therapist. He was warm, understanding, and highly empathetic. However, he could find no answer to the question of what the older bully made the little boy do except that it was "bad, dirty and terrible."*

"Dennis" preferred the third chair technique to any other technique that the therapist tried and therefore it will be periodically employed. Hopefully his resistance will eventually lessen and some clue as to his repressed sexual trauma will emerge.

7. Homework

Once the survivor has learned relaxation to where he can enter that state on a simple cue-word, the therapist can assume that the survivor is actually practicing *self-hypnosis.*

At that juncture, I utilize relaxation and self-hypnosis subliminal cassette tapes to assign homework in the area of the repressed trauma. While I do not personally believe that these cassettes produce a state of hypnosis, they appear to be useful as aides for the frightened, nonconfident and resistant survivor since they relieve him/her of some of the responsibility for consciously remembering the frightening or guilt and shame producing repressed material. This is especially true when dealing with young children who are survivors of a sexual abuse that contained threats to their lives or the lives of their families, especially their mothers. The survivor is encouraged to practice relaxation and self-hypnosis daily and if possible always at the same time. The chosen time should be such that there are no pressing appointments, disruptions or fears of disruption from others. Usually the best time for this is at the end of the day, just before bedtime. This is also the best time for the self-confrontation technique to be practiced as discussed in Chapter 13.

Concerning the specific repressed memory that the survivor should search for in the guided imagery technique, the *least frightening* and *least anxiety provoking* materials should always be suggested first. Asking the survivor to go home and use this technique to uncover the repressed trauma that is causing his/her major symptoms is absurd. I primarily utilize this homework to facilitate the survivor's entering a relaxed state easily and quickly in the office and also to build self-confidence in his/her own ability to deal with the simple daily problems of everyday life.

I suggest that the technique be used to find answers to confusing or upsetting personal behaviors that occurred during that day. For example to find answers to questions such as:

- "Why didn't I say what I wanted to say to my supervisor at work when I was blamed for what someone else did?"
- "Why did I let my wife criticize and demean me without saying a word for simply forgetting to do something she asked me to do ?"
- "Why did I say yes to a request for a favor that I really did not want to do and that interfered with my own personal plans? Why can't I say No?"

. . . and a myriad of other simple daily situations.

As the survivor utilizes this technique to gain more and more insight into his/her own behavior and to make changes in his/her life, self-confidence and self-esteem will begin to increase. Then the therapist can use the relaxation, hypnosis and guided imagery techniques to deal more directly with the repressed material. Of all of the problems that the therapist will face in working with survivors of sexual abuse, repressed trauma is the most difficult to find and resolve.

11

Specialized Therapy Techniques in Homosexual Abuse and Sexual Assault

Once the principles in Chapter 9 and 10 are followed, there remains a need to discuss specialized techniques for the four major categories of sexual abuse: (1) homosexual abuse; (2) sexual assault; (3) incest; and (4) long-term child sexual abuse.

I will discuss each type of abuse-treatment in some detail. The format will be to present a series of problems that tend to occur during treatment with each type of sexual abuse and then to suggest *treatment techniques* that I have found successful for each type.

HOMOSEXUAL ABUSE CASES

In Seductive Homosexual Abuse

The First and Most Serious Problem. When the survivor experiences sexual pleasure, orgasm and/or ejaculation as a result of the seductive homosexual abuse a serious problem occurs. Often, he/she then experiences *severe guilt* and *self-image* damage. What appears to occur is that the survivor mistakenly judges his/her physical/sexual response as evidence of either:

- cooperation or
- homosexual identity or
- unwanted desires/fantasies to have the experience again which so often leads to the survivor eventually *initiating* the sexual behavior with the abuser.

What the therapist or counselor must consider is the principle of *positive imprinting,* which I define as: *When a first orgasm* occurs as part of a sexual molestation and is perceived as pleasurable or the overall experience is perceived by the survivor as pleasurable, positive imprinting usually occurs. (Imprinting was discussed in full detail in Chapter 5.) In addition to an imprint occurring, the survivor often misinterprets his/her physical reaction as *cooperation* with the abuser and therefore deserving of equivalent guilt.

Treatment of this situation first demands a thorough and specialized sex education discussion in order that the survivor is able to understand the *imprint* that occurred during his/her molestation. Topics must include a discussion of the body's physical reaction to sexual stimulation as being a normal physiologi-

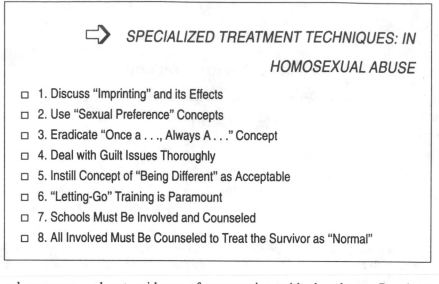

SPECIALIZED TREATMENT TECHNIQUES: IN
HOMOSEXUAL ABUSE

☐ 1. Discuss "Imprinting" and its Effects

☐ 2. Use "Sexual Preference" Concepts

☐ 3. Eradicate "Once a . . ., Always A . . ." Concept

☐ 4. Deal with Guilt Issues Thoroughly

☐ 5. Instill Concept of "Being Different" as Acceptable

☐ 6. "Letting-Go" Training is Paramount

☐ 7. Schools Must Be Involved and Counseled

☐ 8. All Involved Must Be Counseled to Treat the Survivor as "Normal"

cal response and not evidence of cooperation with the abuser. Resultant possible present attractions, fantasies, obsessive thoughts, etc., towards peers and/or adults of the same sex is also a normal and expected reaction, especially in long-term seductive homosexual molestation and is a direct result of the imprint process. In some cases, these reactions may occur after only a few same-sex contacts.

This specialized sex education must also include the concept of *sexual preference* as opposed to *sexual identity*. Sexual preference permits a constant *choice* of both present and future sexual behaviors/partners while sexual identity, on the other hand, implies that once an identity is established (as early as two years of age in some psychoanalytic schools of thought) it cannot be altered. For survivors in this category, if they experience any degree of *pleasure* during the molestation, it is very easy for them to conclude, due to their immaturity and naivete, that their *identity* must be homosexual and that it can never be changed.

It is also extremely important to stress to survivors in this category that choosing heterosexuality (*"I want to be straight and have a family and children and never think about guys/girls again"*) as a therapy goal is usually impractical, in my opinion. In my experience with hundreds of survivors of this type, the positive imprint is permanent and if they catch themselves looking at same-sex peers or adults and becoming aroused, (as happened to "Chuck," in Chapter 8 or to "Todd" in Chapter 5) they will then feel that they failed both in therapy and in their new goals. It is far better for them to accept the fact that they will always be *bisexual* (in order to cover any possible same-sex attractions, thoughts or fantasies) with the understanding that they never again have to perform an overt homosexual act since any future sexual behavior will always remain their *choice.*

One possible choice the survivor may elect is to remain heterosexual in behavior, dating, relating with the opposite sex, marrying and having children. He/she can concurrently become sexually attractive to same-sex partners *without acting out on it* and even masturbate to same-sex acts without ever becoming involved overtly with a same-sex partner. Thus, the survivor's sexual preference, by choice, may remain strictly heterosexual on the behavioral level while in fantasy, attraction, and in masturbation the survivor may remain bisexual and experience homosexual attractions and fantasies. It is *always* his/her choice.

A second choice may be to become bisexual in behavior while making his/her heterosexual relationship the primary one and even marrying. On a secondary level, he/she can experience homosexual relationships that contain less commitment, less love, and without a live-in relationship, etc. The *caveat* in this choice is that they need to inform their heterosexual partner of this decision or suffer anxiety, fear of exposure, and severe guilt on a daily basis. Sharing this choice and its origins or causes may involve risking the loss of their primary relationship, although in my experience, if the relationship existed for several years, and the significant other is assured that *true love* (however each individual survivor defines it) will not be involved, most partners choose to remain in the relationship.

It may be surprising or even barely credible to the reader to accept the *fact* that as high as 85-90 percent of all of the significant others that I have dealt with in these circumstances accept the situation rather than lose a husband, wife, lover, or friend. What appears to be cognitively involved in the partner is that he/she realizes that he/she cannot compete sexually when the need is for the sexual behaviors that only a same-sex lover can provide. However, were the fantasies or attractions of the significant other to involve another individual of his/her own sex, he/she could not and would not accept the situation. Thus, while a wife may accept the bisexuality of her husband and his attractions to and fantasies of other men, she would probably never accept his attractions to and fantasies of another woman. The same applies to husbands or male significant others being able to accept their female partner's attractions to and fantasies of other women but would never accept these attractions or fantasies if they involved another man.

One striking difference in the sexes is illustrated in the following scenario. In a lesbian situation, where the survivor chooses to live as a bisexual female, there is even more acceptance. The male partner often has a sexual turn on to thoughts of his female partner being with another woman. Often he will suggest a "menage-a-trois" since a majority of males voyeuristically enjoy seeing women in sexual encounters and do not become homophobic towards such behaviors. The danger, of course, is that the male in the relationship may (and at times does) become attracted to the lesbian partner.

The third and final choice is to choose a homosexual lifestyle. In many of the long-term homosexual pedophilic/hebophilic abuse cases where the relationship lasted for many years and either did not end or ended in a highly positive way (the younger partner moving either due to attending college or university or of finding employment in a different city or state), or the older partner dying, etc., the young survivor chose to continue in a homosexual lifestyle and was both adjusted and happy with his/her decision. The trauma that is experienced by the other two groups does not occur in these cases and these survivors live healthy and adjusted adult lives. However, for a married survivor, this usually involves terminating the former heterosexual relationship, adding to the problems in the overall treatment scheme since guilt and loss issues develop, especially when there are children.

Caveat: Where child and adolescent survivors choose a homosexual preference, thorough exploration of the reasons, thought processes, and values that this decision was based on is essential. Also, a discussion of all of the societal consequences and prejudices towards such a decision must be a paramount consideration and discussion. This area must be handled in as *neutral* a manner as possible with the therapist taking great care that his/her own prejudices in this area are not exposed to the survivor. In these cases, supportive therapy during late childhood and into adolescence is essential since identity confusion and possible conflicts with parents too often occur.

Regardless of the survivor's choice, *proper guidance without infringing on the right of the survivor to make an informed decision for himself/herself, must always be paramount.*

The Second Problem involves the old concept of *"once a —, always a —"* This subjective-judgment or perception must be eradicated or no changes will occur. While this *subjective-judgment* usually occurs in survivors of long-term, seductive homosexual abuse, I have also seen it in survivors of a single homosexual molestation, especially if reciprocation, by the survivor, occurred and orgasm resulted.

Too often, a survivor in this category who has, on at least one occasion, initiated and enjoyed homosexual behavior with his/her abuser, will make the decision that he/she now *must* remain homosexual for the rest of his/her life. This infers that he/she believes that *change* is impossible and therefore therapy of any kind cannot help, since all therapy intrinsically implies change of some type or other.

The most damaging result of this type of subjective-judgment is that this group of survivors blocks any normal heterosexual feelings, attractions, or relationships from developing and focuses *exclusively* on same-sex thoughts and fantasies. Many of the adolescent survivors that I have treated in this category report beginning interests and attractions toward the opposite sex that they *cut off* as being inappropriate or unrealistic *for them* since they are now permanently homosexual.

Here again, effective sex education with an emphasis on the concept of sexual preference is the primary technique recommended, followed by a positive self-image emphasis with *guided* value-reassessment exercises.

Positive self-image work is one of the primary methods that I have found successful in changing the defective, negative judgments and defective self-image that results in the survivor of seductive homosexual abuse. The specific group technique that I have found most successful with these survivors is a new *self-confrontation technique* that is described in complete detail in Chapter 13 and that I call *NOW* therapy.

DENNIS, whom we met in Chapters 4 and 6, is a perfect example of this defective self-image problem. In therapy for more than three years, "Dennis" continues to berate, put down, and condemn himself as "no good, worthless, disgusting, so terrible I can't look at him in the mirror, ugly" (untrue), and other derisive descriptors. When asked why these negative judgments are true, he cannot give a single reason. Some repressed trauma, that we have been unable to expose, must be producing these reactions.

Unless self-image changes and self-confidence improve, no other therapeutic goals can be realistically set for the survivors of homosexual abuse.

The Third Problem involves *subjective-guilt* issues. While associated with defective self-image, subjective-guilt is a separate and distinct issue. Survivors who experienced pleasure or orgasm during their sexual molestation often experience severe *subjective-guilt* reactions afterwards. The former teachings and values of parents, religion, school, friends, society, etc., about homosexual behavior come into play. The result being that they then often perceive themselves as *queers, faggots, weirdoes, abnormal, different, etc.* This reaction is most severe in adolescents and in male adults who already had doubts about their masculinity prior to the sexual molestation and especially if they are subjected to anal intercourse, which they often perceive as "being used as a woman" primarily due to the words of the abuser. In these cases, *guilt* must be perceived as the most destructive force in the universe. The effects of this guilt include: depression, isolation, and loss of all motivation in school and everywhere else. If the guilt is severe enough it can easily lead to suicidal ruminations and even overt suicidal behaviors. In incest survivors, the guilt and other negative reactions tend to be even more severe. DONNY and JUDY, whose tragic case will be discussed later in Chapter 12, are good examples of this reaction.

The primary treatment technique that is most effective and necessary with this problem involves allowing the survivor to *accept his/her part of the responsibility* in the molestation. This is always necessary when there was a long-term relationship with the abuser, some positive feelings toward the abuser developed that still exist, and the survivor did not report the abuse (cases where someone else discovered the relationship or caught them in an act). Parents, investigators, social workers, and therapists asking:

- "Why didn't you tell someone what was going on?"
- "Why did you wait so long to report the abuse?"

- "Why did you let him/her do those things to you over and over?" etc.

Such questions reinforce the doubts and guilt that survivors have already experienced by themselves.

Just as damaging are the instances where well-meaning therapists, parents and others involved with the survivor *insist* that the *total responsibility* is that of the molester. While legally, morally and technically, this may appear true, the survivor does not perceive it that way. While the survivor externally tries to project all blame on the offender, internally he/she often experience personal and subjective guilt for what is perceived as *his/her part* in the behavior, especially in long-term, seductive sexual abuse. As stated above, in almost every case I have dealt with over the years, *there has been at least one occasion* when the survivor either deliberately returned to the molester and initiated the sex act or set himself/herself up in a position of availability for the offender to repeat the act. Rarely is this reported to the authorities or to parents or friends. The reasons survivors do not report include:

- 1. They knew at the time that what they were doing was either wrong or unacceptable to their parents, friends, teachers, etc.
- 2. When other sexual abuse is reported in the newspapers, on television, or in discussions at home, in school or with peers (especially in "locker room gossip") the survivor has witnessed everyone's reaction to the molester and the names he/she is given ("pervert, sickee, criminal, queer," etc.)
- 3. Since the survivor already feels *different* than his/her peers, he/she does not want this difference to be recognized by anyone. This is a most important factor to be aware of when working with adolescents.

Once a *realistic sharing* of responsibility is established, then *guilt reduction* becomes an immediate priority. The most effective technique that I have used to accomplish this goal has always been a *distancing between the old person (the victim) and the present person (the survivor)*. This difference in persons may be accounted for by the trauma that results from exposure, sharing, or even first disclosing the sexual abuse in therapy. The survivor we see in our offices is very different from the child/adult who was abused. It is the therapist's obligation and responsibility to *discover this difference* and reflect it to the survivor. The fact that he/she *survived* and is in an office for therapy is certainly proof of a difference between the old person who was totally subjugated, controlled, and frightened of reporting/discovery, and the present person.

Finally, use of the new value *human equals imperfect* is utilized. All of us have made mistakes in our lives and learned from them. Once the survivor accepts this fact it will help him/her to return to the human fold and no longer feel like an outcast. When this acceptance occurs, behavioral changes are practically automatic and always observable.

I will often ask these survivors to try to explain to me why "All failures are positive!" Most will answer that we can learn from our failures and that becomes the secondary reason that all failures are positive. However, what they do not realize is that to fail one must *take a risk/chance* and that this is the more important reason that all failures are positive. Once this principle is accepted, survivors fear failure less and are more willing to begin risk-taking behaviors when the time is appropriate.

The Fourth Problem deals with *socialization needs.* The social life of these survivors is usually either very poor or nonexistent. Their fears of being found out are a constant preoccupation and *safety through avoidance* becomes their method of dealing with this fear.

Survivors in this category fear that others can *see* their *weirdness,* their being *different* from their peers, their *abnormality.* Avoidance and isolation become their best defenses against possible exposure. On some level, sometimes consciously and sometimes unconsciously, these survivors *want to tell someone what is going on* but they fear rejection, hatred and punishment from all of their so-called normal parents, relatives, and friends. The distorted values involved in all of these perceptions must be dealt with.

Once guilt reduction has been accomplished, for any effective self-image change to occur, *Socialization Skills Training* is the next important step. This is especially true where either making new friends or dating is concerned.

FIVE ESSENTIAL STEPS IN SOCIALIZATION SKILLS TRAINING

There are five essential steps in socialization skills training. Each will be discussed in some detail.

A New Self-Image

As stated previously in this chapter, the post traumatic self-image is negatively and defectively perceived and must be abandoned. The easiest way to accomplish this, in my experience, has been through self-confrontation mirror techniques (Now Therapy which will be discussed in Chapter 13). While the therapist should *not* participate or contribute to the choices of the makeup for the new self-image, he/she must supervise these choices very carefully. There are several specific dangers involved in these choices that we have already discussed in Chapter 9, p. 116 (New Image Formation Dangers) and these should be reviewed and carefully monitored.

Newfound Self-Confidence and Risk-Taking Behaviors

Along with the many other damaging effects of sexual abuse is a loss of self-confidence. This factor is clearly visible in the survivor's difficulty in making decisions, taking risks with new behaviors, or in meeting new people. In addition, any and all behaviors requiring positive motivation are also affected. These survivors no longer trust their own judgment since trusting their molester was a personal judgment that they made with negative and often disastrous consequences.

As a new self-image forms, *risk-taking behaviors* are initiated at the therapist's suggestion but always with the survivor's agreement. Care must be taken to initially set risk-taking goals at a *minimum* to ensure success. The danger to be aware of here is that the survivor may want to take risks that are too difficult at this stage of treatment and that will most likely result in the self-fulfilling prophesy: *"I know I'll fail!"*

For example, for a survivor in this group to immediately look for another long-term relationship with an older same-sex individual is absurd. The first step would be to reestablish some minimal social activity at school or work that was abandoned either during the abuse period or following the exposure period. Casual relationships are usually preferred to intimate relationships for a new risk-taking behavior since they do not require long-term commitment and can be easily terminated with minimal emotional damage, since they do not involve the deeper intimacy or intensity of long-term relationships.

Increasing the level of difficulty in the risk-taking behaviors is totally dependent on the progress and reactions (perceptions and feelings) of the survivor. The survivor should determine his/her own *readiness* for each succeeding level.

Daily decision making should also be used as a technique to reestablish the survivor's self-confidence in his/her own ability to make correct decisions that are important to his/her life as well as to his/her happiness. Even the most minimal decisions help in this area since "Nothing succeeds like success!" In each therapy session, reviewing the past week's decisions activates this technique. Scheduling decisions, clothing choices, purchasing decisions, leisure time choices, etc., all apply and help to reestablish both a new and positive attitude towards decision making and an acceptance of and learning from erroneous decisions. It is essential that the survivor begin allowing himself/herself to make everyday mistakes and then to be able to say "It's Okay" or "So what, I'm only human" or some similar accepting phrase.

A New Definition of "Friend"

Survivors soon realize that their former definition of "friend," in some way contributed to their old problems and eventually to their abuse. Additionally, an over willingness to *trust* contributed and will never again be the same. It will take longer to establish trust and even once established the trust will never be as absolute as it was in the past. *It is important for the therapist to be sure that the survivor realizes that this new caution is a positive value change.* Learning to test friends becomes a new, appropriate, and approved skill for the survivor to learn and to practice. The survivor's speed in trusting or calling someone "a real friend" is affected and will be much slower, which under the circumstance is both understandable and more than appropriate.

The easiest method to help the survivor establish a new definition of "a real friend" is to have him/her make a list of the traits and qualities that he/she feels others look for in him/her in order to call him/her a "a real friend." Whatever traits the survivor lists will usually be appropriate and important in deciding on who will be called a "friend" in the future.

New Values About the Molestation

Following the discovery and exposure of the molestation, all of the survivor's values about his/her molestation are usually initially negative. He/she is too often bombarded with negative feedback from everyone whom he/she comes into contact with. The therapist must separate himself/herself from these negatively judgmental individuals and their reactions. Helping the survivor to identify any *positive aspects* (in seductive molestation these always exist and are also usually found in incest) becomes the therapist's task. The easiest way to begin is to let the survivor know that the therapist is happy and thankful that he/she is able to see the survivor in the office as opposed to being dead or so severely physically or psychologically injured that he/she could not become involved in treatment.

The second positive aspect of the survivor being in the office is that he/she chose to get help for the effects of the molestation/abuse rather than repressing and trying to forget them as so many others do. As simple as this positive approach is, it is often overlooked by even long-term professionals in this field.

Helping the survivor to find other positive aspects of the abuse follows and is easier than one would expect, especially in long-term seductive homosexual abuse. These include the fact that the survivor had to have *some positive feelings towards the abuser* for the relationship to have continued over any period of time. These feelings need to be exposed, discussed and resolved, that is, either accepted or rejected. Allowing the survivor to *separate the positive elements from the negative elements of the abuse* is an important therapeutic task that will result in more positive dividends than expected. In most survivors, if the sexual molestation/abuse had not occurred as part of the relationship with the abuser, the overall relationship would have been considered healthy, desirable, totally positive, and probably would still exist.

Helping the survivor to see that he/she is capable of choosing good relationships but that these relationships must be *free* and not have a price attached provides the survivor with the realistic goal of finding new friends, whether peers or older individuals with whom he/she can relate *without being abused.*

Letting-Go Training

These survivors tend to *hold onto the past* with all of its horrors, guilts and anxiety provoking memories. The result is often isolation, depression and dysfunctional behavior. Frequently, the referring cause in seeking sex therapy is the sexual dysfunction(s) that they are experiencing in their adult lives.

Letting-Go Training through distancing techniques is the main method I use to deal with this factor. Helping the survivor to learn to *distance* between the old self (the victim who was molested) and the present self (the new person in treatment) is a relatively easy to teach method of letting-go of the past with all its attendant emotions, dysfunctions and other "baggage."

Having the survivor choose a *different name* for the old self versus the new self often facilitates this distancing process. A *nickname* that he/she disliked and saw as somehow negative is ideal in situations where the old self is to be abandoned. A name he/she always wanted to have is appropriate and useful where the old self is to remain, at least for a period of time.

THE PROBLEM OF FAMILY INTERFERENCE

Too often family interference with treatment occurs through well-intentioned "feeling-sorry-for" behaviors or "special treatment" and "spoiling" behaviors. Both of these defective family choices hinder rather than help the treatment process.

The family must be *retrained* in dealing with the survivor and his/her new personality. The most important concept that must be conveyed to both family and friends is that the survivor must be treated *normally* and with the same expectations placed on him/her that are placed on all other family members or friends. The family must also be made to understand that the survivor feels *different* as a result of the molestation now being known by everyone and needs help in order to feel the *same* as everyone around him/her once again. The more normally he/she is treated, the faster he/she will return to their approximate former self, although the survivor will never be exactly the same as before the abuse. Well-meaning family and friends can prolong the problem and cause the survivor to become a serious treatment case. This *family retraining* becomes necessary for all family members, relatives and others living in the survivor's home environment. This retraining must include a discussion of suggestions for helpful (versus damaging) behaviors that they need to utilize with the survivor, if they are to aid in the treatment process.

As stated above, the most important emphasis here is that the survivor needs to be treated normally and not as an invalid, or a child who needs to be overprotected or to be spoiled by being allowed to break any and all family rules and principles. The faster the survivor's environment returns to normal, the faster the therapeutic progress will be.

Where small children are concerned (those under five years of age) the therapist will usually need to spend more time and effort on the survivor's parents than on the survivor.

Where adult survivors are concerned, for current sex partners and/or lovers, this retraining must also include sexual counseling regarding:

Who Initiates Sex?

For at least the first several weeks or even months of therapy, sexual behavior must be initiated by the survivor, not the significant other in his/her life. Also, the significant other must be careful not to cause this initiation by playing martyr, by producing guilt feelings in the survivor, or by implying termination of the relationship if sex does not resume. Discussing with the survivor how he/she feels about restarting the sexual relationship is paramount.

Nudity

In situations where in the past, the significant other practiced nudity as part of his/her normal nightly ritual, (by sleeping nude, walking around the bedroom nude before or after showering, etc.) following the sexual molestation/abuse of the partner, this practice may have to be temporarily altered. As with all aspects of the former relationship, open discussion and acceptance of the survivor's wishes, at least during the early stages of treatment and recovery, is essential if the relationship is ever to return to any semblance of its former state. Return to these former nude behaviors should be restarted as soon as possible but only when the survivor feels that he/she can tolerate it.

Specific Act Sensitivity

In instances where a specific sexual act was one of the most traumatic elements of the sexual molestation/abuse, the significant other's initiation of that act can easily *retrigger* memories or an actual reliving of the sexual molestation/abuse. As in all other interpersonal situations, open and frank discussion as to the survivor's feelings and wishes on the subject are paramount.

Timing of Restarting Sexual Relations

The above three factors all involve a *timing factor.* If the relationship is to continue and the sexual part of the relationship is to return to its former level, *when* this occurs must be the right of the survivor.

All of the above factors are best dealt with in consultation with the therapist and often in a joint session with the survivor, the therapist and the significant other.

Too Often, Survivors Are Not Believed

Besides parents and relatives, too often, well-known or respected individuals in the community, including priests, ministers, teachers, scoutmasters, big-brothers, attorneys and even judges, do not believe the survivor and even punish him/her for reporting the sexual abuse.

Where adult survivors are concerned, parents and significant others often accuse them of lying in order to gain attention or sympathy. Even worse are the cases where child survivors report the abuse to parent(s) and the parent(s) either punishes the child or does nothing about the situation. The child survivor then assumes that the abuser has the parent's permission or approval to abuse him/her and even more damage results.

A major dynamic in the disbelief of parents, relatives, teachers, administrators, etc., is that if they accept the fact that the sexual abuse did occur, then they must take some of the responsibility for allowing it to happen. This especially applies to parents who sign permission slips or forms for their children to go on hikes, camping trips and other school activities with a teacher that they know little or nothing about. It also applies to parents of boy scouts, girl scouts, big-brother kids, and all other situations where the parent or guardian *surrenders* control and protection over their child.

School administrators should feel the same responsibility about teachers or coaches they hire, pastors over priests and ministers they appoint to child oriented activities, etc.

An example will clarify.

- KYLE *was molested from age 10 to 15 by a Catholic priest who was a friend of the family and who often stayed overnight at their home. The priest was allowed to sleep in the same room with "Kyle" and would fondle him, rub up against his buttocks and masturbate him but never to orgasm. The priest would also intrude on "Kyle's" showering to perform the same behaviors. While "Kyle" knew that the sexual behaviors were wrong, he also knew that the priest was both liked and respected by his parents. The priest also told "Kyle" that he had **"permission from God"** to do what he was doing and that if he ever told anyone that he would never be believed and would be "punished for lying about a priest of God."*

  When "Kyle" was 14, he heard from other boys that the priest was molesting altar boys and other boys from the parish school. "Kyle" thought he was the only one that the priest liked. "Kyle became quite angry and out of jealousy, "Kyle" told his mother what was happening. His mother's reaction was an angry outburst in which she replied "Well, if it's happening, don't do it any more." However, nothing changed. The priest was still a regular guest of the household and continued to both sleep in "Kyle's" room and to molest him.

"Kyle's" anger towards his family for allowing and facilitating his molestation still exists to some degree today as a functional adult. Not surprisingly, he chose to become a psychotherapist and specializes in treating sexually abused children. "Kyle" is an excellent therapist who has helped many children, especially boys, to recover from sexual abuse. He continues to deal with his own molestation problems in sex therapy with a certified practitioner.

Education of parents and supervisory authorities must be undertaken to resolve this horrible, escalating situation. The conflict over whether children lie or not interferes in the process. Trained sex therapists, psychologists involved in sexual abuse cases, and other trained personnel can usually determine the truth of the accusations to a relatively high degree through specialized interviewing techniques. Parents *should always assume that the child is telling the truth until proven otherwise*. It is better to err on the side of safety for the child rather than to allow the abuse to continue or worsen. The accused adult's rights are well protected by law and, in most cases, the real truth will surface during investigations by both the prosecution and the defense.

Had "Kyle's" mother taken immediate action, how many other boys could she have prevented from becoming victims of this priest's deviant attentions?

Where Can Victimized Children Go When They Are Not Believed at Home?

Child victims of sexual molestation/abuse need other avenues of finding help when none is available at home. To expect boys like "Kyle" to walk into a police station and report a priest for sexually molesting him in his own home is ridiculous. This is an area that the entire community must become involved in. The schools must become more involved. Too often, I have heard from teachers, school psychologists, principals and even school administrators that their *fears of law suits* prevent them from becoming involved in cases such as "Kyle's." The reality is that state and federal child abuse reporting laws all protect the informant from this type of legal problem unless the report is a deliberate fabrication aimed to hurt someone.

Returning to School

Returning to school is a difficult task involving all sorts of risks for the survivor (both children and adolescents). They will not be the same student that they were prior to the exposure of the sexual abuse. Often, they become behavioral problems for attention and/or self punishment. Concentration problems may affect grades as well as oral performances.

The school personnel, where the survivor attends, must be involved in the treatment process and counseled regarding new behaviors and problems to anticipate and how to handle them. They also need to be trained in how *they should react* to the returning child survivor of sexual abuse. Too often I have heard in therapy that not only the children resorted to name calling and rejection but that the *teachers and other school personnel were also involved in similar subtle putdowns, scurrilous rumors, and rejection of the returning survivor.*

A special caveat applies to young boys just entering school who were molested at very early preschool ages, 3-5 years old, typically. For reasons as yet not fully understood, these young boys have been known to:

- expose themselves to other boys and girls,
- undress younger same-sex children in the lavatories,
- remain preoccupied with genitals,
- unconsciously fondle themselves while daydreaming,
- use sexual language atypical for their age, and
- draw sexually explicit pictures and show them to other children.

Without forewarning and adequate training, schools may *overreact* to these behaviors or become punitive to the point of labeling the child sexually deviant, suspending them, or even expelling them from school.

Teachers need to be made aware of these potential problems and how to both prevent and handle them in the simplest and most effective manner. Three simple methods that I have suggested to school personnel for these problems follow.

- 1. Gently interrupt the survivor's unacceptable behavior without shock or scolding.

- 2. Inform the school psychologist of each incident as it occurs and what may have precipitated it.

- 3. Communicate about the problem with the primary therapist in the community who is treating the child. This can be done either directly or through the child's parents.

An example will help to clarify these suggestions.

- RYAN, *one of my youngest male survivors, upon entering Kindergarten, his first school experience, developed the following ritual. When it was time for the children to use the toilet facilities, "Ryan" would "inspect" each boy's genitals, without saying anything to them.*

  When they were finished urinating but had not yet returned their penises to their pants and zippered up, he would turn them around, look, and smile without saying a word. Eventually, one boy told the teacher. A clever solution to the problem was made possible since the teacher first consulted "Ryan's" therapist, whose suggestion was to assign him as the monitor outside the toilet until all of the other boys in his class had returned to the classroom. It was then his turn to use the facilities. In this manner, the young child was never aware that he was being monitored himself.

This discussion concerned only *seductive homosexual abuse* since homosexual assault cases will be covered under the section on sexual assault survivors since the molester's behavior in these cases was *sexual assault* and not seductive sexual molestation/abuse.

SEXUAL ASSAULT CASES

Before beginning this section, a word is necessary as to why the word "Rape," for the most part, will not be used in this section. Rape is too often legally defined as forced penile vaginal penetration and only that. There are other forced sexual acts that are as demeaning and degrading and also as damaging as that defined by rape that also need to be considered including forced sodomy, forced oral sex, forced fondling and masturbation and many, many others. "Sexual Assault" includes any and all forms of forced or nonconsensual sexual behavior.

In addition to experiencing a majority of the personal problems and effects listed above, survivors of sexual assault have several special problems that need to be considered.

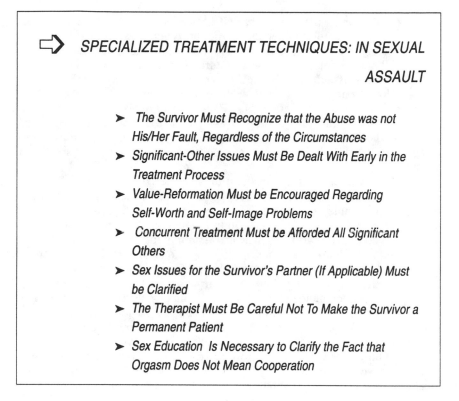

SPECIALIZED TREATMENT TECHNIQUES: IN SEXUAL ASSAULT

➤ The Survivor Must Recognize that the Abuse was not His/Her Fault, Regardless of the Circumstances
➤ Significant-Other Issues Must Be Dealt With Early in the Treatment Process
➤ Value-Reformation Must be Encouraged Regarding Self-Worth and Self-Image Problems
➤ Concurrent Treatment Must be Afforded All Significant Others
➤ Sex Issues for the Survivor's Partner (If Applicable) Must be Clarified
➤ The Therapist Must Be Careful Not To Make the Survivor a Permanent Patient
➤ Sex Education Is Necessary to Clarify the Fact that Orgasm Does Not Mean Cooperation

Self-Blame

A special problem too-frequently emphasized by survivors of sexual assault is *self-blame*. These survivors often become "Monday-morning-quarterbacks," finding and inventing ways that the assault could have been avoided and then assigning guilt to themselves for not using these methods. Several example statements from survivors whom I have treated come to mind.

- "If I hadn't gone out for milk so late at night, nothing would have happened."
- "If I hadn't worn so tight a dress/skirt, he might not have become excited."
- "If I had fought harder, I might have been able to stop him."
- "If I hadn't agreed to go camping alone with my scoutmaster, this wouldn't have happened."
- "If I hadn't agreed to shower alone with the coach, he couldn't have played with my penis, it wouldn't have felt so good, and I wouldn't have gone back for more."
- "If I had worked out more in the gym like my friends do, I would have been able to fight him off and then he couldn't have used me like a woman."

The number and variety of these self-accusatory and recriminating statements is as infinite and as varied as are the survivors themselves.

The primary treatment guideline for the survivors of the sexual assault group
is that all therapy contacts must be structured in such a way as to convey the
message that the assault was *not the survivor's fault, regardless of the circumstances.* Nothing he or she could have done would cause or justify the assault.

The sexually assaultive person (S.A.P.) will do all in his/her power to place
the responsibility and blame for the assault on the victim. In a shocked
condition, the survivor is highly vulnerable to any and all suggestions, comments or criticisms and the abuser, *aware of this,* uses it to his/her full
advantage.

Any therapy or counseling must aim to *undo* the self-blame as well as any
other damage resulting from the sexual assault. Even if the survivor had been
running around nude, it did not give the abuser the right to assault her/him. I
often use the example of the "Lady Godiva" story to illustrate this point with
female as well as male survivors, who are assuming full responsibility for their
own assault. Circumstances such as jogging alone in a park late at night,
walking alone in a high crime rate area, hitchhiking and accepting a ride from
a stranger, allowing an alleged utility repair man into the house or apartment
without checking credentials or calling the company, agreeing to either play
strip poker or go "skinny-dipping" (nude swimming) with a lone adult, etc.,
while all *examples of poor judgment and definite risk taking behaviors,* do not
give the abuser the right or excuse to sexually assault anyone.

Each of the above examples are from real case histories and each contributed
to the survivor's severe guilt, depression and even to attempted suicidal
ideation as well as actual suicidal incidents. A specific example will clarify.

* *Remember* DIANA, *whom we met in Chapter 10, who after watching a late movie on
T.V., went to the refrigerator to get something to drink and realized that there was no
cream or milk for the next morning's breakfast. Throwing a raincoat on over her
negligee, she drove to the local shopping center where a 24-hour convenience outlet
was located. Except for the clerk, no one was anywhere to be seen. "Diana" jumped
out of the car, leaving the driver's door open and the engine running. She ran into the
store with the correct monies and purchased her milk. She returned to the car and
began the drive home when a young man arose from crouching behind the driver's
seat. After thanking her for the invitation, he threatened "Diana" with a knife, forced
her to drive behind the shopping center complex to a deserted area and sexually
assaulted her there, making her first fellate him and then forcibly penetrating her.
When he was finished, he ran off into the neighboring woods.*

  *During her first session in my office, "Diana" was unable to make any eye contact
with me. Her opening statement to me was "I stupidly went out and got myself
raped!"*

Certainly, "Diana" used poor judgment in going out after one a.m. wearing
only a negligee, and leaving her car door open and the engine running. In no
way, however, did this give the attacker (S.A.P.) the right to take advantage of
the situation and sexually assault her. The hospital nurse certainly contributed

to the post traumatic shock and depression by not believing "Diana's" story and then the husband's lecture when they returned home, focusing on her using better sense and taking better safety precautions, all convinced "Diana" that the attack was *primarily her fault.* No one had mentioned or discussed the responsibility of the attacker at all.

The most important and urgent task in "Diana's" therapy was to get the story straight and to put the responsibility where it belonged. This does not mean that her part in the incident should be minimized or denied. She needed to accept her part of the responsibility in order to ventilate the resultant personal guilt realistically. Too many untrained individuals would deny "Diana" any and all responsibility, insisting that it was *all* the offender's fault. This is an unrealistic approach and prevents the survivor from dealing in therapy with issues that she/he feels are pertinent and important.

Misinterpretation of Normal Physical Reactions During the Assault, Including Orgasm and/or Ejaculation

When an orgasm or ejaculation occurs during the sexual assault, the survivor will often come to the faulty conclusion that it meant *cooperation* on her/his part and therefore it was not a case of real assault. A great many cases that never are reported are due to this faulty value/conclusion.

In sexual assault, the offender will often *insist* that the victim enjoyed the act. He/she will quote erection or lubricating, movement of hips, moaning, smiling, not complaining, etc., as *proofs* of the survivor's enjoyment and cooperation. The conclusion that the offender reaches (and desperately needs to reach) and then forces on the victim is that these behaviors prove that the victim *wanted* the assault to occur and enjoyed it. One of the most frequent offender statements to the victims is *"You were asking for it and you know it!"* or some other variation with a similar meaning. All of these justifications, rationalizations, and projections are utilized to reduce the degree of responsibility and guilt that the abuser experiences after the sexual assault. These defenses become a major resistance in the offender's treatment. The reader is once again referred to volume one in this series *Treating Sex Offenders in Correctional Institutions and Outpatient Clinics.*

In sexual assault cases as in cases of other forms of sexual abuse, sex education is necessary to clarify and explain the physiological fact that having an orgasm does not mean cooperation or that the victim liked the sexual assault and therefore also liked the abuser. Most survivors have had little or no sex education and do not understand that, once orgasmic, their bodies will function on an autonomic level ("Auto pilot"). *Under most circumstance their bodies will respond physiologically regardless of whether they cooperate or not;* females may lubricate, males may get an erection, both may experience orgasm.

A special case comes to mind that bordered on the ridiculous.

- *Driving on one of the state's superhighways,* ANTHONY, *a 41-year-old male salesman, stopped under an overpass to check his map for directions to the location of his next customer. Out of nowhere, two women came up to the driver's window brandishing a pistol and forced their way into the car, one in the front and the one with the pistol in the back seat. After robbing "Anthony" of his wallet and credit cards, they decided to sexually assault him as well. He was moved to the rear seat and told "**Either you get it up and give us a good time or we'll shoot it off and you'll be a dead man!**" Although frightened to death, "Anthony" managed to get an erection and performed on the first woman, as commanded.*

  *When he had satisfied her and while the two women were switching seats, the opportunity arose for the salesman to grab the gun. Holding them at bay, he drove off the highway's next exit and took them to the nearest police station where he was **laughed at**. Beside that humiliation, the officer in charge told the two women that they could charge him with assault and false arrest, if they wished. Undaunted, "Anthony" left the local police station and next took them to the State Police barracks where he was finally aided. However, the county prosecutor refused to press for an indictment against the two women when the salesman admitted that he did **perform intercourse on the first woman**. The prosecutor insisted that "**If you were really forced and frightened you would not have been able to get an erection or to complete intercourse.**" Laughing hysterically, the two women were released from custody, free to continue their assaults on innocent males with impunity.*

All Other "Significant Others"

Husbands-wives, girlfriends-boyfriends, or other significant others too often misunderstand the situation, harbor their own judgmental feelings, or, although well-intentioned, blunder in their dealing with the survivor of sexual assault.

All of the significant others mentioned above should (I prefer *must*) be involved in the treatment process where any survivor is concerned. This rule certainly applies to the survivors of sexual assault since while some issues are the same as in other types of sexual abuse, other issues are totally different.

The most important areas that must be discussed and resolved with the significant others include *treating the survivor as if she/he has a terminal disease*. This problem exposes itself in behaviors such as:

- a. fear of talking about the event,
- b. fear of touching the survivor physically, often seen in refusing to kiss the survivor on the lips after an assault,
- c. not dealing with questions that are bothering them (the significant others) about the circumstances of the sexual assault,
- d. terminating social relationships, visits, company, going out to dinner, etc., to *protect the survivor.*
- e. avoiding discussing their feelings regarding the survivor. This especially applies to the male partners of female survivors of sexual assault who now might feel that the survivor is *dirtied, sullied, used, or diseased* (especially when AIDS phobia is present), *possibly pregnant,* etc.

The significant others need to be able to see the therapist whenever necessary and express whatever they feel without the therapist becoming angry and judgmental in a survivor-advocate manner. While this is sometimes difficult, considering the ignorance associated with sexual assaults, the therapist will accomplish little for the survivor by becoming adversarial with individuals that the survivor must live with and deal with on a daily basis. *Re-education rather than recrimination should be the rule.*

This same situation also applies to parents and others in the household who are in close daily contact with the survivor. Involvement of these individuals assures that treatment will become a family affair and be life-oriented rather than an isolated exercise that applies only to the therapist's office.

Subjective Judgments

Distorted subjective judgments (discussed in Chapter 9) and *self-recriminations* are all too common in sexual assault survivors and must be dealt with as early as possible. This is a very critical problem area since these negative self-evaluations affect self-image, self-confidence and all other areas of therapy.

Value reformation, especially regarding self-worth and feelings of being dirtied, sullied, used, unworthy of a positive or good relationship, etc., must be a consistent focus until behavioral evidence of changes occurs. *Distancing techniques* are a major aid in this process, when correctly utilized. Separating how the survivor perceives herself/himself into the victim of the sexual assault and the person in treatment today allows the survivor to become much more objective and reality critical about the sexual assault.

Utilizing the *third chair technique,* discussed fully in Chapter 10, accelerates the distancing as well. As stated previously, in the third chair technique, the survivor is asked to imagine that another survivor is sitting across from her/him in an empty chair. The therapist then replays all of the criticisms, putdowns, punishing phrases and statements that the survivor used on herself/himself but now making these derogatory statements the verbalizations of the survivor in the third chair. The therapist then asks the present survivor to talk to or counsel the survivor in the third chair. What usually occurs is that she/he does an excellent job. She/he is caring, empathic and appropriate with the invisible survivor in the third chair. The therapist then challenges the survivor to say the same things to themselves, not as the present person but as the survivor at the time of the sexual assault.

Once this stage is reached, *letting-go techniques* follow. The therapist uses the truism that there is nothing that can be done about the past but that a great deal can be done about the present and the future. *Letting-go* will be one of the most difficult changes for the survivor to make. It may take a long time and have to be focused on weekly. With young children and adolescent survivors, I usually exaggerate this area and allude to the fact that we do not have time machines that can return to the scene of the assault and change what happened. I also stress that all of the punishment in the world will never change one aspect of the remembered assault. The goal is not to have the survivor forget the facts of the assault but to let-go of the associated feelings and guilts that are intimately attached to the memories of the assault.

Sexual Issues

Sexual issues for the husband-wife, boyfriend-girlfriend, males-females living together, or gay individual-partners are often a major concern of the sexual assault survivor and need to be addressed as early as possible in the course of the treatment.

Arrangements should be made, with the survivor's permission, to hold a separate session with the sex partner of the survivor. Following answering whatever questions the partner may pose, several important issues must be discussed and suggestions made for handling these problem. These include:

- 1. that there should be no initiation of sexual behavior unless it comes from the survivor and only when she/he is ready! The partner needs to understand and accept the fact that this initiation of sex may not be for quite some time. The therapist must make sure that the partner understands the reasons. This will be one of the therapist's most difficult tasks.

- 2. that, once sexual activity is resumed, the survivor must also be allowed to choose the type of sexual behavior and the specific act. Also that this situation will remain for some time. Intercourse, oral sex, or any act that occurred during the sexual assault may not be advisable in the beginning. Substituting intimacy, touching, holding, etc., appears more appropriate for the first month or so or until the survivor suggests or permits going further. Acceptance of these conditions, on the part of the partner, will be of paramount importance to the overall treatment of the survivor of sexual assault.

Rapid Promotion

Too often, survivors become professional patients, either due to their own dependency needs that are tolerated or due to the conscious or unconscious personal needs of the therapist.

Care must be taken not to make the survivor a *permanent patient* and in this manner to revictimize the survivor. Long-term unnecessary therapy will convince the survivor that she/he really is *sick, "nuts," mentally damaged, permanently ruined, etc.,* fears that she/he already has. A *weaning process* should be begun as soon as the therapist feels that the major issues have been at least identified, touched upon and are in the process of being resolved or when the therapist senses a dependency situation developing.

In my experiences, the best method to utilize with all survivors is to promote them from weekly to bi-weekly sessions for several weeks or months, then to monthly sessions for a reasonable time span, then to quarterly contacts (every three months), and finally to PRN ("pro-re-nata") or "call in when necessary" status. The survivor does not have to leave therapy *"cured"* (a word I despise). Of course, the understanding should exist that should an emergency occur or should a setback develop that the process can be reversed for an agreed upon time period. Naturally, any and all promotion should be with the discussed and explicit consent of the survivor.

In my private practice with survivors of sexual abuse and/or sexual assault, I never promote to termination. I leave all survivors at the PRN level. This provides the survivor with the additional security that she/he still has a right to call-in or ask for a situational session. It also assures the survivor that she/he has not been *rejected* by the therapist, a fear that most of them have from the beginning. In my early years of treating both offenders and victims, I did "terminate" cases. When the first few failures returned to former patterns, *without ever having called in for help or additional therapy,* I asked each one:

- 1. If she/he had any *"warning signs"* that a recurrence was in the offing. — The answer was always affirmative.

- 2. When these "warning signs" occurred, why had she/he not called in for help? — The answer that the failures gave was that they did not want to disappoint their therapist or their group by letting them know that she/he was not *cured* and that she/he was again experiencing symptoms.

These two factors determined the need to eliminate even the impression that a "cure" had occurred or that the survivor would remain symptom free, for the rest of her/his life. The PRN solution resolved this dilemma and the above two reasons for not calling in were never used again, although certainly there were additional failures.

12

Specialized Therapy Techniques in Incest and Long-term Child Sexual Abuse

Having discussed the specialized techniques necessary for the first two categories of sexual abuse: homosexual abuse and sexual assault, this chapter will deal with the last two categories of sexual abuse: incest and long-term child abuse..

INCEST CASES

It is important to remember, as I have mentioned elsewhere in this work, that I only consider incest to have occurred when a *biological* parent or relative is involved. Where foster parents, adoptive parents, or live-in significant others are concerned as molesters, I see them as fitting more appropriately into either the pedophilic or hebophilic categories. The dynamics of these individuals differs greatly from those of the biological parent, especially where "rights" and "ownership issues" are concerned.

The first consideration in incest is that in all incest cases, but most importantly those occurring during adolescence, the survivor is *doubly damaged.*

- 1. She/he becomes a survivor of sexual abuse, and
- 2. She/he becomes a victim of one or both of his/her own parents. The effects in this second factor involve:
  - a. Betrayal
  - b. Violation of the love trust relationship between parent and daughter/son and, finally
  - c. Identity problems affecting self-image and self-esteem, too often lasting for the rest of her/his life.

Incest survivors, while experiencing many of the same reactions to their sexual abuse that the other two groups of survivors experience, have additional problems specific to their abuse that must be addressed separately.

Unresolved Questions

There are often *unresolved questions* that neither the therapist nor anyone else except the abuser is able to answer or to help the incest survivor to resolve. These questions, if left unanswered, will disrupt therapeutic progress and personality change. The most frequent of these questions, in incest cases, is always *"Why me?"*

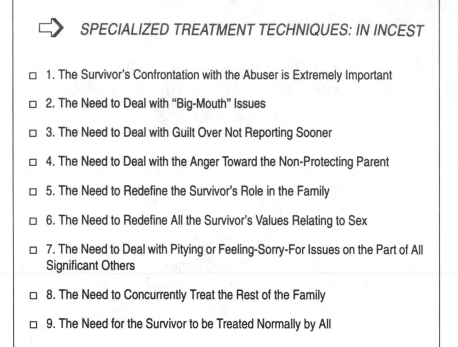

SPECIALIZED TREATMENT TECHNIQUES: IN INCEST

☐ 1. The Survivor's Confrontation with the Abuser is Extremely Important

☐ 2. The Need to Deal with "Big-Mouth" Issues

☐ 3. The Need to Deal with Guilt Over Not Reporting Sooner

☐ 4. The Need to Deal with the Anger Toward the Non-Protecting Parent

☐ 5. The Need to Redefine the Survivor's Role in the Family

☐ 6. The Need to Redefine All the Survivor's Values Relating to Sex

☐ 7. The Need to Deal with Pitying or Feeling-Sorry-For Issues on the Part of All Significant Others

☐ 8. The Need to Concurrently Treat the Rest of the Family

☐ 9. The Need for the Survivor to be Treated Normally by All

This question occurs primarily in multi-sibling families where the survivor is the only known victim of one or both parents. However, it may also occur in an only child family when the survivor is comparing herself/himself to other children or peers with whom she/he associates or visits.

Face-to-face confrontation with the incestuous father/mother is extremely important, especially when there are other siblings in the family. Only the offending parent(s) can provide an answer that will be accepted to the "Why me?" question. It may surprise the reader to know that the incestuous offender's most frequent response is *"Because I loved you the most!"* Also surprising to those not involved with these cases is the fact that the offender's answer is probably the truth due to his/her distorted values and perceptions, especially the "Love equals Sex" value.

Ambivalence

In incest survivors, *Ambivalence* (love/hate) about how they feel about the abuser is a second and very upsetting reaction that needs to be confronted directly with the offending parent(s). Disclosing these feelings to anyone but the offending parent(s) does not fully ventilate them. These feelings then remain an issue in therapy repeatedly, sometimes for many years.

In cases where direct confrontation is impossible, what the therapist can do is to help the survivor to clarify the issue. Survivors, as a group, do not give themselves permission to feel ambivalent. They hear from the nonoffending parent, friends, and often authority figures that they should be angry and hate the incestuous parent and want them punished. As a result, they see their ambivalence as a problem and are unable to resolve it one way or another.

Value reformation techniques help a great deal in this area. Helping the survivor to separate those personality and behavioral traits in the offending parent(s) that she/he *loves* and those that she/he *hates* appears, over a period of time, to settle the confusion for most survivors of incest. In the majority of cases, it is the *sexual behavior, the control and the threats* that are hated while the remaining behaviors and traits are loved. Establishing *a new value* that permits judging all people that the survivor is in contact with in this manner will help to establish better future relationships as well. The former black-and-white thinking that the survivor held and his/her all or nothing perceptions are abandoned and replaced with a more moderate and reasonable set of values. These new values will eventually apply to herself/himself, as well.

Role-playing techniques may also be utilized with the therapist playing the role of the offending parent and allowing the incest survivor to ventilate his/her feelings, especially the anger, onto the therapist. There is a danger in this technique of the survivor becoming *physical* and causing injury to the therapist.

Revictimization by the Incest Survivor's Own Family and Friends

Too often, the incest survivor becomes *revictimized by her/his own family,* including the nonoffending parent and the siblings. This occurs since more often in incest than in any other sexual abuse, the entire socioeconomic base of the family is altered (for the worse) by the incestuous parent's imprisonment or being forced to leave the household and establish a new residence. This is more true when the father is the abuser than when the mother is, regardless of whether the survivors were females or males. In father incest, even if the mother is employed, it is rare that her income equals that of her husband's. The family's economy that was based on a two-salary income no longer exists.

Regardless of the reasons, the surviving family of incest must often move to a less desirable neighborhood, give up many of their former luxuries (golf/country club, summer camp, vacations at the shore, etc.) and concurrently lose long-term friends and schoolmates (for the siblings). The children must change schools and lose their teachers, friends and extracurricular involvements (sports, drama, music, etc.). Their anger is then turned onto the incest survivor and she/he often becomes known as *"Bigmouth."* An example will clarify.

• *While working with an incest case in a mental health clinic in a wealthy community, I was assigned to counsel a 16-year-old, bright and extremely beautiful young lady, CONNIE, who had been sexually abused by her father over a three year period. His threats to leave the family and to harm her mother and younger sister kept "Connie" silent until she caught her father beginning the same pattern of molestation on her 12-year-old sister. It was then that she went to the school psychologist and told the whole story, including what had happened to her in the past.*

The father was a well-liked, successful businessman in the community who had a home improvement business. Through his work in the area as well as his active involvement in the Rotary and Elks organizations, he was both respected and liked by all with whom he came into contact. He was an officer in the school's PTA group and volunteered for sports activities: coaching and supervising in his daughter's high school. As a result of his sports involvement in the school, he was also known by most of his daughter's schoolmates.

*Her mother, friends, community organization members and "Connie's" school-mates all believed the father's story of his **innocence** which made "Connie's" life a pure hell! She dropped out of school and could not even walk down the streets of her community without harassment, insults, and even threats. The school authorities also believed the father and allowed him to continue in his work at "Connie's" school with the other children.*

*The horrible thing about the whole affair was that the father had admitted his offenses to us at the mental health center. By law, we had reported it to the appropriate DYFS (Division of Youth and Family Services) agency who informed us that the prosecutor's office found our report of the father's confession to be **"insufficient evidence for referral to the grand jury."***

"Connie's" situation became so unbearable that she became severely depressed and entertained suicidal thoughts. In desperation, we contacted relatives of her family and were fortunate in finding a maternal grandmother in Florida who would take "Connie" into her home and give her a chance at a new life. The parents too willingly agreed. "Connie" was eventually able to adjust and, through continued therapy in Florida, began a new life.

Re-education of all family members by involving them in the treatment process with the survivor (if they are willing) appears to be the most effective treatment technique in cases of this type. They need to know the terrible feelings, the extent of the emotional damage, and the overall destructiveness that the incest behavior wrought upon the survivor.

Role playing also helps in the process of sensitizing the family members to understand what the incest survivor is experiencing. The process involves having the nonoffending parent (if one exists) and each of the siblings *switch places* with the survivor and then having the rest of the family or the therapist make the same comments, doubts, accusations, etc., to him/her. Having him/her imagine how he/she would feel and what he/she would most want from his/her family instead of the putdowns and negative judgments, is really both dramatic and effective. This is a highly emotional and powerful technique, and the therapist has to prepare and be ready for a multitude of possible reactions from members of the family, both positive and negative. Often, the other family members, once they realize what they have done to their sibling or child, develop their own guilt problems and may need therapy themselves. If therapy for other family members is necessary, it should be done either situationally or with another therapist rather than by the one treating the incest survivor. This will avoid a conflict of interest and the doubts or suspicions of revealing information from one patient to another. If the survivor's primary therapist is considering treating other family members it should occur only with the survivor's explicit approval.

Finally, focusing on *empathy and family cohesion* is essential. Utilizing all the outside community resources that the therapist can find will also improve the family situation and take much of the pressure off of the survivor. This often includes referrals to several social service agencies to aid the surviving parent to cope with financial problems and to obtain better employment and housing and contacts with the school board where it is deemed essential that the remaining siblings continue in their same school even if they have moved to another district. Referrals to family therapy agencies for situational support for the whole family may also be necessary.

Guilt

There is a need to deal with the *guilt and self-recriminations* that the survivor feels for not reporting the incest sooner, especially in cases where a younger sibling is now being molested. This guilt often results from innuendo and improper questions. Parents, investigators, even therapists, often exacerbate this problem by asking persistently "Why did you let it go on for so many years?" or "Why didn't you come to me sooner?"

The survivor needs to know that the therapist understands the situation that she/he was in. This could involve several situations. Where believable threat was involved (a knife, threats to kill the mother or other siblings, threats to kill a pet, etc.) the situation is fairly easy to deal with and is usually understood by everyone.

However, one of the most common factors found to explain the delay, when fear or physical threat were not present, is the *fear of loss of the secondary benefits* that the abuser so cleverly used to obtain cooperation or silence. These "perks" are often difficult to abandon, especially in cases where feelings of acceptance and love were involved. The survivor, once again, needs to *separate the acts from the actor*. While the therapist should agree with the survivor that the behavior was either morally or legally wrong, that does not mean that the survivor was totally evil, bad, unworthy, etc. This distinction must also be made clear to the nonoffending parent and all other parties involved with the incest survivor.

Secondly, since nothing can be done about the past, once it is ventilated with all the attached emotions, then the survivor must find a way to *let go* of it. Even though placed in her/his inactive memory banks, the memory can always be recalled at will. Since it is the emotional reactions that did the damage, they must be ventilated and resolved completely, as we have stated so often before.

In cases where the incest has been repressed for a long period of time, a short and simple explanation of repression mechanisms might help. (One of my active cases involves eight adult survivors of the same incestuous father who had repressed the sexual abuse for a minimum of 40 years until one of the siblings under hypnosis remembered it and then triggered the remaining seven siblings' memories.) Where repression is suspected, I like to use the analogy of a locked file cabinet drawer where the damaging memories are stored. There are still cracks and openings around the outside of the drawer that permit the emotions and feelings to escape while the actual content of the drawer remains securely sealed. This analogy often explains unexpected and unwanted emotional reactions, phobias, unreasonable outbursts, sexual dysfunctions, and even illogical fears that the survivor may have been experiencing.

Anger and/or Rage Toward the Abuser as well as Toward the Nonoffending Parent

The guilt issues mentioned above often block anger or rage toward the abuser from surfacing. This is especially true in incest survivors who still feel ambivalent toward the offending parent and are still finding ways to blame themselves for the incestuous abuse. An example will clarify.

- JOEY, *whom we met in Chapters 2 and 3, was brutally and forcibly sodomized by his father. Later that evening, while lying in bed, unable to sleep, "Joey" kept replaying the tapes of the sexual assault by his father and asking **Why?** over and over. He suddenly came up with (forced) an answer. Whenever "Joey" was in the shower, his father would find an excuse to come into the bathroom. "Joey" was afraid that his father would see him naked with an erection (either from the flow of water or from his masturbation habit) and, anticipating that his father would pull back the shower curtain (as he always did), he always faced the wall. When his father did pull back the shower curtain, he always saw "Joey" from the rear. Remembering his father's comments after the assault about his "tight, boy pussy," "Joey" reasoned that the sight of his wet and naked buttocks must have "turned his father on" each time that he saw him naked in the shower. **Therefore,** (a quantum leap!) the assault was his, "Joey's," fault and he had no right to feel angry at his father.*

Many of the incest survivors I have treated had similar reactions, *all* based on the comments, rationalizations, or projections of their incestuous parent(s).

Anger Toward the Nonoffending Parent

There are always mother or father issues in these cases, especially feelings of *anger* over not being adequately protected. There is often a deep suspicion that the nonoffending parent (if both were not involved) knew what was going on all along and permitted/allowed it. This *knowing* could either mean actual knowledge of the incest or a suspicion it was happening and not wanting to find out the truth. Either is equally damaging and anger producing for the survivor. Here again, "Joey" is an excellent example.

- *Coming home, after being assaultively sodomized by his father at the father's paramour's apartment, "Joey" entered his house in shock and bleeding rectally. His mother took him into the bathroom, undressed him, cleaned the blood and the inserted cotton wading into his anus, a second painful penetration. She then told "Joey" to go to bed and "You'll be all right in the morning."*

    *"Joey," lying in bed and replaying the tape of his arrival home, interpreted his mother's non-questioning and nonreaction to mean that not only did she know what his father was doing but that she **condoned** his father's behavior. What "Joey" wanted and needed was for his mother to comfort him and to put the blame on his father by calling the police and having him arrested (punished). Rage and anger toward all mother-figures resulted and "Joey" became a violent rapist in later life.*

Reality therapy is the approach of choice for this problem. Survivors, especially children of incest, have a right to be angry for not being protected from the sexual abuse. When the survivor is *ready*, a confrontation session with the nonoffending parent (if she/he agrees), will help to, at least, bring the feelings of anger to the surface and ventilate them. To what degree this confrontation will resolve the problem depends on the willingness of the involved parent to accept some of the responsibility and of the survivor to "let-go" of as much of the anger as she/he can. Several sessions of this type may be necessary before any resolution occurs.

If this type of confrontation session is to take place, a preparatory session with the nonoffending parent alone is necessary to prepare her/him for what may occur. Here again, the therapist must be prepared for a lengthy and highly emotional session. The therapist's role in these sessions is that of *referee* or *mediator*. The therapist's primary responsibility is to make sure that the session does not harm the survivor more than help her/him. Most nonabusing parents that I have worked with handle this session quite well. This is primarily true since they have already told themselves the same things that they will hear from their surviving child and the exacerbation helps relieve their usually intense guilt as well as their self-recriminations. Thus the confrontation session can benefit both the incest survivor and the nonoffending parent.

In cases where the nonoffending parent refuses to become involved in the survivor's therapy, role-play techniques, with the therapist assuming the role of the nonoffending parent may be employed. Letter-writing therapy techniques are also useful in these cases, regardless of whether the letter is ever delivered. Both of these methods provide limited ventilation of the anger/rage.

Redefining the Survivor's Role in the Family

There is now a need to *redefine the survivor's role in the family*. She/he is no longer *special* to the incestuous parent or to the rest of the family in either a positive or negative way especially in the manner that she/he was *special* during the incest.

This issue must be dealt with on a Family Therapy basis with *all* members of the family involved. Here again, the therapist plays the role of the moderator, teacher, and, if necessary, the referee.

The nonabused family members need to be given *permission* by an authority figure outside of the home (the therapist), to treat the survivor in their usual and normal pre-incest discovery manner. In a majority of incest cases that I have worked with, once exposure of the abuse occurred, the rest of the family was constantly *walking-on-eggshells.* Feeling sympathy for the survivor, becoming overly permissive, going out of the way to protect the survivor, etc., all were positive and love motivated but had the effect of increasing the survivor's feelings of being *different.* These family reactions need to be avoided at all costs. As stated repeatedly, the more quickly the survivor begins to feel *normal* or the *same* as their siblings or peers, the quicker recovery will occur.

Distorted Sexual Values

There is a need to *redefine all values related to sex.* This especially applies in cases where the survivor formerly used sex to earn or buy love, acceptance, gifts, companionship, or, often in incest, to protect another sibling or the entire family from the threats of the incestuous father/mother.

When the survivor has resolved the above listed seven problem areas (pages 170-176) and is ready, *sex attitude restructuring exercises (S.A.R.)* should begin. Complete sex education is often necessary since a majority of these survivors (especially the younger children and the more immature or naive adolescents) were taught all of their sexual facts and values by the offending parent in a manner designed to accomplish his/her goals of molestation and to justify his/her deviant behaviors. While "sex equals love" dominates a list of these distorted values, there are others including the value of the parental right to teach their children proper sex education *by explicit example,* so often found in incest cases. These and all other discovered distorted values regarding sex need to be replaced with positive and healthy sexual values.

Desensitizing Techniques

In some cases of sexual abuse, whether incestuous or not, *specific body part or specific sex act phobias result.* In these cases, special desensitizing techniques to either the body part or to the act need to be developed and assigned as "homework" exercises with a caring, sensitive and involved partner. A specific example involving both elements will clarify.

- LAUREN, *whom we met in Chapter 6, due to her father's violent, painful and traumatizing sexual abuse, over a long period of time, developed a **penis phobia.** She could not even tolerate seeing a picture of a nude male in a nudist magazine without having* *an hysterical, terror reaction. She developed an absolute aversion to thinking about or discussing heterosexual activity and in particular fellatio.*

After several months of weekly therapy, focused on desensitization, and once "Lauren" began relaxing more in therapy and became more capable of dealing with the more difficult aspects of her case, the subject of her reaction to seeing her new husband BILL'S penis as he returned from showering in the honeymoon suite at Niagara Falls, was broached. She very much wanted her marriage to succeed and also to become capable of having normal sexual relations with her husband without remembering her father and panicking.

After seeing "Bill" privately on more than one occasion, it became more than obvious that he truly loved "Lauren" and wanted their marriage to work. He offered to do *"anything at all that I thought might help her and that might reestablish their marriage."* In her next session, I prepared "Lauren" for "Bill's" involvement in her treatment. Up to this point, "Bill" knew nothing about "Lauren's" molestation by her father but was willing to help without knowing why.

Once "Lauren" was relaxed and ready for the desensitizing process, I asked "Bill" to come into the office and to not say anything throughout the session. I instructed him to stand in a corner diagonally across from where "Lauren" and I sat and then asked him to undress to his underpants. "Bill" did as he was asked without the least hesitation and with no question. Once he was undressed to that level, I turned to "Lauren" and asked her to look at "Bill" from head to toe, several times. Up to this point, upon hearing my instructions to "Bill," "Lauren" had immediately lowered her head, almost into her lap. Now, after several minutes of hesitation, she looked at "Bill's" feet and then slowly moved her gaze up his body until she was looking into his face. "Bill" smiled. I waited until "Lauren" had done this several times and until I felt that she was comfortable and not about to panic. I then said to her "The rest is up to you."

"Lauren" almost panicked but gained control of herself since she knew that she could end the session right there and not be criticized by either "Bill" or myself. Slowly, gripping my hand until she almost cut off the circulation, she told "Bill" to remove his underpants and again averted her gaze. "Bill" did as requested, again not saying a word. After what seemed an eternity, "Lauren" again looked at "Bill's" feet and ever so slowly moved her gaze up his body until again she met his face. She then jumped up out of her chair and ran over to "Bill," crying and hugging him as tightly as she could. I left them together in the office for some 20 minutes and then returned to find them on the floor in each others arms, smiling and crying at the same time and telling each other of their love.

Three sessions later, "Lauren" happily informed me that they had had their first intercourse and that she enjoyed every moment of their sexual encounter. Further desensitizing homework was used involving "Bill's" return to his normal post-showering nude behavior. Bill was also given the caveat to allow "Lauren" to initiate any sexual encounters for the time being and also, more importantly, to allow her to choose their sexual scripting. Also "Bill" was warned not to expect oral sex for a long, long time and he happily agreed.

"Lauren" was promoted rapidly and has now been on PRN status for over a year. She calls in regularly with a *progress report* and comes in for a session as new material regarding her incestuous abuse surfaces. Prognosis for total recovery in a seemingly hopeless case is now excellent.

Another case needing desensitization therapy involved:

- LEROY, *a 24-year-old male, who was a survivor of mother-son incest. After his father deserted the family when "Leroy" was 10 years old, his mother made him sleep in her bed. In the beginning, she fondled his genitals and had him fondle her breasts. Eventually she masturbated him to orgasm and he thoroughly enjoyed it. She then taught him to reciprocate and he didn't mind the game she called "Stinky-finger."*

    When "Leroy" began ejaculating at around 12 years old, his mother fellated him rather than "waste it." When she forced him to reciprocate orally on her, "Leroy" vomited. His mother was not a very hygienic person and her vaginal odor was overpowering. From then on, "Leroy" did all that he could to avoid any contact with his mother. She, however, beat him mercilessly with the buckle end of a belt, a broom handle, ironing cords and anything that she could find in order to force him to perform cunnilingus on her. Each time he did, "Leroy" became ill and vomited. He eventually ran away from home when he was 14 years old and when apprehended, his mother refused to take him back. He lived in one foster home after another until he was old enough to find employment and a place of his own to live in.

    At 24 years of age, "Leroy" met a girl and fell madly in love with her. When they decided to have sex and he saw her naked, "Leroy" ran into the bathroom and vomited violently. His family physician, finding nothing physically wrong, referred him to me for sex therapy. "Leroy's" desensitization involved the necessary cooperation of his fiancee and nightly homework. The homework involved several stages. First, showering together, then lying in bed naked and simply talking. Touching and sexual activity was prohibited at this stage. "Leroy's" first goal was to be able to simply be in bed naked with a woman and to look at her without becoming ill. Removing the 'threat' of potential sexual activity, made this possible. Once "Leroy" felt comfortable at this step and no longer felt like he would become ill, the second step was initiated. This involved mutual body exploration but again with sexual behavior prohibited for the same reasons stated in the first step. Once the second step was mastered, then step three was initiated and involved mutual masturbation and "Leroy" once again played 'stinky-finger' without becoming nauseous or ill. In step four, intercourse was permitted, when "Leroy" felt comfortable enough to attempt it. Everything went well and "Leroy" was ecstatic.

    At this stage a hiatus occurred. Although "Leroy" wanted oral sex from his fiancee, he was unable to even consider reciprocating so he never suggested it. This hiatus lasted about six months. Finally, at the therapist's suggestion, a total body oral sex session occurred without emphasis on any particular area and "Leroy" enjoyed this stage with no negative reactions. Cunnilingus has still not occurred and his fiancee understands that it may take a long time or that it may never occur. She is satisfied with the sex life they now enjoy. The couple has an August date for their marriage.

The School's/Employer's Reactions to Learning of the Incest Situation

The *school* (where children or adolescents are concerned), including the administration, the involved staff, the nurse, and the school psychologist must also become peripherally involved and informed of pertinent facts about the incest survivor's treatment in order to prevent the same permissive, pitying attitude to be used or to set lower goals for the incest survivor. *Communication* with the school psychologist or the guidance counselor must be maintained by the therapist to retain consistency of handling these children. Where the survivor is treated one way at school, in a totally different way at home, and yet in another totally different way in therapy, the only result can be incredible confusion.

Behavioral changes may also be observed by school personnel especially where acting-out behaviors or overt sexual behavior is reported. The therapist needs to prepare the school authorities, psychologist, teachers and other school personnel for these possibilities in the incest survivor and to make appropriate suggestions for handling them.

Where older survivors are concerned, if they are in a college or university, similar contact must be made with an advisor and other involved staff. Where adult survivors who are employed are concerned, there is often a need to communicate with their employer through either the personnel department or through a counseling service if one exists at their place of employment. Nothing, of course, can be communicated to these individuals without the explicit permission of the survivor through a written release form. Even with such a release, no details of the abuse should be communicated, only what the survivor wants the school/employer to know or what she/he now needs from her/his school/employer or fellow students/workers. In this regard, encouraging the survivor to return to school/work as soon as she/he feels able to face it should be one of the primary therapy goals. The longer she/he is away from her/his school or place of employment, the more difficult the return and adjustment will be.

LONG-TERM SEDUCTIVE CHILD SEXUAL ABUSE TECHNIQUES

Since this area is a particularly sensitive and difficult one, a summary of several caveats must precede our discussion of each treatment technique presented.

A form of conditioning occurs in these survivors.

They become passive/compliant and wait for orders rather than make decisions. The therapist must give them responsibility and control for their therapy as discussed in Chapter 9.

These survivors have a great deal of trouble believing that change is possible for them and are not sure they really want to change, since the "status-quo" is safe.

The therapist must find ways to *prove* to them that change is possible and desirable. Using daily behavioral change successes appears to be a most effective method.

There is ambivalence regarding the feelings about the abuser in these survivors.

Therapy must assure them that this is normal and acceptable. This is a good place to change their old values on love from either "love equals sex" and/or "love equals obedience" to "I can love a person and still hate something they do," and/or "I don't have to pay to be accepted or loved."

Same-sex abuse survivors often feel that their sexual identification has been permanently established by these acts and therefore cannot be changed.

Sex education and the concept of *sexual preference* will clarify this issue intellectually, then they must internalize it through behavioral means.

They feel guilt and blame for the abuser's problems, including his arrest, job loss (if applicable) and incarceration (if applicable) and wish they had just left things as they were.

Reality orientation and proper focus on adult responsibility is necessary at this juncture. Even in sexual assault, it must be pointed out that regardless of the survivor's role, whether passive compliant or nonresistant, that did not give the abuser the *right* to sexually assault her/him. The examples that the therapist will use to defend this argument depend on the circumstances of each survivor's abuse and are ideally presented in *story form* using someone that the survivor knows: a friend, sibling, etc.

A method that has worked many times for me in the past with this group is to ask for the survivor's help with another survivor with similar problems. After explaining the details of the abuse and the other survivor's negative reactions, I ask this survivor what he/she would say to the other survivor if he/she made certain negative statements about themselves. Often I play the role of the other survivor and ask this survivor to be the therapist. They always say the right things.

I then use the survivor's own statements from the role play about his/her problems and he/she usually is able to see the double-standard being used due to "subjective judgment elements" (discussed in detail in Chapter 9). From here on, therapy becomes easier and more productive. This technique can be used whenever the situation calls for it.

These survivors continue to feel different than their peers, regardless of how their peers respond.

"Different" here means unequal in an inferior way. They perceive that the abuse has left them dirtied, sullied, shamed, damaged and undeserving of being accepted equally by their peer group. A typical statement, illustrating this

⇨ NEGATIVE EFFECTS OF INCESTUOUS ABUSE

BOYS	GIRLS
• Repeat the offense in a ritualistic manner on younger siblings or sibling substitutes.	• Stress being adult. This change occurs as a sudden-onset occurrence.
• If forced, painful sodomy was involved, they often chose rape to deny their femininity and also to project their rage against their perceived nonprotecting mother.	• Overmakeup and overdress as seductive to satisfy their need for attention and sometimes for the father's continued approval.
• Display generalized rage at females throughout their lives that they cannot justify or explain.	• Start using their body and their looks for gain (learned from father).
• Tend to be aggressive and pain-producing in their sexual encounters.	• Become teases to boys and often to older men.
• Often have unresolved bisexual feelings and tendencies that frighten them and that they need to deny.	• Become outrageous flirts; partially to confirm their attractiveness, partially out of anger.
• Lose interest in school grades and often become school behavioral problems.	• Lose interest in school: want money, gifts, jobs, travel.
• Feel ambivalent towards the father: love and hate him at the same time.	• Consider the incestuous father their boyfriend or lover. This is usually the father's idea.
• As parents, fear having children since they might pass on their deviation or, even worse, become sexually abusive towards them.	• Become physically and emotionally abusive parents, but not sexually abusive. At times, this abuse ends in the death of a child.

reaction might be "If they knew what happened to me or what I have done, they'd never talk to me again!"

Here again, role playing to expose the double-standard works along with all of the self-esteem and self-image techniques described above. One role-play method I use includes asking for the name of their best and closest friend, and then suggesting that this exact same scenario has happened to that friend and now the friend has told their best friend, the survivor. I then ask several questions that reflect the anticipated negative response that the survivor predicted would occur if his/her friend knew the secret. "Would you drop them and tell them to stay away from you?" The usual response is "No!" "Would you call them names and tell them it was all their fault?" The usual response is "Of course not!" To the question "Would you go running around the school and tell all of the other kids what happened?" the usual response is "That would be crazy, mean and hurtful!" or something similar.

Usually, by the third or fourth question, the message has gotten through and the survivor sees the absurdity of her/his fears. Of course, if the survivor had labeled individuals "friend" who were really not friends, the outcome could be different and this possibility must be anticipated and discussed before the technique is used.

Self-confrontation, discussed in detail in Chapter 13, will also usually work with this issue of feeling *different*. The therapist can always help with the proper questions but never with any suggestions or answers.

These survivors often prefer to "forget the whole thing" rather than deal with it.

Young children, tend to *repress* the details while older survivors tend to *minimize and leave out details that embarrass them* or that they consider *"too bad or too dirty."* The therapist must make sure that this *forgetting* does not occur. Repetition of the factors and events of the abuse at regular intervals (a form of desensitization) helps to prevent the *forgetting* as do value reformation exercises, especially where subjective-judgment concepts are concerned.

The survivors of long-term seductive child abuse crave an inordinate amount of attention and acceptance.

In doing so they often *"test"* parents, teachers, peers and even therapists to the limit and beyond. The therapist must find a way to let these survivors know, through value reformation, questions and examples, that *testing* is normal in all relationships and that the survivor should communicate her/his intention of testing to a prospective friend, parent, etc.

Also, when they truly do need some *attention,* learning to ask for it becomes extremely important since it implies that they deserve it. When this occurs, it is an excellent sign that progress is being made and that therapy is on the correct course. This is another example of *behavioral confirmation,* a necessary and essential ruler with both survivors and their abusers where any reported change is concerned.

This group of survivors tends to act out their anger on everyone around them, especially parents and others whom they felt should have protected them from the abuser.

These survivors often become behavioral problems, acting out their anger anywhere and everywhere, especially at school. Often their siblings will receive the brunt of this anger since they are perceived as having been spared the abuse and since the survivor is usually incapable of directing the anger at the abuser.

The treatment goal here is to get the survivor to vent the anger *appropriately* and to direct it at the real cause of the anger, not onto an innocent victim. Of course, *finding* the real source of the anger becomes the hardest part. It could be:

- 1. the abuser,

- 2. the negligent protector (parent, foster-parent, principal, pastor, etc.),

- 3. the survivor, herself/himself, or

- 4. the peers who either harassed or rejected him/her.

Helping the survivor to identify the object(s) of his/her anger now becomes the primary goal and then the secondary goal becomes finding a method of *appropriately* expressing this anger.

If the abuser is the target of the anger, if at all possible, this expression of anger should occur during a confrontation with the abuser, in person. Where it is impossible to confront the abuser due to the abuser's death or if he/she is in prison where the survivor may not be permitted to visit, a *written confrontation* (which I have the survivor compose for homework and then read aloud in my presence in her/his next therapy session) provides the next best outlet. Whether the letter is sent or not does not appear to be as important as the fact that it is written and has been *ventilated outloud.*

This group of survivors will find ways to punish themselves when others won't.

These punishments may range from failures to isolation to pain to suicide. This is a particularly important and dangerous area that the therapist must constantly monitor. Clues from outside sources as well as from the survivors themselves must be paid attention to and be dealt with as each occurs. When the possibility of suicide is discovered, family members, especially parents or guardians should be made aware of the situation and suggestions should be given as to how to identify the warning signs and prevent the attempt.

Reality therapy has always worked best for me where punishment needs exist. I ask the survivor *if punishment will undo the sexual abuse or destroy the memory* or *make them feel better when it is over.* If they say "Yes!" then it would be an acceptable alternative. Not a single survivor in my 30 years of experience has ever agreed that punishment met either of these three conditions.

Once the survivor has reached this conclusion, then a *substitute behavior* for the punishment that will produce positive results is recommended. The therapist may help the survivor find such a substitute behavior but may not choose or suggest one for them. The best method in accomplishing this is to have the survivor make a list of all the possible alternatives that he/she can think of and then discuss each one during the next session. One of his/her choices will usually result in far more positive behavioral changes than one that was thought of by the therapist, parents, or friends.

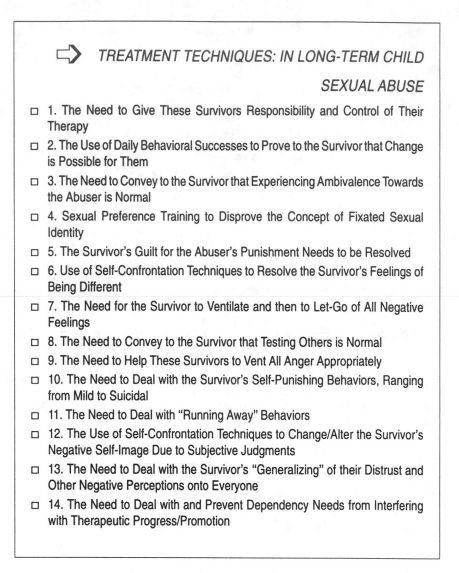

⇨ *TREATMENT TECHNIQUES: IN LONG-TERM CHILD*

SEXUAL ABUSE

☐ 1. The Need to Give These Survivors Responsibility and Control of Their Therapy

☐ 2. The Use of Daily Behavioral Successes to Prove to the Survivor that Change is Possible for Them

☐ 3. The Need to Convey to the Survivor that Experiencing Ambivalence Towards the Abuser is Normal

☐ 4. Sexual Preference Training to Disprove the Concept of Fixated Sexual Identity

☐ 5. The Survivor's Guilt for the Abuser's Punishment Needs to be Resolved

☐ 6. Use of Self-Confrontation Techniques to Resolve the Survivor's Feelings of Being Different

☐ 7. The Need for the Survivor to Ventilate and then to Let-Go of All Negative Feelings

☐ 8. The Need to Convey to the Survivor that Testing Others is Normal

☐ 9. The Need to Help These Survivors to Vent All Anger Appropriately

☐ 10. The Need to Deal with the Survivor's Self-Punishing Behaviors, Ranging from Mild to Suicidal

☐ 11. The Need to Deal with "Running Away" Behaviors

☐ 12. The Use of Self-Confrontation Techniques to Change/Alter the Survivor's Negative Self-Image Due to Subjective Judgments

☐ 13. The Need to Deal with the Survivor's "Generalizing" of their Distrust and Other Negative Perceptions onto Everyone

☐ 14. The Need to Deal with and Prevent Dependency Needs from Interfering with Therapeutic Progress/Promotion

Besides functioning as an escape mechanism running away becomes a method of dealing with people they know and from whom they fear judgment.

Running away may actually be a *running to* someone or someplace where the survivor feels that she/he will be safe, accepted, and loved. Reality therapy, here also, regarding the prices and outcomes of such behavior needs to be discussed. Then the survivor should be given the choice of whether to continue with the "running away" behaviors or not. My rule has always been: *"Do whatever you carefully choose, as long as you're willing to pay the full price for it."* Prices have to be fully discussed since most survivors are unaware of all of the consequences of their behaviors, especially the dangers of running away. At this point, they may be simply acting on impulse or from panic. In this area and in all other areas as well, as long as the survivor is made to see that the choices are his/hers, then they get the credit for the result or are responsible for the payment for the choices they make. In other words, they are again in control of their lives.

Survivors of long-term child sexual abuse often project their own judgmental views about their abuse onto everyone around them and, too often, choose avoidance rather than communication with parents, authority figures, therapists, etc.

Here only self-confrontation works. Until the survivor's personal views and judgments of themselves change, no one else's views (including those of the therapist) have any meaning or significance. The whole world can love them but as long as they despise and hate themselves, their behavior and feelings will remain negative and no change is possible.

One of the three requirements for change to occur is *"I deserve to change."* As long as their self-perceptions are negative due to perceived shame and guilt, no change can be asked of them or be expected to occur. A re-reading of the problems that "Dennis" is having with his therapy (discussed in Chapter 6) will clarify the extent and seriousness of this type of damaging and often highly resistant problem.

ADDITIONAL MALE SURVIVOR PROBLEMS

All male survivors have problems that are specific to their being male and that are quite different from female survivor problems in many respects while sharing other common reactions. To begin with, males report sexual abuse even less frequently than do girls but for many different reasons and, as a result, less attention is paid to the problem of male sexual abuse. Finkelhor (1984) suggests that this is

> ... not due to an absence of male victims, per se, but rather the result of a) investigator assumptions regarding the 'typical' abuse case (i.e., an older male victimizing a young girl), and b) social phenomena that discourage male abuse disclosures, such as expectations of self-reliance and avoidance of implied homosexuality (most sexual abusers, regardless of the gender of the victim, are male).

Referring to the illustration entitled: Special Effects of Sexual Abuse on Boys (p. 187), the reader is given ten of the special reactions that boys have to sexual abuse that result in behavioral acting out, loss of motivation to succeed, depression and even suicidal thoughts and behaviors. Thus, Elliot and Briere (1992) state that:

Research suggests that the victimization of boys and girls differ in the following ways: Boys are more frequently molested outside the family than girls. The onset of abuse tends to occur at a younger age for boys and to end at an earlier age. Physical force is used more frequently against male victims. Since the majority of sexual abusers are male, boys are more frequently abused by someone of their own sex, while girls are typically abused by someone of the opposite sex. Males tend to minimize their victimizations or view it less negatively than do females, despite studies indicating equivalent levels of later psychological damage. One of the most striking gender differences is the male's greater reluctance to disclose the sexual abuse during childhood or adulthood, which may make him a 'hidden victim,' susceptible to a number of somatic and emotional disorders years after the abuse.

Unrealistic myths and beliefs, some engendered by the abuser(s), others by peers feigning knowledge, lead to unbelievable conclusions in these survivors. For example, the first "effect" listed often results in avoidance of locker room and gym activities or any other situation where changing clothes or showering is involved. I have had many pre-adolescent and post-pubertal boys as well insist that "if other boys or instructors see me naked they will know what was done to me." This belief is often partly responsible for their non-reporting.

These boys also realize that a medical examination would be part of the reporting procedure and then, either:

- 1. there would be no evidence that they were sexually abused (as in fondling, masturbation and even fellatio), or

- 2. there would be evidence of sexual abuse (as in anal penetration) and then their parents and the whole world would know that they were *used as a girl.* A "Catch-22" results.

Feeling different in these boys is highly magnified and results in social isolation and avoidance as well as serious damage to their changing and developing self-image.

Self-blame is frequent in these cases and it appears to be a direct result of statements made by the abuser, coupled with the male survivor's demanding need to know "Why me?" More often than not they find a reason to blame themselves (as "Joey" did). The resulting self-blame and self-recrimination damage all motivation to succeed.

Undoing by repeating the identical abuse on younger and more vulnerable boys is a constant and ever-present danger. The previously mentioned *fear of being the only one* is present in these cases. The outcome is always negative in these cases since the "undoing" never works and through trying over and over again the behavior eventually becomes *compulsive* and a new sex offender results.

Where incest is concerned, males report even less frequently than do girls but for different reasons. The incestuous abuse may have been at the hands of the father, mother, older brother or sister, uncle, aunt, grandfather or grandmother, or male or female cousin, etc. As stated elsewhere in this work, I only consider sexual abuse to be incestuous if there is a direct bloodline involved.

Foster or adoptive parents, siblings, and relatives as well as live-in males or females are more appropriately considered either pedophilic or hebophilic sexual abusers.

In my experience with incestuous parents, they consider *all* of their children to be their possessions and will use any of them for their deviant sexual needs. If their primary victim is not available when their wants or needs arise, then they will use any of their children who are available. The old adage of "any port in a storm" aptly applies.

INCEST HAPPENS TO BOYS TOO

This factor must be taken into consideration when a girl, who has brothers, reports incestuous sexual abuse. Too often, parents, police, youth bureau investigators, social workers, etc., see incest as a father-daughter occurrence and don't bother asking the boys (or even other female siblings who did not report) if they were also abused. Boys, especially, will not volunteer the information since their reactions are different as is the price that they will pay for reporting. In my thirty years of experience, I have found that *boys have different problems following an incestuous relationship with either parent and therefore need different and very specific treatment than that used with girl incest victims.*

A distinction must be made between males molested by males (whether parent or not) and males molested by females (parent or not). Other relevant factors to be considered include the relationship of the abuser to the survivor, age disparity between the survivor and the abuser, and whether seduction or force was used. Each factor will be discussed.

In Chapter 11, I have already discussed seductive homosexual abuse and homosexual assault. What remains in this section is to discuss father-son incest, mother-son incest, older brother/sister incest and relative incest (male or female).

FATHER-SON INCEST

While all other incest survivor problems apply, there is a major difference in male survivors of father-son incest where *identity problems* are concerned. This is especially true when an incestuous father chooses sodomy (anal penetration) as the incestuous act. (This also applies to other types of male-male sexual assault.) In the boy's (or older male's) confused mind, where there already may be some self-doubt about his masculinity, this form of violation is subjectively perceived as *being used as a woman!* If the boy has any knowledge of sexuality (and most adolescents and even many preadolescents today from age nine on have such knowledge), then the boy realizes that his father normally should be having sex with his wife (the boy's mother) or with some other woman and not with him. The father's choice of his son as a sex object *in preference to a woman* is often perceived by the son to mean that he

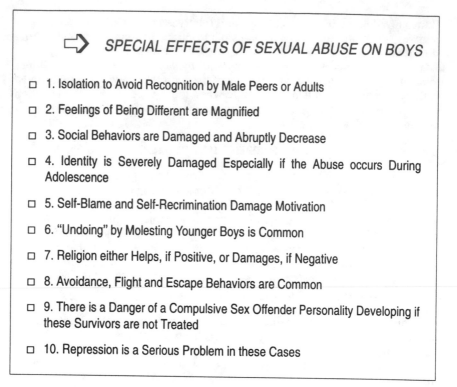

SPECIAL EFFECTS OF SEXUAL ABUSE ON BOYS

☐ 1. Isolation to Avoid Recognition by Male Peers or Adults

☐ 2. Feelings of Being Different are Magnified

☐ 3. Social Behaviors are Damaged and Abruptly Decrease

☐ 4. Identity is Severely Damaged Especially if the Abuse occurs During
     Adolescence

☐ 5. Self-Blame and Self-Recrimination Damage Motivation

☐ 6. "Undoing" by Molesting Younger Boys is Common

☐ 7. Religion either Helps, if Positive, or Damages, if Negative

☐ 8. Avoidance, Flight and Escape Behaviors are Common

☐ 9. There is a Danger of a Compulsive Sex Offender Personality Developing if
     these Survivors are not Treated

☐ 10. Repression is a Serious Problem in these Cases

must be more feminine, in some way, and more sexually exciting than the other women that the father had available to him.

An even worse scenario exists when the father, during or after an anal sexual assault, comments in a highly complimentary manner on the quality of the sex with his son, using references or comparisons to women he has been with and rating the boy as better. The damage is magnified even more. The following statements were taken from actual incestuous fathers or from their survivor sons.

- "That was the best sex I've ever had!"
- "Your 'pussy' was the best I've ever been in!"
- "No woman has ever made me feel so good!"
- "No woman has ever turned me on the way you have!"
- "Your mother never made me feel like that!"

The damaging effects of statements like these and a hundred more just like them that may be even more damaging, is obvious. The self-image, identity and self-esteem of the boy/male is terribly damaged, potentially for life. His shame and guilt as well as his fear that others may also see him as *feminine* or worse, often prevents him from reporting or seeking treatment. These personal and subjective-judgment reactions often equal or exceed the fear of his father's threats, which usually involve the family status or the safety of other family members, including younger siblings. A tragic example, at this point, will clarify:

- DONNY *and* JUDY *were both the long-term victims of an incestuous father. One of the most shocking facts in this case was that the incestuous father was a well-known physician and a member of his community's task force on the prevention of sexual abuse on children. Image was everything in his life and the image he projected was false to the core.*

    From their earliest memories, both children remembered their father as a dictator who ruled his family with an iron fist. Corporal punishment was swift, sadistic and frequent. All family members feared their father intensely. There were several other siblings in the family who were older than the two but "Donny" and "Judy" were special to each other and had the closest relationship that any brother and sister could possibly develop. There was almost an extrasensory link between the two.

    *When "Judy" was only six years old, the first sexual assault on her occurred and left a permanent mark in several ways. Arriving home from some social affair where "Judy" had to act like the loving and wonderful daughter of this "great man," "Judy" was made to wait for him in the living room. She sat, in terror, wondering what she could have done wrong and anticipated the worse, a beating. Her father returned to the room after some time, wearing his pajamas and robe and told her to undress. Now she was sure that she was going to be beaten for some unknown transgression. Instead, he began to fondle and kiss her and then laid her down on the living room rug and **raped her**. During the sexual assault, her mother entered the room and screamed at "Judy," "You little bitch! — You're trying to take my husband away from me and he's too weak to handle your seduction." The father never paused for a moment but continued the sexual assault until he had been satisfied. "Judy" later received one of his **special beatings** for upsetting her mother.*

    The mother left the room and several days later abandoned the family without explanation. Over the next ten or more years (before "Judy" finally ran away from home), the beatings and the sexual assaults continued on a three-to-five times a week basis. When "Judy" protested or did not appear (act) pleased to see her father in a sexually excited state, she would be beaten on the head with a miniature baseball bat and/or have large and damaging objects inserted into her vagina. She often was beaten into unconsciousness.

    On more than one occasion, "Judy" had to be taken to the emergency room of the local hospital for treatment. Naturally the father took her to the hospital where he was on the staff and had many friends. His usual explanation to the emergency room staff was that she was a "klutz" and had fallen down the stairs, off a bicycle, etc. The staff of the hospital believed him or acted as if they did. In order to protect herself from questioning, "Judy" would act so obnoxiously that no one who offered help remained interested in talking to her or taking her side for very long.

    Unbeknownst to either "Judy" or "Donny," their perverted and corrupt father was sexually molesting each of them and getting them to submit by saying that if the one didn't do what he wanted, he would go to the other. Due to the closeness of their relationship, each of them protected his/her sibling by submitting to his perverted sexual desires. On one occasion, when "Donny" did not perform up to his father expectations, his father took a scalpel and cut "Donny's" penis deeply stating that the next time he would "cut it completely off!" "Judy" heard "Donny" crying in the bathroom and found him naked and bleeding on the floor. She 'butterflied' the wound and helped him to clean up and dress since "Donny" refused to go to the hospital with this type of wound fearing that he would be seen as a "faggot" or "pervert."

Both children felt helpless and depressed and sincerely believed that no one would believe what their father was doing, were they to seek help. They leaned on each other and both found a great deal of consolation in music. "Donny" loved music so dearly that he began a career (unknown to his father) in music in a neighboring city where he composed beautiful music which he performed and sang to great acclamation.

However, the sexual, physical and emotional abuse did not stop and, unable to take any more, "Donny," disgusted with how he saw himself and his inability to break loose from his father, committed suicide.

"Judy" ran away from home and *survived on the streets* of a major metropolis with no help from anyone in her family. Her college career was abandoned and she also considered suicide. Some inner strength made her a survivor wanting revenge on the "monster." She also determined that as soon as possible she would find a career where she would be able to help other children like herself and in this way to make up in part for failing "Donny" (her perception). Slowly but surely, "Judy" found work and a place of her own to live and began to rebuild her life. She volunteered for "hot lines" that aided sexually or physically abused children and teenage runaways and made up her mind to find a way to do more. Eventually, she began teaching in a special school for children who could not adjust to regular classes or were considered to be pre-delinquent.

Today, she is teaching in another school in her hometown and has returned to college to finish her degree. She still suffers depressions and has not totally eliminated the guilt. She needs intensive therapy but is not willing at this point to trust anyone sufficiently to take this risk. Problems continue with her remaining siblings who continue to blame her for all the problems in the family and *who still disbelieve her allegations about their father.* There is a strong possibility that her remaining brothers were also victimized but either suppressed the memories or deeply repressed them. Either way they are in heavy denial. "Judy" still has had no real contact with her mother who also has never stopped blaming her for all the tragedies in the family. What happens to "Judy" in the future is now "Judy's" choice. Help is available and has been offered. All she has to do is fully commit herself to the risk of trusting someone again and believing that she is worth the effort.

"Joey," whom we met in Chapters 2 and 3 and who was brutally sodomized by his father, has been released from the treatment center and is once again

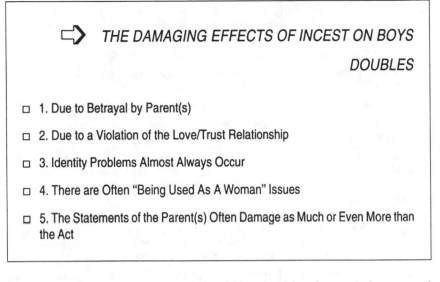

living with his wife and children. He is involved in after care therapy and reports from his family indicate that he is doing well.

The primary need in these cases is to let boys (and girls as well) know in any way possible that they have a *right* to report their abuse and that they were in no way the cause of the incest.

Most statistics indicate a much lower incidence of male incest than actually occurs. Over 90 percent of the pedophiles and hebophiles that I have treated over the last 30 years were themselves victims of some form of sexual abuse, a large majority of them survivors of incestuous molestation. As stated before, while their own abuse never *justifies* their abusing innocent children, it certainly helps to *explain* it.

MOTHER-SON INCEST

Of all child sexual abuse statistics, mother-son incest is probably the least ever reported and I feel that it will remain the least ever reported abuse for many years to come.

There is a special relationship and bonding that exists between mothers and sons that does not exist between fathers and sons. A loyalty and *need to protect* results that transcends the boy's personal needs and sexual or psychological health.

In 30 years of working with offenders and victims, I have had only a dozen or so male survivors ever admit to mother-son incest and then only under the strictest confidentiality conditions. Even a one time incident will leave a permanent mark on the boy and affect all male-female relationships until the shame and guilt is adequately resolved in therapy. Where long-term mother-son incest is concerned, the shame and guilt magnifies, especially where sexual pleasure was experienced.

Several common factors in these cases should be noted.

- 1. No woman can ever live up to the boy's memories of his mother's idealized assets.

- 2. As an adult, the boy now looks for a woman to *replace* his mother in his life.

- 3. The adult male incest survivor constantly compares any woman he has a sexual relationship with and, usually, finds her lacking (compared to his mother).

- 4. Womanizing often results since no woman meets the unresolved needs from his relationship with his mother. These needs may be his desire to possess her, to marry her, to never be separated from her or to simply continue his relationship with her *forever.*

- 5. Sharing the secret of the incestuous relationship with anyone is nearly impossible since the survivor fears damaging his mother's reputation (the above mentioned protectiveness). He also fears the dramatic negative reactions of his peers, friends and especially his father whose wife he had an affair with.

In all of the cases of this type that I have personally dealt with, I have **never** been allowed to discuss the situation with the mother herself. This is not true where fathers are concerned. Most male survivors want the incestuous father exposed, confronted, and even punished. Not true where mothers are involved.

Finding a method of bringing these mother-incest male survivors into treatment is a major challenge to all involved in this field.

SIBLING INCEST

Another form of incest that is being reported more frequently in the last ten or more years is that of sibling incest. Sexual behavior between siblings is often a normal developmentally experimental behavior. This might involve brother-brother, sister-sister (less frequent) or brother-sister sexual behavior. These cases usually involve consensual or seductive sexual behavior with siblings close in age to the initiator.

However, there are cases that go beyond these parameters. These would include brothers sexually assaulting younger siblings, male or female, and father provoked sibling assault. In these cases, the father not only initiates the sibling incest but often *directs* the assault, in person. Several specific cases come to mind and are relevant to this discussion: "Todd," raped by his brother at age 10 and discussed in Chapter 9, "Philip" and "Rachel" who imitated their parents' sexual behavior and were severely punished, as discussed in Chapter 3, and "Tim" who was masturbated by his brother at age 10, as discussed in Chapter 6. In each case a *trauma* resulted and surfaced in deviant sexual behavior in later life. The difference in these cases and in those that were not traumatized but developed normally was the existence of a negative result, whether rejection, beatings, pain, ridicule, shame and guilt, feelings of femininity in boys and immorality in girls, etc.

What appears, therefore, to be the essential factor that differentiates these cases from positive to negative is not the sexual behavior but the personal or authoritative reaction to the behavior, the result. An example of father-provoked sibling incestuous assault is necessary at this juncture.

• PETER, *is an incestuous father who molested all of his eight children, two boys and six girls. "Peter," himself, was molested from age five to age nine by his own father who sodomized him at every possible opportunity. "Peter," in turn, sodomized his two sons, **always** in the shower. During each sexual assault on his sons, "Peter" continuously raved on about how much better the sex with his boys was than with any woman, including their mother. After "Peter" was finished assaulting one of the boys, he would tell him the following: "Now that I've taken your manhood from you, why don't you get it back by fucking one of your sisters. You have my permission." At least one of the boys accepted his father's invitation. The boy forcibly sexually assaulted at least four of the six sisters. On several of these sibling assaults, "Peter" accompanied his son and **directed**. He then rated the boy's performance, adding suggestions for the **next encounter**. At least the one boy compulsively continued these incestuous encounters with his sisters but was sensitive, loving, and kind in complete opposition to his father's angry, forced, and always painful attacks on the same sisters.*

*Surprisingly, two of the sisters today feel that without these sexual incidents with their brother(s) they would not be as sexually well-adjusted in their marriages. I concur with their conclusions based on interviews with their husbands who confirm their present sexual **normalcy**, unexpected in incest cases like these.*

MALE SURVIVORS OF RELATIVE-INCEST (MALE OR FEMALE)

A final category of incest that severely affects male survivors is that of *relative-incest*. Sexual abuse by uncles, aunts, grandfathers, grandmothers, etc., is more frequent than one would suspect from sexual abuse statistics and often occurs in conjunction with parental abuse. The old adage *"It runs in the family"* applies in quite a large number of incestuous families and follows the undoing and normalizing behavior patterns of other sex offender groups.

In the large incestuous family discussed above, the incestuous father who molested all eight of his children, both boys and girls, was also incestuously abused himself by his father. As therapy with the children progressed and more and more repressed memories emerged, several of the female children began to remember sexual molestation by their *grandfather,* the father who molested their father. The patterns of the molestation with the grandchildren were almost identical to those with his own sons.

Boys frequently become survivors of relative-incest when either their own fathers are missing (deceased, divorced, or deserted) or when their needs for male identification and bonding are stronger than usual. Unsuspecting mothers often become involved in fostering a relationship with male relatives as a substitute for the missing father and unknowingly hand their sons over to a pedophile/hebophile. This often involves either the grandfather or an uncle.

Relative-incest can also involve an aunt or grandmother. These cases appear less frequently or simply are less frequently reported for the same reasons that mother-son incest is so infrequently exposed. Also, the misperception that sex with a female is normal, positive and should be appreciated comes into focus, the *Mrs. Robinson Syndrome.*

As in parental incest, the trauma in relative incest doubles since there is an implicit trust in a relative that does not exist with a stranger. A sense of personal betrayal results, especially when the sexual behavior is discovered or the survivor is caught in *flagrante delicto* with his uncle/aunt. Anger often ensues since the child had assumed that the attention from the relative was motivated by sincere concern and love. After exposure or abrupt cessation of the relationship, the child/adolescent realizes that he/she was "conned" and "used."

Treatment is identical to that for parental incest survivors with an emphasis on the value that being a relative in no way prevents problems, sickness or perversion from occurring. The remaining treatment techniques are identical to all sexual abuse.

Caveat: It is imperative that all of the anger is ventilated and that a new self-image is in existence prior to promotion to PRN status.

ADDITIONAL TREATMENT CONSIDERATIONS

In addition to offering survivor-oriented sex education, self-esteem exercises, assertiveness training, S.A.R. (Sex attitude restructuring) courses, social skills training, risk-taking training, and anger ventilation, group therapy with other peer-age survivors offers the best treatment modality for male survivors. While individual therapy may be necessary in the beginning, as quickly as the survivor is ready, he should be transferred to an adjunctive, professionally monitored, self-help group.

Networking with other incestuously abused males is a most important factor in the overall rehabilitation of these damaged males. These *self-help* type groups work excellently with incest survivors (both male and female) as long as they are properly supervised by a trained and experienced professional.

Successful treatment for these survivors is definitely possible and must be made available if there is to be any hope of decreasing the number and seriousness of incestuous crimes, adult sexual dysfunctions, failed relationships and marriages, severe depressions, suicidal fantasies and attempts, etc.

A SPECIAL APPROACH FOR REACHING MALE SURVIVORS OF SEXUAL ABUSE

The pressing problem today is how to reach these molested male children and adolescents before they possibly become young adult male sex offenders, repeating their abuse on other males as a method of normalizing or undoing their abuse as discussed in detail in Chapter 4.

One New Jersey community, Monmouth, found a simple but effective method of accomplishing this task. They developed a program called *It Happens To Boys Too!* The prosecutor's office formed a male victimization committee to handle this project and invited individuals from treatment agencies, probation, DYFS (Division of Youth and Family Services) and private practice therapists involved in child sexual abuse to participate. A simple poster placed on school and clinic bulletin boards and the same poster enlarged on community billboards brought in more calls than were ever anticipated. Most of the callers were male victims of all ages who simply did not know:

- 1. that they had a *right to report* or

- 2. did not know *whom* to report to or *where* to report.

The next step was to recruit therapists from the community to treat the cases, either "gratis" or at a special reduced fee. There are very few private practitioners who cannot afford to open one or two treatment slots per week for this kind of community work. The response was overwhelming and sufficient to allow both *screening* of the therapists to be sure they were qualified and *training* of the approved therapists in specific techniques to work with these young males. Little or no financial expense was involved.

Training was provided on an all day basis for three different groups: the professionals (psychologists, psychiatrists and social workers actually involved in treatment of these young males), the paraprofessionals (including investigators, social workers and others not directly involved in treatment) and finally educators (teachers, guidance counselors, school nurses, administrators, etc.) All three training sessions were well attended and well received.

If one community in New Jersey can make an effort of this type why not other communities in all of the states? With an effort of this type, no one knows the exact percentage of sex crimes in the future that might be averted. If we accept the fact that each pedophile or hebophile molests anywhere from 50 to 100 victims before being apprehended (*if he ever is!*) and that each undiscovered or untreated male has more than a fifty-fifty chance of becoming a child molester himself in later years, the overall figures could become astronomical. Additionally, early discovery and treatment could eliminate the incredible number of depressions, male sexual dysfunctions, and even suicides that often result from undetected and untreated/unresolved child/adolescent sexual abuse.

FIVE ESSENTIAL THERAPY TECHNIQUES

A summary of five important therapy techniques that should be used with *all* survivors of sexual abuse must finally be discussed.

Ask Questions, Don't Suggest Anything

Therapist's tend to *suggest* too often. For example, statements such as "Some survivors feel . . ." is one suggestion that is definitely unacceptable. Survivors will grasp at any straw to avoid dealing with their real issues, feelings, or facts.

Assuming that the therapist is capable of knowing what feelings the survivor attaches to which occurrences is dangerous and may prevent the survivor from ever expressing her/his true feelings. For a therapist to assume that the survivor is angry at the sexual behavior of the abuser and therefore makes a statement such as *"That really must have made you angry!"* when, in reality the survivor was about to state that she/he enjoyed the sex, betrays what the therapist expects the correct answer to be. Survivors, still needing acceptance and approval, will usually follow the lead of the therapist and agree.

Elicit Problem Areas Through Gentle Probing

The therapist should take the stance that he/she knows nothing about sexual abuse or its effects on the survivors and therefore every statement of the survivor must be *picture clear* so that the therapist will understand her/him and her/his problems.

Survivors tend to speak in vague generalities or abstractions that leave the therapist to fill in the missing facts, a dangerous practice. Survivor's statements such as *"He made me do things with him,"* or *"He undressed me and then he did it to me,"* leave a great many possibilities open and do not clearly define the abuse. The first statement above was made by a ten-year-old boy who was made to dress in girl's clothes and dance as the molester masturbated. Did that possibility occur to you? The second statement involved a nine- year-old girl being given an enema by her incestuous father while he was nakedly erect. Did that possibility cross your mind when you read the statement?

Be Wary of Patronizing Statements

The therapist should never make statements such as *"I understand how you feel"* or *"I know what you went through"* unless she/he is a survivor and is willing to disclose that information to the client. Instead, when the timing is right, a statement such as *"I can't imagine how it must have been but I'd like to. Won't you help me to understand?"* or *"How do you feel about . . . ?"* or *"How did you feel when . . . ?"* is more appropriate and is also more acceptable to the survivor.

Timing and Readiness Issues are Critical

Pushing the survivor into any area or topic too soon may damage rapport and increase defensiveness, thus taking longer to get to the important issues.

Since *trust* was immeasurably damaged by the abuse and its aftermath, it will take time to again trust another adult. This is true for both children and adult survivors. Allowing the survivor to pace themselves and to take risks (like trusting) when he/she is ready will accelerate the treatment process.

The Therapist Must Remain Nonjudgmental Toward the Molester

Until the therapist is sure of the survivor's true and complete feelings about her/his abuser, *caution* must be exercised. Often therapists make the error of feeling that judgmental statements demonstrate support for the survivor. However, where *ambivalence* and a love/hate relationship with the abuser are suspected, talking disparagingly about the molester can push the survivor away and stop him or her from telling the therapist about any positive feelings for the abuser that may have existed at the time of the abuse or that may still exist. Questions that are neutral in this area are essential. A simple *"What did you feel about . . . then?"* or *"How do you feel about . . . now?"* are more effective ways of dealing with this issue.

SUMMARY

From the complexity of the issues presented, it should be both clear and obvious that specialized training by a highly experienced professional in the field is *absolutely necessary* before any counselor or therapist attempts to treat survivors, regardless of academic credentials or years of clinical experience.

13

Self-Confrontation and New
Image Formation

Resistance to change in many survivors of sexual abuse is most often the primary barrier to therapeutic insight or progress. Part of the reason for this resistance is the survivor's *guilt* and his/her major use of *denial* as a primary defense mechanism. A simple principle results: *The more intense the guilt that he/she is experiencing, the stronger the denial will be and consequently the greater the resistance.* In my 30 years of experience in both institutional settings as well as in private practice, I have encountered this resistance in innumerable cases. As a result, the need to develop a method of eliminating this barrier became paramount.

THE CHILD-WITHIN

After years of dealing with resistant child and adult survivors, I came to the conclusion that a unique syndrome was mostly responsible for this resistance to change and the overwhelming guilt that was preventing any changes from occurring. What appears to happen in long-term seductive sexual abuse, whether seductive or assaultive, stranger involved or incestuous, is a *developmental-fixation* at the age of the onset of the sexual abuse. Emotionally and psychosexually, the survivor appears to stop growing psychologically, while physical development continues at a normal rate. Outwardly this developmental-fixation is not easily seen and is often completely missed by even the most competent therapist. I call this process, including the fixation, *the Child-Within Syndrome.* Several diagnostic elements exist in the "child-within syndrome" that make identification and discovery possible.

- 1. The main feature of the syndrome is the survivor's inability to see himself/herself in any positive way while seeing family members, friends, and even the abuser in positive ways.

- 2. Concurrently, the survivor is unable to accept any positive comment or feedback from anyone, including the therapist, without great discomfort. Often, he/she will do something self-destructive immediately following positive compliments to prove how *bad, evil, or rotten* he/she really is.

- 3. This discomfort remains unchanged regardless of what technique the therapist employs and is considered by the survivor as ridiculous and illogical ("makes absolutely no sense"). Still the survivor insists that he/she cannot alter the condition.

Two examples will clarify.

- DENNIS, *whom we met in Chapter 6, has been in treatment now for almost three years. No really significant changes have occurred, especially in regards to self-image and self-esteem. "Dennis" refuses homework assignments that include doing self-confrontation mirrors (discussed in detail later in this chapter) stating that "I can't stand looking at that piece of shit in the mirror! — I won't look at him. He makes me sick!" When asked what he sees when he looks at himself in the mirror that so terribly disturbs him, "Dennis" cannot answer or explain. If asked what other people looking at him would see, he states "A regular guy, I guess! They wouldn't see anything different than if they were looking at anyone else." When asked to reconcile the difference in his reaction to his mirror-image and his anticipated reactions from others, "Dennis" states, "They just don't know what a piece of worthless garbage that guy in the mirror really is!"*

- RUDY *arrived at the treatment unit in almost a catatonic state. He had been severely traumatized in the state hospital from where he was transferred but no one knew exactly how. The suspicion was that he had been sexually assaulted there by either another patient or a staff member.*

  Slowly, as he became more comfortable, "Rudy" came out of his shell and began to communicate with other members of his group and his living area. After some six months, he sent me a letter, expressing an interest in working in the video-studio complex and listing some former electronics experience. I had him tested and he was assigned as a trainee. Within a very short amount of time, "Rudy" proved to be a fast learner and developed a special skill in videotape editing, a complex and delicate assignment.

  After completing an important and difficult edit, I went into the control booth and congratulated "Rudy" on his work and stupidly (hindsight) told him that if he continued progressing in video work that someday soon he could become the booth director. Strangely, "Rudy" did not look at me or respond. He simply left the booth and returned to his room.

  The following morning as I arrived at work, I saw "Rudy" being led out of the studio complex by two officers. Asking what was going on, I was told that "Rudy" was being taken to lock-up and that I should go into the control booth to understand why. As I entered the booth I saw the destruction that had taken place. Several videotape recorders had been seriously damaged and the booth looked like it had been hit by a tornado. The damage was later estimated to be approximately $5,000. I quickly left the booth and caught up to "Rudy" and the officers and asked him what had happened. His shocking reply was "Now tell me how great I'm doing!" "Rudy" had not let go of his many guilts and simply wasn't ready for the compliments that I had heaped upon him and proved to me just how wrong I was.

A seeming contradiction occurs in these survivors. If the therapist asks this type of individual what his/her reaction would be to a close or best friend performing the identical deviant acts or behaviors that he/she did, he/she begins to defend the friend, justifying his/her behavior and insists that he/she would help him/her in any way possible. Something he/she cannot do for him/her self.

Child-Within Theory

What appears to occur is that the child who is abused, at some later time, usually the evening of the occurrence or the next day, reflecting on and *judging* what happened, blames himself/herself for the abuse. Through this *subjective-judgment phenomenon,* discussed in Chapter 9, using parental or authority "rulers," the child then puts himself/herself in the lowest-of-low category and accepts both the responsibility and the guilt for the sexual behavior. This is especially true concerning those behaviors or incidents in which he/she might have *reciprocated, enjoyed, and/or returned to many, many times.* This reaction is very frequently seen in long-term seductive-molestations.

DISTANCING TECHNIQUE

In cases of this type, I use a *distancing-technique* that I call the *"third or empty chair technique."* This technique was fully discussed in Chapter 11 and it is suggested that the reader review this section before attempting the technique. "Distancing" will often result in a breakthrough in the resistance. A summary of the steps in the "Distancing" technique follows.

- 1. Ask the survivor for a *nickname* that he/she was called when he/she was a child or would have preferred to be called. If there was none, have him/her make one up. I discourage the use of "little" as a prefix to his/her present first name since true distancing does not occur with this choice.

- 2. Using his/her imagination, have him/her visualize himself/herself as the child at the age at which the initial abuse experience occurred. Then use an empty chair in the office and ask the survivor to visualize this abused-child sitting in that chair.

- 3. From that time on, when the subjective-judgment phenomenon or the extreme resistance to positive feedback occurs, have the survivor talk to the abused-child sitting in the empty chair using the nickname. Repeat, in a role-play, whatever the survivor has just said to degrade himself/herself but as if the child victim in the empty chair were speaking. Then ask the survivor to respond to the child victim in the empty chair. His/her responses are most often something healing and positive.

- 4. Maintaining the distance between the survivor and the now-established child-within, ask the survivor to accept the hypothesis that the child-within will always be inside him/her. Then add that this situation is okay as long as he/she never again gives the child-within control of his/her body, thoughts or actions.

- 5. The therapist must keep track of who is speaking in the therapy session and respond appropriately, using the nickname if it is the child-within and using the survivor's present name when it is the present adolescent or adult.

An example of this technique follows.

- DENNIS *is highly sensitive to losing friends and/or being rejected. He consistently feels like he does not belong. These feelings originated in grammar school and continued through high school. Whenever someone from work or his college fraternity calls to* *invite him to a baseball game, a party, a trip, etc., while desperately wanting to go, his **child-within** panics and he sadly and painfully declines.*

Now that "Dennis" has begun the distancing-technique from DENNY, *his child-within, he still hesitates but then accepts the invitation and usually has a good time. He recognizes and accepts the fact that it is his child-within, "Denny," who is so frightened of rejection and/or of losing new friends. He is learning to control the urgings and panic of "Denny" to play-it-safe. Unfortunately, "Dennis" is still unable to make this separation in other areas of his life on a consistent basis but is working on it.*

In my opinion, it is doubtful that the *fixated* child-within will ever change. It appears that sexual-trauma permanently fixates the thoughts, feelings, reactions and self-judgments of the child-within *for life,* especially in the long-term or severely physically traumatic cases. Distancing from the child-within allows true progress to occur in these highly resistant survivors. A frequent bonus to regaining control from the child-within is a *quieting* and lessening of the child-within's panics and fears. It is as if the battle as to who is the boss has been won by the survivor and has convinced the child-within of his/her *strength* and ability to protect the child-within from future harm. Once the first .success occurs, the entire atmosphere of treatment changes. This technique works just as well in combination with the NOW mirror, self-confrontation technique. The child-within distancing technique is a four-step process.

- 1. Identification of the existence of the child-within.

- 2. Training the survivor to distance himself/herself from the child-within.

- 3. Risk-taking behaviors to break the control of the child-within.

- 4. Repetition of the procedures in all areas of heavy resistance, especially those involving self-image, self-judgment and self-esteem.

Another example will clarify.

- KITTY *has a little girl-within whom she calls* BETTY. *When "Kitty" first began therapy, she had several disabling problems: she could not look at or use sharp kitchen knives. They had to be locked in drawers. Secondly, "Kitty" could not drive over bridges without debilitating panic and terror.*

  As therapy progressed over a six month period, "Kitty" related the following encounter with "Betty." On a recent holiday, "Kitty" was expecting guests for dinner and her husband called stating that he had to work overtime. Thus, he would be unable to cut the veggies for a salad or the roast for dinner. "Kitty" went to her bedroom and did a NOW confrontation mirror, telling "Betty" that they ("Kitty" and "Betty") had to prepare dinner and not to be afraid since their abuser (her father) was not in the house and, even if her were, that she, "Kitty," would protect "Betty" from any harm.

  Mustering all of her courage, "Kitty" entered the kitchen, unlocked the drawer and removed a sharp paring knife and began cutting the veggies. All the while she continued calming "Betty" and guaranteeing her protection. Slowly, "Betty," the child- within, calmed down and eventually simply stopped panicking or sending frightening thoughts and messages to "Kitty." "Kitty's" children and her husband were amazed and very happy for her accomplishment. Never since that day have the kitchen drawers been locked.

Once the first success occurs, the entire atmosphere of treatment changes. Several weeks later, the same technique worked on her bridge-phobia and "Kitty" drove herself to therapy for the first time, a trip that required crossing a major bridge over a river that was quite high. Positive gains transferred to other risk-taking behaviors in "Kitty's" life as therapy progressed.

Another adjunctive technique for the most highly resistant cases is that of *self-confrontation* or *NOW* therapy.

SELF-CONFRONTATION

When therapist confrontation methods did not work with the most highly resistant cases, I had to develop a *pre-therapist confrontation method* that the individuals could do by themselves. As a result, *NOW Therapy,* a method of self confrontation was begun.

After many frustrating hours of trying to break down the resistance and minimize the denial of these highly resistant individuals, the task at first appeared hopeless until one patient made the following casual remarks in the heat of an emotional outburst.

- *"How can I learn to like or care about myself when I did those horrible, disgusting, dirty things?"*
- *"How can I remember all of what happened without reliving the fear, pain, disgust or dirtiness that I must have felt then?"*
- *"I don't want to go through it again!"* or
- *"If you knew all the things that happened and how I really felt, you wouldn't want to have anything to do with me!"*

Once this problem was identified, the solution came as a direct result: *self-confrontation in a private and safe setting where no one could hear or observe what the individual was saying or could see what he/she was doing.* Since "admitting it to myself" appeared to be the key, it also became the essential and primary element of the technique. Expecting the individual, no matter how motivated, to *"bare- all"* in the first self-confrontation session, even to himself/herself in total privacy, was as senseless as expecting the individual to "cure" himself/herself. Therefore, a slow, gradual approach to complete openness had to be built into the system.

Additionally, since *identity* was also an issue, the first assignment was to stand in front of a full-length mirror (at home in his/her bedroom or bathroom) and to distance from the person in the mirror, making their reflection his/her "best-friend in the whole world who knows every secret there is to know about you." Then, by using *"You"* statements rather than *"I"* statements, the distancing should be complete. After several months of experimenting, two other major requisites were incorporated into the technique.

- 1. The technique worked best in the *nude.*

- 2. The technique had to be done *out loud.*

The first condition, *the nudity,* resulted from an interesting incident with one of the most resistant individuals I have ever worked with, "MARK," whom we discussed in Chapter 9. "Mark" was a participant in the advanced sex education program. A major module of that program was the "Body-Image Exercise" of Doctors William E. Hartman and Marilyn A. Fithian (Hartman, William E. and Fithian, Marilyn A., 1987). In this exercise, usually conducted in a group setting, each individual member of the group stands nude in front of a three-paneled mirror (dressmaker/tailor's mirror). The individual is then asked to:

- touch each part of his/her body, and
- state a like or dislike for that part of his/her body and the reasons behind the decision.
- When he/she is finished touching and judging all parts of his/her body, he/she is asked to perform three additional tasks.
  - 1) Rate the body he/she is looking at in the mirror on a 0 to 100 percent scale, judging his/her body against all others in his/her sex and age group.
  - 2) Choose one part of that body to change, specifying the change and the reason for his/her choice.
  - 3) Choose one part of that body to take to a totally new body, specifying the reason for his/her choice.

Once finished with this part of the technique, he/she is asked to turn around and face the group, giving the rest of the members of the group *permission* to both look at his/her body and to comment. Each group member then gives the person-in-the-mirror a rating of that body and the reasons for the rating. The group members also answer the remaining three questions above.

When the entire group is finished giving feedback, the person-in-the- mirror is then asked if he/she wishes to change his/her rating or choices for changes. Not surprisingly, many individuals, following the group's evaluation and suggestions, *improve on the rating of their bodies and also alter the changes that they had previously made.*

Even when used alone instead of as an adjunct to traditional therapy, the Hartman-Fithian Body Image Exercises improve self-image and self-esteem, increase interpersonal communication and facilitate involvement in treatment. Primary therapists have reported these changes in both sex offenders and survivors of sexual abuse/assault with each sex education class held.

Back to "Mark." The day following his turn at the mirror in sex- education, "Mark" asked to see me privately, and made the following comments.

That mirror stuff was really something. — I never felt like that before. — I went back to my room and I really felt like a new person. — Instead of laying on my bunk and watching T.V., I went to the recreation room and played pool, and even played cards with guys I never talked to before, and really had a great night. — The only problem with it (the mirror technique) is that it doesn't go far enough. — It deals only with your body. — I wish I could have talked to that guy in the mirror about himself and his problems.

Within a half-hour, "Mark" and I returned to the Video Studio Complex, where the sex-education classes were held, set up the mirrors and a camera and the first *NOW Therapy Session* (Mirror-self-confrontation) took place.

Where the nudity-condition is concerned, shorts, underwear, bathing suits, etc., were all tried for a six month period at the suggestion of some of the more conservative members of the treatment staff. The participants in the NOW program reported that their defenses remained as *strong or stronger* and that blocking and resistance continued to occur. Once a NOW member had experienced the technique in the nude, when he/she was asked to try it with even minimal clothing, he/she reported feelings of discomfort and frustration.

Where the *talking-out-loud* is concerned, thinking or mental confrontation also failed. Apparently all of the lies, fantasy materials and distortions that the survivors learned from their abuser and used daily, kept intruding. But, *if he/she looked himself/herself in the eye and spoke out loud,* it became impossible to lie; he/she would actually interrupt himself/herself and confront any attempted lie or distortion, such as minimizing or denial. The important factor was that the survivor *hear with his/her ears what was being said with his/her mouth (voice).* What others said about or to the survivor had no impact on his/her true feelings, but what he/she said to or about himself/herself did! A simple but too often overlooked factor.

An unexpected bonus also occurred in all survivors using the technique: *a noticeable increase in self-confidence and a slowly-emerging new self-image* developed, although no direct work had been done in these areas. Others in the survivor's life (parents, wives, children, work supervisors, primary therapists, wing personnel, etc.) reported the changes as did the survivors, themselves.

Theoretical Considerations

What appears to happen is as follows. From the time of the initial abuse, the survivor felt he/she had been out of control or, at least, perceived that others controlled all of his/her decisions. The list of *controllers* ranged from parents to teachers, to friends, to associates and employers, to wives or lovers, etc., even to their own children (where applicable).

In the self-confrontation technique, the participant *must* accept *credit* for any change, insight, or confronted-experience. Prior to the NOW self-confrontation technique, positive feedback, although desperately wanted, could never be tolerated. Once motivated to attempt the technique, the technique and the individual appear to take over. Most of what occurs is *unplanned,* regardless of the amount of rehearsal that precedes the actual session. In fact, it is quite a common occurrence that little if anything that was rehearsed in preparation for the confrontation session is ever actually discussed during the *mirror.*

In a majority of cases, the greatest fear of the survivors is facing the fact that he/she is a *victim* and standing there telling his/her "friend" in the mirror that he/she *was* a victim and that *NOW, It's Okay.* Once this hurdle is passed, a permanent value change usually occurs that quickly internalizes. This value change involves letting-go of the old value that *"You're worthless and undeserving of love, friendship and acceptance"* and replacing it with a new value that *"MAYBE, you're really not so bad after all and MAYBE you do deserve to be loved."* Unless the survivor is still involved in the abuse-behavior, there will usually be some positive behaviors and occurrences to discuss with their "best friend."

This "MAYBE" disappears as daily evidence accrues that confirms the new value. The therapist must use homework to ensure that the survivor finds evidence of worthiness on a daily basis. This is a new habit for the survivor to learn and will take time, patience and practice.

THE NOW-THERAPY TECHNIQUE

Where resistance is so great that even the self-confrontation mirror technique, in the format described above, does not work, a further *rule* is added to the technique to insure success.

> *From the moment that you enter the mirror, nothing may be mentioned or discussed except those behaviors, feelings and personality traits that existed after you awoke this morning. No past memory, act, guilt, or feeling may be included.* Thus the title: NOW therapy.

Since most of the problems regarding change stem from the survivor's *beating himself/herself* with what he/she did or did not do in the past, finding a method of *letting-go of the past* becomes an essential and necessary part of the treatment process.

I am convinced that the survivor that I am now seeing *is not* the same person that was involved in the abuse. By this I mean that the exposure, the legal-action (if any), friends and parents discussing the case, etc., have all had a profound effect on the survivor. His/her personality is altered, rarely for the better, more often for the worse. Thus, distancing from that old personality becomes essential. Adding this new boundary to the self-confrontation causes a great deal of conflict for many survivors. It involves letting go of the past (at least for the "mirror" session), and letting go of the guilts and accompanying self-punishing behaviors that resulted from involvement in the abuse. These are the two most difficult and resistant "letting-go" changes that any survivor has to make. Here again, time, patience, and daily practice are essential. This also is a stage of therapy where *backsliding* is most likely to occur in the form of regression. The therapist must be prepared for this possibility. An example will help.

- MARK, *discussed earlier in this chapter, when given this new instruction stopped doing confrontation mirrors for six weeks. His threat was "if you insist on this new rule, I'll quit therapy!" My response simply was to repeat, as I often did, that it was his therapy, his life, and thus his choice. Eventually, he returned to doing NOW mirrors and broke through this very difficult level of change-resistance.*

A Special Procedure with the Most Resistant Survivors

For a small percentage of survivors, even the NOW technique does not work and, for these, an additional exercise is necessary at the onset of self-confrontation treatment. The new steps are as follows.

- 1. These resistant survivors are permitted to begin the confrontation mirror with a negative judgmental statement or a negative self-criticism. *BUT*
- 2. Before they are permitted a *second negative* comment or criticism of their "friend in the mirror," they must find a positive or complimentary statement.
- 3. Then they may use a *second* negative comment or statement which must be followed by a *second* positive comment before going on to the next negative, etc.

Using this *balancing-technique* for the first time will require a great deal of time and patience, since there may be a silence of as much as 15-20 minutes after the first negative-statement before they make a positive statement, *and that's "Okay!"* Once this pattern of balance is established, it becomes a mandatory, conscious procedure until the survivor can balance his self-confrontations spontaneously. This usually takes from four to six sessions.

Caveats

Several caveats regarding the NOW self-confrontation-mirror technique must be discussed.

- 1. Minimally, the session should always be at least audio-taped. Video-taping is the ideal but not usually available to survivors in their homes. However, if the NOW technique is to be used in a group setting, then video-taping should be a mandatory requirement. The reason for this mandate is that the most traumatic and shocking revelations and/or accusations usually occur while doing a NOW mirror but often can be re-repressed following a session; thus the need for at least an audiotape recorder to be used. The therapist should carefully explain that the taping is for the survivor, not for the therapist or for anyone else. This is an important instruction aimed at preventing *performance-oriented* sessions. It should also be explained to the survivor that no one else ever has to see or hear the tapes, including the therapist, *unless the survivor so wishes.* The survivor should listen to the tape preferably before retiring for the night or, at the latest, upon awakening the morning following the NOW session, otherwise the impact is lost. If not, the danger exists that the re-repressions of important revealed materials may become lost.
- 2. The therapist must ensure that these sessions do not become *self-punishment* sessions, a real danger with the guilt-ridden survivor. His/her negative self-image is bad enough at the start of therapy and care must be taken that this negative self-image does not become enhanced. Weekly reports from the survivor on the self-confrontation sessions are used for this purpose. In my experience in using this technique for over 20 years, survivors will often volunteer a tape of a session that they were either pleased with or that disturbed or confused them. Listening to the tape *in their presence* becomes highly therapeutic and revealing as well since all survivors utilizing this technique run a *commentary* on their performance as

the tape plays. This playback session also affords the therapist an opportunity to provide *guidance* for future self-confrontation sessions through the use of subtle suggestions or highly directive suggestions, depending on the circumstances.

- 3. *"Mirrors,"* then, become a major homework assignment *with the content left entirely up to the survivor.* The reason for this is that the current issues in the survivor's therapy may be overshadowed by an immediate and pressing problem in his/her life. Should he/she feel the obligation to do a mirror on a subject that the therapist has assigned, he/she may use this directed-homework as a means of avoiding his/her more pressing, real-life daily problems.

- 4. As the survivor becomes more comfortable with self-confrontation, the therapist, either in an individual or group setting, can also begin to become more directly confrontive.

The overall major benefits include *a new self-confidence* and a *lessening of the almost-complete dependency* that these survivors have on the therapist. More risks will be taken and more new behaviors attempted. Here, as in all therapy modalities, *"Nothing succeeds like success!"* An example of the progress of a survivor utilizing the mirror-self-confrontation or NOW technique will clarify the overall procedure and the benefits.

- MARK, *discussed several times in this chapter, has been in therapy over 18 years with, at least, six different primary therapists. While being one of the most-liked survivors that I have worked with, and the friendliest, most helpful group member that I have encountered, no real progress for himself had ever occurred. His first "mirrors" were so negative and self-degrading that I almost stopped him from using the technique. Then, one day, he did a private (versus group) mirror-session that lasted for almost two hours. When he was finished and returned to his room, everyone around him noticed that he was **different** but they didn't know in what precise way. For a day or so he was rather quiet and, when asked what was happening to him, he simply stated that he was "not-himself." Then, in his next group therapy session, he suddenly and shockingly became confrontive with a close friend, who was lying to the group. He unmasked the "game" that his friend was playing and the purpose behind the deception. The effect was electric. I couldn't understand this change in his long-standing passivity.*

    *In an individual therapy session, a few days later, "Mark" asked me to review the videotape of his last NOW session with him. To say the least, I was both shocked and thrilled by what I saw and heard. For the first time "Mark" showed care and concern about and for himself. He was balanced in his comments and criticisms of his "friend-in-the-mirror" and gave him both praise and encouragement as well. The session ended with several realistic and positive goals to be accomplished before the next session. "Mark" had finally **let-go of the past** and accepted himself for who and what he was today. He was on his way to a new personality and a new life. More importantly, he was truly happy for the first time in more than 18 years. He no longer needed to **buy** his friendships. Most importantly, he no longer needed to rape in order to feel like a man. "Mark" was now ready for other therapy modalities and this time they would work, since he "NOW" deserved to succeed.*

Self-Confrontation therapy works with all survivors with a resistance-to-change problem. It is especially helpful with sex-offenders and survivors of sexual abuse who have had years of unsuccessful therapy attempts. In any case where self-image and self-esteem problems are the primary cause of therapeutic resistance, this technique should be considered one of the methods of choice. Once positive results are obtained with self-confrontation, then other forms of traditional treatment modalities can be utilized and will have a much better chance of succeeding.

14

The Triple Damage of Religion
and Cults in Sexual Abuse

In previous chapters, I have discussed the *doubling* of the trauma of sexual abuse when parents, relatives, and authority figures such as teachers, scoutmasters, big-brothers, policemen, foster-parents, etc., were concerned. In this chapter I will discuss the *tripling* of the trauma when the added element of the *supernatural* is added to the sexual abuse effects through involvement of a priest, minister, rabbi or other religious authoritative figure who either directly or through implication adds "God," the devil, or any other religious entity as the authority for the abuse or as the punisher should his/her wishes not be complied with or should the survivor *dare* to tell anyone or report the abuse.

RELIGION

Before we can intelligently discuss this topic, we need a working definition of religion:

The *American Heritage Dictionary* (1989) defines religion as "an organized system of beliefs and rituals centering on a supernatural being or beings." Religion can be a highly positive or a highly negative experience for a small child, depending on the *perception and focus* of the particular religious sect. In my experience of treating both offenders and the survivors of sexual abuse for over 30 years, *sin-and-damnation* type religions did the most serious damage to both children and adults under the guise of the highest good. Humanistic-type religions, on the other hand, focus on acceptance of man as imperfect and offer forgiveness and hope for happiness. The latter provided the most therapeutic and effective good for both of these groups.

There is a highly positive correlation between both types of religion and the outcome of sexual abuse cases, especially where the survivors of sexual abuse by priests, ministers and other religious personnel are concerned. This correlation is always found in survivors of sexual abuse. The correlations indicate that:

- 1. Survivors with a religious background that is positive and forgiving appear to adjust the fastest and appear to be the least permanently damaged by their sexual abuse.
- 2. Survivors with a religious background mired in sin and damnation are the ones who are most seriously damaged by their sexual abuse and have the greatest problems with "letting-go" of any *guilt feelings* associated to their perceived role

in the sexual abuse. These negative effects are magnified and doubled or tripled when the survivor's parents are deeply mired in negatively oriented religion. Two cases will support these correlations.

- DAVID *is a 41-year-old incestuous father who molested his now seven-year-old daughter over a period of several years before discovery. He was offered treatment rather than prosecution for reasons unknown to this writer, although the court asked me to be his therapist. Guilt and a severely damaged self-image were the two most obvious and serious problems that he brought to his therapy.*

  *"David" came from a stern, Roman-Catholic home, **where he could do no right.** He was constantly criticized and put-down for the least thing and **sin, damnation and hell** were constant topics in the lectures he received on an almost daily basis. The harder he tried to please his parents, the more he failed and the more he was criticized. Now, at 41, "David" has no formal religion and has not practiced his old Catholic faith for over 20 years. His philosophy tends to be humanistic for everyone **else in the world except for himself.** He is intellectually bright and a successful computer trouble-shooter and program designer.*

  *Intellectually, "David" understands the need to let go of the guilt and to forgive himself for an extremely long list of real and exaggerated transgressions, beginning with **being-born.** However, emotionally he is unable to rid himself of the guilt, self-hate, self-recrimination, and the feelings of being a sort of "Satan incarnate" (his label). The negative, religious conditioning he underwent for his entire formative childhood and adolescence has been indelibly imprinted and, while he makes progress in all other areas, "David's" guilt remains nearly as strong as when he first began therapy over nine months ago.*

  "David" can list the positive changes he has made, especially where self-image and self-esteem are concerned. However, when dealing on an interpersonal level with either co-workers, supervisors, or male and female friends, he immediately becomes "unworthy" (his term) and finds a way to destroy or end the relationship "before they find out what a real rotten piece of shit I really am."

  The result is loneliness, revolving depression, and every escape defense mechanism know to man. The most recent escape defense was to volunteer to be one of the first employees to be fired in an upcoming takeover and merger of his company. The moment he learned that several managerial posts would have to be "cut" to ensure the economic survival of the company, he went to his immediate supervisor and told him to place his name at the top of the list.

  "David's" plans are to buy a motorcycle (he has already accomplished this goal) and to spend a month or two traveling around the country, possibly joining a biker's group (with a notorious reputation for meanness and evil), "the place I really belong!"

  Periodically, out of nowhere, religion becomes the topic of the session. "David's" mood changes abruptly, his attitude toward himself becomes hypercritical and negative, and depression begins. It takes an hour or more to break the mood and to return "David" to the mood he felt at the beginning of the session. Even then, he has lost ground rather than made any gains.

As a general rule, the longer the indoctrination and conditioning of the negative-religion exists, the more difficult it is to help the survivor find self-forgiveness and happiness. Another example will further clarify.

- KYLE, *whom we met in Chapter 11, was triply traumatized since his abuser was a Catholic priest who was a long-term friend of the family. The "tripling" involves firstly the abuse, secondly the adult authority figure and thirdly the religious and supernatural element. The reader will remember (from Chapter 11 where the total story was told) that the priest told "Kyle" that "he had permission from God to molest him" and that "God would punish him if he told anyone and would protect the priest." All the priest's predictions came true in "Kyle's" confused and traumatized perception.*

   While "Kyle" has made tremendous gains and is now a practicing therapist helping other child and adolescent survivors of sexual abuse, he remains in therapy and is never totally free of the guilt from his involvement in the abuse nor is he ever completely happy or secure. He has to be convinced that he is a good person and that he deserves anything: success at work, a wonderful girl who wants to marry him, the right to go on for advanced degrees, the right to speak on the subject of sexual abuse at conferences, etc.

How long it will take for "Kyle" or "David" to fully let-go of the guilt and the self-recrimination is impossible to predict. All that therapy can provide is support, encouragement and reinforcement of positive gains and changes while value re-evaluation takes place.

While the examples above involve Catholic families and Catholic clergy, I have also treated survivors of sexual abuse who were involved with Protestant ministers from several denominations. In 30 years, I have not only worked with several Catholic priests, two Protestant ministers and an evangelical preacher who molested children but have also read of cases of sexual abuse involving leaders or every organized religion including Baptist ministers, Episcopalian priests and Jewish Rabbis.

MULTIPLE-PERSONALITY DISORDER AS A RESULT OF RITUAL, CULT ABUSE

All of the cases of cult abuse that I have encountered, minus one, developed multiple personality disorder (MPD) as a defense mechanism. The reader is referred to Chapter 4, where this phenomenon and its treatment are discussed in detail. Most writers on the subject have had the same experience; however, the treating professions are only now beginning to accept MPD as real and a true response in sexual abuse cases, particularly in incest and cult abuse.

One might go so far as to hypothesize that MPD is a distinguishing characteristic of incestuous and cult abuse. In Chapter 4, I discussed the *distancing technique* that I have successfully used in treating these cases and the reader should review the technique before going further. There are also other specific treatment techniques for this disorder that we must now discuss.

SPECIAL TREATMENT CONSIDERATIONS

While these survivors are treated in the same manner as all other survivors of sexual abuse, there are several necessary additional elements involved in their overall treatment. Before true progress and a return to former behaviors and positive attitudes towards themselves can be achieved, *religious re-educa-tion* must be included in their treatment program. Several steps are involved.

Personally Perceived Guilt Must be Resolved

It is important to state here that the survivor's perceived guilt must be respected if healing is to occur. There are still well-meaning individuals, including therapists, who insist to the survivor that all of the guilt belongs to the offender and they, the survivors, are totally innocent of any wrong doing. *Not so!* Many survivors, including the two in the cases cited in this section, felt personal responsibility and severe guilt for some portion of the abuse. There can be several survivor situations that can produce these perceptions.

- The survivor who didn't resist or fight off the abuser. This frequently occurs where authority figures are concerned and definitely applies to "Kyle's" case.

- The survivor who reached orgasm during the sexual abuse or enjoyed the sexual manipulations of the abuser. This situation occurs more frequently in abused boys than in abused girls, although it is present in both groups of survivors. It even applies in adult survivor cases and produces even more guilt in the adult survivor than in the child or adolescent survivor. The guilt of this pleasure reaction increases dramatically in all survivors when the abuse is homosexual in nature and the survivor considers themselves "straight" or heterosexual.

- The survivor who felt a deep emotional attachment, including "love" for the abuser. Very frequently this reaction occurs in cases of a single parent survivor or a child/adolescent survivor from a totally cold, negative, and unloving home environment who has replaced a non-loving parent with the abusive religious individual. Adult survivors also are included in this group and usually have developed a "crush" on their priest, minister, rabbi, etc.

- The survivor, whether child, adolescent, or adult who desperately craved accep-tance and was willing to do anything to get that acceptance often submits to the sexual advances and abuse of anyone who shows them the least form of accep-tance. Sexually abusive, religious individuals, both male and female, are experts at spotting these individuals in their congregations, churches, etc.

All of the above factors produce personally perceived guilt that must be ventilated, forgiven by the survivors themselves, and then learned from for future behavior. For this reason, allowing the survivor, his/her guilt is essential to the treatment process. The therapist's acceptance of the survivor, *before, during, and after* these guilt confessions is also essential not only to the treatment process but also to the religious re-education that is essential to these individuals.

A New Attitude Toward Religion Must be Encouraged

Once the guilt is ventilated (confessed) and the survivor has forgiven themselves for the sinful/bad behavior and feels that "God" (supernatural being) has also forgiven them, then a new attitude towards religion must be pursued.

In all of today's religions, even the most restrictive and prohibitive, there are positive elements that can be found. The most important of these is *forgiveness*. In some religions, this is accomplished through confession to a priest or minister followed by contrition for the perceived "sinful" or "bad" behavior. In other religions, the confession is directly to "God" as is the contrition. Regardless of external procedures and formats both elements are essential to the recovery process of the survivor.

The therapist cannot permit the survivor to set expectations of *perfection* upon themselves if a healthy adjustment is the goal of therapy. Making sure that the survivor's religious beliefs and affiliations allow for some form of confession and forgiveness and that these are readily available should a new transgression occur, is an important element in treating the survivor of a religiously connected sexual abuse. This is especially true in cases where the sexual abuse has not been reported and the religious abuser is still in the community and still affiliated with the survivor's church, synagogue or congregation. In "Kyle's" case, the priest involved remained a friend of his family and continued to spend weekends at his home, still sleeping in his bedroom and still abusing him. Therapy was aimed at finding reasons for "Kyle" to be away from home on these priestly weekends as often as humanly possible. Four years later, when "Kyle" was 15 years old, the priest left the church and "Kyle's" life and recovery really began and continues today.

CULTS AND RITUALS

The phrase "ritualized abuse" was coined in 1980 by Lawrence Pazder, M.D. at an American Psychiatric Association annual meeting in New Orleans. Dr. Pazder was attempting to understand this phenomenon and to distinguish it from other forms of sexual abuse since the treatment techniques for *ritualized abuse* are different and distinct. The definition he presented follows.

> Ritual abuse involves repeated physical, emotional, mental, and spiritual assaults combined with a systematic use of symbols, ceremonies, and machinations designed and orchestrated to attain malevolent effects. [Pazder, 1980]

My experience in this area, until recently was limited to involvement in two very different and very dramatic cases that left a lasting fear on this writer of ever accepting a third case. Both clients were offenders and self-proclaimed satanists. Since that time, however, I have learned to work with these survivors of sexual ritual abuse (SRA) and want to offer the reader some impressions and some references. First, a distinction and caveat must be made. While some of these ritual offenders truly appear to believe in a diabolical force, Satan and/or his minions, others simply use the trappings and Hollywood-type settings of the satanic cults seen in movies and fictional literature as a rationalization and excuse for their deviant needs and desires. The therapist, *if* he/she chooses to become involved in cases of this type will need to carefully distinguish between the two. Let us look at two cases that I personally was involved with and discuss the serious implications for the survivors afterwards.

• *The first case involved* MARTY, *an intelligent, friendly, sociable and quite likable young 22-year-old man who was arrested for raping a 60-year-old widow, after breaking into her bedroom through a window. No elements of cultism or satanism were detected in the offense and the case was considered simply another sex offense in the community.*

Almost from the first group-therapy session, "Marty's" intensity, especially a penetrating **stare** *with cold, steel-gray eyes, was not only visible but actually frightening. No one could hold that gaze for too long without becoming extremely uncomfortable. "Marty" used his stare to control both the therapist and the group, especially when questions were asked in areas that he did not want to venture. He would simply stare the person down until a terrible silence filled the group therapy room. After a few minutes, "Marty" would smile sardonically and ask "Any more questions?" Of course, there were none. Some of the group members were so upset that they actually had to leave the room and not return for the remainder of the session.*

After almost a year of intense work, "Marty" began to take therapy more seriously. He also simultaneously began to show emotional reactions, which up to then he would never allow. He requested adjunctive, individual therapy in addition to his assigned group therapy and also joined several other ancillary programs including sex education, social-skills training and the education program where he took college classes and did quite well. One evening, in an individual-therapy session in my office, he revealed that he had a **dark secret** *that was causing him terrible guilt problems especially since he had returned to his original religion, the Roman- Catholic faith. The chilling story he related follows.*

"Marty" ran away from home when he was 16 years old. His father was both alcoholic and abusive and his mother both weak and an alcoholic. He denied any memory of being sexually abused, at first, but felt "there might be something there" (in that area).

Hitchhiking from state to state, he ended up in a major metropolitan area where he was picked-up by a wealthy older man in a limousine for sexual purposes (he was prostituting at the time "for survival," his term). The man took him to his apartment in a high- rise apartment complex and, after their sexual episode, offered "Marty" a job and a place to live, the older man's apartment. "Marty" accepted even though the man did not discuss what kind of job he had in mind, but it was winter and he felt he had little or no choice.

After a week of buying clothes, being taken to nice restaurants and to the theater, "'Marty" was driven to a warehouse in a deserted section of the waterfront. They entered a dark room filled with lockers where there was an attendant in a long black robe that reminded "Marty" of a priest's black cassock. "Marty" was told to completely undress and put his clothing in a locker. He was then given a black robe of his own with a hood that extended beyond his face, totally enclosing his head. The obvious purpose was to conceal any and all identity of the person wearing it. By this time, the older man had disappeared and the attendant ushered "Marty" into a dimly but colorfully lit auditorium with a table made out of white marble, set up on a stage. There was incense burning all around the room and the odor was almost overpowering. "Marty" was told to sit and wait.

In a short time, others began to enter the auditorium, all dressed in identical black robes that did not allow "Marty" to see their faces or even to distinguish whether they were male or female. "Weird music" (his term) began to play and from behind the table the old man appeared dressed in a long purple and black robe that was trimmed with gold and silver braid.

The attendant then led a young teenage girl (who looked to be about 13 or 14 years old) into the room. The girl was naked and obviously drugged. He tied her to the table, legs and arms spread, with strong ropes that appeared to be permanently attached to the table.

At this moment, "Marty" realized that this was some form of **cult** *and that something* **evil** *was about to occur. As he correctly suspected, chanting in a strange ritual language began and was repeated over and over, as the group sang and danced themselves into a frenzy. The more frenzied they became the more they revealed of themselves, many tearing off their robes and dancing in the nude around the girl on the table. After what seemed an eternity, the man, now seen by "Marty" as the high priest of the cult, threw off his robes and violently sexually assaulted the girl while cutting strange "symbols" into her chest and onto both breasts. The other participants continued in their frenzied chanting and singing. When the high-priest was finished with her, one by one the others raped, sodomized, and orally copulated with the girl, or urinated and defecated on her body. "Marty" had never seen anything like this and, while he was in shock, he was also sexually excited as well. When he was invited to take his turn, he also raped the victim. When everyone was finished, the girl was led away and "Marty" never saw her again.*

"Marty" was now considered to have been **initiated** *and to be a full member of the cult. His benefactor, the older man, was the "high priest" and cult leader. "Marty" also recognized some important and influential people in attendance as members. Within a month or so, "Marty" was promoted to "enforcer" of the cult. His major function was to procure the victims: runaways at bus or train terminals, or street-people (homeless) living in alleys and boxes. A major requirement for each victim was that she/he was all alone in the world and not family-connected. "Marty" easily obtained the trust of potential victims with food, money, and proffered friendship and literally interviewed each one. If any indications of potential danger to the cult were detected, he gave them some parting money, wished them luck, and disappeared. If no danger was elicited, he would offer them a place to "shack-up" for a few days and take them to the warehouse, owned and utilized by the cult. There they were literally* **imprisoned** *in prepared cells, often being chained-up when "Marty" had to leave them alone. During their imprisonment, "Marty" prepared them for the impending weekend ceremonies. He rehearsed the ceremonies almost fully, being careful to leave out the fact that they might be sacrificed (murdered!) when all of the cult members had used them for their most deviant needs.*

By this time, I was totally shocked and did not know whether to believe any of the story (which in subsequent sessions became even more horrible!) or to decide that "Marty" was either making all of this up or was psychotic and/or delusional. I made the serious error of telling him my feelings about the stories of the cult and, *after staring me down,* he left the office without saying a word.

About ten days later, I received a phone call at my home about one in the morning. The first thing I heard was *weird music* playing that sent chills up my spine. Then a deep and powerful male voice said "I understand that you don't believe what "Marty" has been telling you?" By now, I was wide awake and quite frightened. The voice then told me everything there was to know about me and my family, including many intimate facts that no one should have or could have known. Some of the facts related to me by the voice were: my wife's and son's first names, all of our daily routines, where my son went to pre-school, when my wife worked in the garden, where we lived, including a description of the house, the room layout, the furnishings, colors of walls, a description of my home office, etc.; facts that only someone who had been inside my home could have known. He even told me my work schedule, day by day. I was then told to *"stay out of the cult's business." I continued treating "Marty" and learned more and more, especially the techniques and manipulations that cults use to control their victims.*

Rules That Cults Impose On Their Members (Victims)

- 1. Once initiated, there is no quitting and the individuals are literally owned by or belong to the cult.

- 2. Cultists' belief in Satan and his minions is often as real as Christians' and Jews' belief in their God.

- 3. Cultists proffer a belief that if they please Satan, they will achieve power, happiness and wealth.

- 4. Terror and threat are major means of preventing betrayal of the cult. In the more bizarre cults (e.g., Manson & Matamoras), both animal and human victims are tortured and even sacrificed (murdered) to demonstrate the punishment for betrayal of any type.

- 5. Membership often includes influential individuals with *power* from all walks of life: professionals, artists, actors, symphony conductors, clergy from all different organized religions, police chiefs and law enforcement officials, as well as others who simply have power through wealth.

Are there *poor cults?* Yes, but these are made up of seriously ill individuals who are either borderline personalities or overtly psychotic who are led by a clever and manipulating individual for his/her own purposes and needs. The members are led to believe that they really are agents of Satan or one of his lesser demons and that they receive the *right* to behave deviantly, break laws and even sacrifice and kill. We have all read about cults like this in the newspapers or viewed a T.V. special on the subject, e.g., the Manson cult's ritual murders of Sharon Tate and her family, the Matamoras satanic- ritual killings and many others.

Why Are So Few Cults Exposed and Prosecuted?

Many law enforcement agencies will categorically state that the entire question of cults and satanism is greatly exaggerated and that there is little evidence of any growth in this phenomenon. The exact opposite appears to be true. Once the operation of the cult is thoroughly understood, then the reasons that so few are ever identified and dealt with becomes strikingly clear. In *all* cults, there is the same mandated directive.

Whenever a cult practice or ceremony takes place, *all* attendees must participate in the scheduled activity. In this way, there is communal guilt. Anyone who is present at the activity and refuses to participate faces dire consequences up to and including death! In this manner, the cult remains perfectly secret and perfectly protected by common guilt.

Secondly, membership includes doctors, priests, lawyers, police officials, morticians, morgue attendants, paramedics, and all other professional occupations that can either tend to the inflicted wounds of the victims or easily dispose of the bodies where death occurred. A reading list on the subject appears at the end of this chapter for individuals interested in exploring this subject in more depth.

The above case focused more on the *physical* dangers and practices of satanic cults. There are other cults that appear more benign but the damage they cause is effectually as long-lasting and serious as the first type. A second example will clarify.

- VIC, *at age 23, was ordained a satanic minister by the famous (infamous?) Anton Levay in the Church of Satan Resurrected, originally based in California. He settled in a wealthy and cultured city in one of the eastern states and founded a satanic church in an abandoned Baptist church building.*

  *Being legalistically oriented, "Vic" obtained written consent and permission (with minimal problems) from the parents of more than 50 teenagers, 48 boys and 2 girls, to join his flock and to undergo **secret, physical initiations** into his satanic religion. Without ever really knowing who this individual was or what he was about, the parents signed the legal permission slips when pressured by their teenagers. (These permission slips were evidence in the eventual case of sexual molestation that brought him to the treatment center.)*

  *These physical initiations were based on **pain tolerance** and had several levels, beginning with a "paddling on the bare buttocks" during which the initiate was not allowed to cry or utter sounds of pain. Masturbation, group sex, anal-receptive sex followed in the intervening stages and eventually, at level 25, the process finished with a satanic ritual led by "Vic" in black robes, with the new member tied naked on a flat marble table. "Vic" in his robes as high priest would then light a black-candle and drip hot wax onto the stomach of the new member, inscribing a **permanent mark** symbolizing that the new member now belonged to both Satan and to him ("Vic"). When the wax cooled and was ripped off, it left a scar in the image that he had described. The victim was now a full member of the cult, **"personally owned"** by "Vic" to do with as he pleased, in private sexual rituals of twos and* threes. "Vic," in these private rituals, sexually molested the victims in any manner that "fit his mood at the time" (his words).

Only after six or more years, did one boy report to the authorities and a second boy eventually volunteered specific information. "Vic" was sentenced only for the sexual molestation of the two boys. During the first six months of his treatment, Vic showed his therapist a cult log, containing the names and rituals performed on almost 600 victims, 98% of whom were adolescent or pre-adolescent boys. Since only first names or coded cult names were used, the other victims were never located or treated even though the authorities visited all of the junior high schools and high schools in the area in an attempt to locate the other survivors and get them into treatment. The potential future damage is obvious.

TREATMENT CONSIDERATIONS

While all of the already discussed effects of long-term seductive sexual abuse apply, there are several specific effects and treatment problems that appear to be unique to the survivors of sexual cult molestation and that require specialized treatment techniques. A triple trauma is involved: first, the same trauma that exists in all cases of sexual molestation, secondly, abuse by an adult authority figure, and thirdly a *supernatural* trauma with fears of revenge from a supernatural deity if the survivor reports.

Effects of The Cult's Total Control and Conditioning: Grave and Long-lasting

Being "owned" by a supernatural deity that is all-powerful and can destroy the survivor or his/her family if he/she disobeys or betrays it is both controlling and terrifying. How does the survivor undo this ownership by a deity or his/her fears of retaliation connected to divulging any of its secrets? Even when these survivors do enter treatment, they find it difficult, if not impossible, to believe that a human, mortal therapist can prevail over a powerful, evil, satanic being. This belief probably accounts for the fact that even after "Vic" was incarcerated, the other victims never came forth, only the two who made the original complaint.

In therapy, *challenge* appears to be one of the only methods of obtaining trust and rapport from the survivor and of calming or alleviating his/her terror. By challenge I mean using everyday positive occurrences in the survivor's life to prove that the purported power of the satanic deity and its threats do not exist. If, for example, in the second therapy session, the therapist checks the previous week's occurrences and finds that no terrible horror or tragedy has happened, this reality can be used to indicate that the threat of betrayal that the survivor feared by coming to therapy and revealing the *secrets of the cult* was an idle and meaningless one. This tactic also allows the therapist the opportunity to *"depower"* the satanic priest and to show the survivor that the rituals, gowns and chants were all *manipulations,* used to obtain his/her cooperation in the deviant sexual needs of either the individual or the group.

As the weeks go by and no supernatural punishment occurs, survivors, themselves, begin to perceive what really occurred and how they were *used* for the sick, sexual needs of the individual or the group and that the rituals and practices only *justified* these sick behaviors by blaming them on the wishes of Satan and his hordes.

If the survivor was raised in a positive, forgiving religious environment, prior to the satanic-cult involvement, this can also be used to assuage his/her fears, nightmares and terrors. All religious denominations have some form of Satan and some form of opposing positive force (God, angels, saints, etc.). However, when the survivor was indoctrinated in one of the negative, hell-and-damnation religions, the damage and trauma again *doubles*. Not only does the survivor have to fear punishment and retaliation from the demonic or satanic powers but also from a Zeus-like, ever-watchful and unforgiving God who demands "an eye for an eye and a tooth for a tooth." These survivors cannot turn to their original childhood religion for help and are lost and in turmoil. Therapy will be harder and longer in duration for this group. It is not surprising to note that the most cult survivors who commit suicide are found in this group.

When the survivor is *ready* and on the road to recovery, *reality therapy* techniques continue to be utilized, with *distancing* techniques appended to allow the survivor to examine and understand his/her former weak, vulnerable and needy personality that the pervert(s) took advantage of.

When asked how he recruited his victims, "Vic" stated that he chose only those who:

- had problems at home,

- appeared and acted passive, weak, and dependent,

- were looking for a male authority figure as a parent substitute and guide,

- could instantly (through simple testing) be ordered to obey the commands of the satanic minister,

- were willing to believe in magical and supernatural forces that had power and control over them, and that could, if obeyed, provide power, money, happiness, and solutions to all of their problems, or

- were in the throes of adolescent rebellion against authority, rules and regulations.

These guidelines, used by "Vic," sound almost identical to the requirements of the seductive pedophiles and hebophiles, except for the belief in magical and supernatural forces. The dangers of long- term games like "Dungeons and Dragons" become obvious.

One of "Vic's" favorite tests was to have the new applicant "wet his/her pants" in front of the entire group of initiated members of the cult. To "Vic" this proved that his power and authority exceeded that of the influence of the initiate's parents, his former religion, and his peer group. He then felt confident that the remainder of his perverted orders would be obeyed and never reported. Unfortunately, 98% of the adolescents he victimized reacted as he had predicted.

Problems with Reentry into Normal Peer Groups

After long-term involvement as a hand-picked, special member of a satanic cult involved in very antisocial and deviant practices in the guise of religion, feeling comfortable in his/her peer group is difficult and seems impossible for the survivor of cult abuse. The feelings of being *different* that all survivors of sexual abuse experience are now *doubled:* once for the deviant sexual behavior with an adult (especially if he/she was the same sex), and the second for membership in a cult that worships Satan, demons, and evil.

In therapy, this appears to be an ideal setting for *support-group* involvement and networking. However, there are *dangers* with SRA cases that do not exist in other forms of sexual abuse. The major danger is that an SRA seeking therapy *may* be sincere and may have actually broken off from the cult. However, one cult practice is to infiltrate therapists who accept SRAs in treatment in order to "set them up" or to gain information on them that can be used against them, a form of blackmail. Networking without being absolutely positive that the SRA is not a "plant" could produce danger for the other SRAs and for the therapist as well. The care and concern that must be taken in this screening and weeding process may take many months and, even then, the therapist can never really be sure.

Once a single member of a satanic cult has truly broken away and reintegrated into his normal peer group, this individual can do more for the remaining survivors of satanic cults than any therapist can ever hope to accomplish (unless the therapist himself/herself is also a survivor of a satanic cult). This support-group involvement should remain *adjunctive* to the individual therapy of the cult survivor and not replace it. This is necessary since in all of the cases I have dealt with or discussed with other therapists *there is always at least one secret or one act or behavior that the survivor will not be able to share in a group setting and that needs to be ventilated and resolved.*

Where *promotion* issues are concerned, this group of survivors is the exception to the rapid promotion rules that were discussed in Chapter 11, page 168. Nightmares, fears, misinterpretation of reality, where misfortunes or problems are concerned, and re-triggered associations to the past involvement and behavior, all must be dealt with over a long period of time. These damaging and traumatic effects will often continue to occur in this group for many, many years. Once PRN status ("call in when necessary") has been achieved, regularly scheduled *checkup* sessions are essential for the survivors of sexual abuse in a satanic cult. All survivors want to believe that they are "cured" and no longer need to be dependent for help on the therapist (which they interpret as a sign of weakness, especially during adolescence). When the therapist makes regularly scheduled checkup sessions as part of the P.R.N. agreement, this problem is avoided and the self-esteem and self-respect of the survivor remains strong and intact.

The Problem of Recurrence of the Abuse: Strong and Definite Possibility, Especially During Treatment and Shortly Thereafter

The *vulnerability* of this group of survivors is far greater than any other group discussed thus far. So is the guilt that they continue to experience for the deviant acts they *"willingly"* (their conditioned perception, placed there by the deviant cult leader) performed for the "master" or high priest. If publicity was involved in the exposure of the cult, other deviates with the same proclivities will come out of the woodwork looking for ex-cult members to recruit for their own deviant sexual purposes. This danger must be avoided. Early discussion of this possibility and the dangers inherent in succumbing over again to a similar influence by another satanic cult leader is the best method of preventing this possible recurrence. Parents, friends, and other group members in a stronger position or more advanced in their own treatment, teachers, and other authority figures should all be involved in this area, and made acutely aware of the dangers.

For at least the first month or two of treatment, the survivor should be left alone as little as possible, especially when in the community (traveling back and forth to school, gym, community activities, etc.). He/she should also have someone sleeping in his/her bedroom (but not in his/her bed!) due to nightmares and night-terrors.

Prevention of recurrence is the major focus with this group. Some of the cult activities and behaviors will maintain a perverted attraction- potential for the survivor for several months after therapy begins. This is especially true where sexual activities and drug use are concerned. These areas need to be thoroughly explored, discussed and resolved with the survivor and then discussed with all significant individuals involved in the life of the survivor including parents, siblings, close friends, school counselors, church leaders, etc.

CONCLUSIONS

While the subjects of religion, cults and satanism had to be included in this coverage, my personal experience and knowledge in this area is new and very limited. In my travels around this country and in Europe, I have begun meeting more and more survivors of satanic abuse as well as more therapists involved in this field. I continue to accrue facts, case histories and treatment methods being used that will eventually reach book length. What I have gleaned from these experiences is that *the damage is long-term and the effects insidious.*

In no other sexual or criminal offenses that I have evaluated or treated have I experienced the loathsome and deplorable acts foisted on innocent human beings than I have heard from survivors of satanic cults. I recently met an 18-year-old female survivor with 17 years of satanic cult abuse, both at home and outside the home. Her abuse began at birth. In fact, the reason the girl was conceived was for her to become *"an instrument to be used for the greater glory of Satan and his minions"* (a direct statement made to the authorities by her own parents). As her memories are brought into consciousness through hypnosis and regression techniques, the rituals and acts that she was subjected to throughout her life continue to surface. The majority of these acts are so horrible that I would not consider retelling them here or anywhere else. The fact that she is a survivor and existing is a *miracle* since she has already made many suicidal attempts. Treatment will be a long-term battle requiring courage and stamina on the parts of both the survivor and the therapist.

Society does not want to know or to believe that these kinds of sexual and physical abuse may exist. Authorities call what few reports are made the *imagination of children and adolescents looking for attention and/or revenge on parents and other authority figures.* In this way, they don't have to face the horrors that really do exist in their area of responsibility. Even when presented with *incontrovertible evidence* such as being taken to the cult meeting room where ritual sacrifices have taken place and being shown the skulls and bones of the many victims, they find excuses and rationalizations to sweep the incidents and reports under the carpet. Why? The reason is obvious. As "Marty," discussed earlier in this chapter stated, the membership of these cults is composed of influential and authority- oriented individuals in society, who suppress evidence as well as hinder, block or even *order* investigations stopped. In the case of the girl discussed in this section, that is exactly what occurred.

Could these reports be hysterical manifestations or a deeper underlying pathology? Of course, they can. However, the consistency of the survivor's stories and descriptions of the ceremonies and practices of the satanic cults are too exact to be imagined with a global unconsciousness of some type or other. I have interviewed victims in several parts of the United States and in Europe who give an almost verbatim account of the practices they were forced to submit to and who also describe the exact trappings of the rooms where these practices occurred. There is no doubt in my mind that the survivors *believe* that these horrible acts were perpetrated upon them. I, therefore, treat them on the basis of their beliefs.

Are there individuals and groups of individuals who use the trappings of cult worship to justify and excuse their deviant behaviors? Of course there are. "Vic" admitted that although ordained a satanic priest, he really did not believe in the powers of Satan since he never profited from them and was not protected from being sent to prison as he was told he would be. Yet, he persisted in his deviant need for sex with teenage boys.

The reader is strongly advised to find more literature and discussions on this topic if presently involved with survivors of this type or ever plan to be and to be sure that he/she has the moral, religious, and personal strength to deal with the gross revelations that will definitely ensue. A list of suggested readings follows:

- Bach, Marcus. *Strange Sects and Curious Cults.* 1992. New York: Dorset Press.

- Davies, Maureen. 1991. *Helping Individuals and Agencies Deal with Problems of Ritual Abuse.* Rhyl-Clywd, Wales LL18 4HA: Beacon Foundation.
- Diamond, Vera. 1992. *Satanic Ritual Abuse Syndrome.* London, England: The Cornelian Trust. (Unpublished paper).
- Kahaner, Larry. 1988. *Cults that Kill.* New York: Warner Books.
- Lavey, Anton Szandor. 1969. *The Satanic Bible.* New York: Avon Books.
- Lavey, Anton Szandor. 1970, 1971, 1989. *The Satanic Witch.* Los Angeles: Feral House.
- Oke, Isaiah. 1989. *Blood Secrets: The True Story of Demon Worship and Ceremonial Murder.* New York: Prometheus Books.
- Otter, G'Zell, Editor. 1989. *Witchcraft, Satanism and Occult Crime: Who's Who and What's What.* Los Ippilotos, CA: Green Egg.
- Pazder and Smith. 1980. *Michelle Remembers.*

15

Conclusions

The following conclusions are offered as an important guide for anyone planning to become involved in the treatment of the survivor.

THE TREATMENT OF SURVIVORS IS A SPECIALIZED FIELD

From my observations and contacts with professional groups, I strongly feel that professional schools, today, are not fully or even adequately preparing psychiatrists, psychologists, social workers and other counselors in the dynamics of the survivors of sexual abuse/assault or in the specific techniques required to treat this group in an effective and successful manner. The professional's only alternative is to seek out and to participate fully in comprehensive training programs, offered by other professionals with experience and expertise in this difficult field.

Once training is complete, then the professional seriously needs to seek out a supervisor with experience and expertise with this group and spend a minimum of 50 hours in supervised training. Ideally, this supervision should range anywhere from 50 to 100 hours. Supervision should present no real hardship since most qualified supervisors allow the trainee to use cases from his/her practice that are current. Supervision can be effected in several ways.

- On-site supervision during an ongoing therapy session. In an agency or clinic setting, this could be accomplished with a one-way mirror arrangement,
- videotaping of the sessions and then a supervised playback, or
- when videotaping is impossible then audiotaping, the least preferred or effective method, should be utilized.

Videotaping is the preferred and more effective method of supervision, since body language and messages sent by the therapist via visual expressions and changes in posture are extremely important and cannot be detected on an audio recording. When audiotaping is the method of supervision, it must be supplemented by more on-site supervision sessions than would be necessary with videotaping.

It should be made perfectly clear that all three methods *mandate* openness of what is being done and having the permission of the client. Covert taping is unethical and, if discovered, could not only destroy the relationship between the client and the therapist but could also result in legal action.

TREATING SURVIVORS IS NOT A FIELD FOR EVERYONE

The *personality of the therapist* is an important factor when considering an individual's qualifications to treat the survivors of sexual abuse. Several specific factors should be weighed.

The Prospective Therapist's Comfort with Sexuality, Per Se

Comfort with sexuality necessarily includes the therapist's sexual prejudices, sexual moralizations, lack of adequate sex education, problems with sexual slang and "street language," rigid sexual preferences, strong religious judgments regarding human sexual behavior, etc. All of the above factors strongly affect the therapist's ability to work comfortably and effectively with survivors or even more with their abusers.

Therapists who have never experienced a full sex attitude restructuring (S.A.R.) training seminar should definitely arrange to participate in one as soon as the decision is made to work with survivors of sexual abuse. If a prospective supervisee has not participated in a S.A.R., all qualified clinical supervisors should make this a *concurrent prerequisite* to their accepting a prospective therapist trainee in supervision.

Ability to Deal with Painful and Shocking Experiences

Working with survivors of sexual abuse *always* involves hearing very painful and often degrading and shocking examples of "man's inhumanity to man." Each time I thought I had heard the most shocking and terrible story of my career, my next client or two proved me wrong, and told an even more horrible or more painful story of sexual abuse.

Therapists are and will remain human! It is not only permissible but also therapeutically positive for the therapist to experience and share the shock and horror as well as the compassion and empathy that he/she feels for the survivor. Not to do so could be interpreted as coldness, indifference, and lack of concern, not as professionalism (as some professionals might think). However, this factor is only part of the problem. The real problem occurs when the therapist is unable to *let-go of* his/her feelings after the session and takes them home to his/her family, friends, etc. When this occurs, the therapist-trainee should seriously consider either getting immediate help from a supervisor in the field or eliminating survivors from his/her caseload. While this may seem to be a drastic solution, it makes no sense to attempt to help a survivor and in the process to damage either the therapist or his/her family.

Prospective Therapist's Ability to Retain a Reality-Oriented Mind-Set

The therapist-trainee must accept the inevitable fact that for some survivors *change* will be very slow and for others it may never occur. If the therapist makes change and success *his/her responsibility* rather than the *responsibility of the survivor,* the outcome can and often will be damaging to both. The therapist must maintain a *distance,* regardless of how small that distance is.

Ability to Tolerate Failure

As stated above, not all survivors will respond positively to therapy. Some will resist, others will never become sufficiently motivated to change, and still others will fail and quit. All of the above possibilities are realistic and subjective decisions and choices that the *survivor, not the therapist* must make.

When failure does occur, while it will be difficult to accept, the therapist cannot assume the responsibility if he/she knows that he/she did his/her best. If the therapist does assume the responsibility for the failure it will be disastrous for his/her psychological health and, in no way help or affect the life of the survivor.

DIFFERENTIAL TECHNIQUES FOR TREATING SURVIVORS OF SEXUAL ABUSE

Several important principles must be followed in dealing with survivors of sexual abuse if therapy is to be successful.

The Therapist Needs to Relinquish Control to the Survivor

As stated in Chapter 9, since *control* is the main element in all sexual abuse on the part of the abuser, returning that control to the survivor must be a primary element of the therapy. Most therapists tend to remain in complete control of all therapy sessions, so this mandate will be a dramatic change and will need to be consciously practiced by new individuals to this field. Not all therapists will be willing or able to relinquish this control and that decision should be made prior to deciding to treat survivors.

The Therapist Needs to be Able to "Promote" the Survivor Steadily

Promotion is necessary before intractable dependence becomes a problem. As stated previously in this work, my own preference is to advance the survivor from weekly to biweekly, then to monthly, and eventually to PRN status (call or come in as necessary). As soon as the survivor begins to respond to treatment and has begun to alter his/her negative self-image, suggesting or even forcing promotion to bi-weekly becomes a necessary step in order to prevent overdependence on the therapist and the therapy situation. Trips, conferences and vacations offer the therapist a practical and realistic method of *forcing* the first promotion, especially when resistance is experienced. The remaining promotions can then be made with the *consent of* and based on the *comfort level* of the survivor.

When PRN (pro-re-nata) status is reached, the therapist can expect a form of *testing* to occur. This testing usually takes the form of several phone calls at all hours of the day and night, or a sudden unscheduled appearance of the survivor at the office. All of these situations can be avoided with careful and explicit instructions as to what PRN involves and the times that the therapist will be available for consultations. *Emergencies,* of course, are an exception to these rules but, here again, care must be taken that the survivor does not use the label "emergency" when one does not really exist (the "boy who cried wolf" syndrome).

The Therapist Needs to Handle Frustration Continually

Survivors have their constant ups-and-downs, highs and lows, productive sessions and seemingly worthless sessions. The therapist must accept these situations as normal and learn how to use them to help the survivor to understand himself/herself in a clearer and more meaningful way. Learning to *predict* his/her own behavior and to recognize the *triggers* that precede or precipitate these negative times is all a necessary part of the overall treatment process. The nonproductive sessions should be used to aid the survivor in learning these essential facts about himself/herself.

The Therapist Needs to Offer Flexible Scheduling Hours

The *moods* of the survivor vary so greatly that regularly scheduled sessions (the traditional fifty-minute-hour format) do not always work, especially in the beginning of the treatment process. This is especially true when a situation occurs that produces panic in the survivor and requires that the he/she see his/her therapist as soon as possible, even when not scheduled.

Flexible hours are also necessary when the survivor begins to unload the *emotional baggage,* resulting from the abuse, that will begin to surface. Scheduling the newer survivors in the last time slot of the day appears to be one of the practical solutions to this problem that will not affect other clients in the therapist's practice.

Money Cannot be a Priority Where Survivor Treatment is Concerned

In my opinion, refusing treatment because the survivor cannot pay or does not have insurance is unconscionable. There are very few full time private practitioners who cannot afford to volunteer, at least one, if not two or three time slots per week for this group of patients. There is also the second option of utilizing sliding fee scales to resolve the money problem since there are therapists who feel that if the client does not pay for his/her services, the therapy will not be as effective or the client will not be as seriously involved. The group may have to be subsidized.

In my own private practice, I utilize the following subsidy system. I treat not only survivors of sexual assault but also sexually dysfunctional couples, adult males with a specific sexual dysfunction and finally sex offenders referred by the courts for therapy as a condition of their probation or parole. I charge all individuals in this last group, the offenders, one and a half times my normal fee and explain to them that the additional monies will subsidize the treatment of a survivor of sexual assault, similar to the one that they perpetrated. I have never had one of the offenders refuse to participate in this subsidy system. While this system works for me, I am certainly not recommending that all therapists use it. However, in one way or another, all treating professions need to offer some time for this group of clients, if for no other reason then as a community service.

Individual and Group Therapy

Where all survivors are concerned, peer support is often more valuable than the support of the therapist in a one-to-one situation. Every survivor needs to know that *he/she is not the only one* who has experienced this type of trauma. Group therapy affords survivors the opportunity to learn, firsthand, that there are others, especially peers, who have also been sexually traumatized and who really do understand how he/she feels, what he/she went through, and what he/she is experiencing in the present. While this group experience is critical in the preadolescent and adolescent groups, it is just as important with very young children and older adults as well. *Survivor groups* provide an *expertise* that the therapist cannot provide unless he/she also is a survivor of sexual abuse and is willing to disclose that information with clients. Survivor groups also provide the potential and the individuals to form a *network* to be available when the therapist is unavailable or out of town.

Comfort with a Degree of Physical Contact

This is especially true where *hugging* is concerned. Survivors have experienced *negative physical contact* from the abuser. They are frightened of, and in the beginning, cringe at even the slightest physical contact. As therapy progresses and rapport and trust are established, the therapist needs to attempt some slight physical gesture, such as a touch on the arm or the shoulder, or even a pat on the back especially when the survivor either arrives for or leaves a difficult and painful session (such as the first time the survivor shares the details of the abuse).

I often use this first touch as a *test* to see just how much rapport and trust has been established and just how far the survivor has progressed in therapy. It also provides a topic for a specific session when the survivor seems to have nothing to say. The therapist, as stated before, needs to help the survivor to restructure values that were distorted by the abuser and the abuse relationship. Physical contact is a good place to begin the process of preventing the survivor from over-generalizing all of the actions and behaviors of the abuser onto everyone else whom he/she comes into contact with.

GROUPS AND NETWORKING

Due to the unique needs of some survivors, the therapist's availability becomes a critical issue. Since 24-hour availability is impractical and unfair to the therapist, some other form of emergency handling must be arranged, in advance. Perhaps a colleague can cover at certain times. However, what I consider an even more practical solution to the problem is the *networking* of a group of similar survivors so that they can learn to work with and to eventually rely on each other. Quite often, when one survivor helps another in an emergency or even in a social situation, benefits occur to both the helper and the individual receiving the help. Networking eliminates a great many problems for the therapist, including the resocialization needs of these clients. Often, survivors in a network find that they have a great deal in common and become good and even close friends. Their *comfort level* with each.other is much greater than with a nonsurvivor and this bodes well for networkers to gravitate towards each other in more than a therapeutic way. These relationships must be known to the therapist so that no negative effects occur.

Additionally, the network, after a period of time, usually produces a *leader* who can then become a para-professional under the supervision of the primary therapist. This individual can handle minor problems when the therapist is unavailable. An example will clarify.

RALPH, discussed in Chapters 2 and 3, was a natural- born leader, president of his class in high school, and the captain of his dirt bike team. Since I had several male survivors in the same school that "Ralph" attended and who all lived in the same neighborhood, I formed a survivor's group with them and promoted networking.

Once or twice a year, I travel to England or to other European countries to conduct training seminars in both sex offender and survivors of sexual abuse dynamics and treatment. During these trips, "Ralph" is my contact person for the group. A notice is placed on the school's bulletin board stating that *"Bill's kids please contact "Ralph" in room xxx."* If a serious problem arises, "Ralph" calls my office and a message is immediately sent to me, wherever I am, so that I can either contact the survivor involved directly or have some other trained colleague handle the problem. In over five years of traveling, "Ralph" has handled all of the minor problems that occurred without the need of contacting me.

FOLLOW-UP IS ESSENTIAL

There can never be true termination of treatment in survivor treatment cases, only promotion to a PRN (call or come in when necessary) status. Part of the PRN procedure should be a method or condition of remaining in contact with the survivor. This process is a form of *follow-up*. There are several ways in which follow-up can be achieved.

- When the survivor is promoted to PRN status, a *condition* is addended for monthly, quarterly, or at the minimum, annual *check-in*. Check-in may be a telephone call at a prearranged hour. I personally use 9:30-10:00 P.M. for all PRN survivor calls since by then my last client is gone and the call will not disrupt a therapy session. An alternate arrangement to the telephone call may be a postcard or letter on a regular schedule. This written check-in should contain a progress update and should also include problems, if there are any. Finally, check-in can be an actual short visit on a prescheduled basis. With my survivors, this "visit" consists of attendance at a Christmas lunch at a local restaurant. This form of check-in is a natural result of the networking discussed above and was suggested many years ago by "Ralph," the adolescent survivor discussed earlier as well as in Chapters 2 and 3.

Two additional situations are covered by the check-in system.

- Survivors have their ups and downs and most likely will, at some future time, experience a *regression* and the need to return to formal treatment. These regressions are usually temporary setbacks and should be treated as such.

- When a temporary setback occurs, it is essential to let the survivor know that this *does not mean that the original therapy failed.* The original changes made are real but pressures or similar situations can retrigger a return of the old bad feelings. Usually, only a brief refresher is needed in these cases. One or two crisis sessions are usually sufficient to put the survivor back on track. However, if the setback involves new memories ("flashbacks") that had not been previously dealt with in therapy, a longer period of time may be necessary before PRN can be reestablished.

YOU-THE-THERAPIST CONSIDERATIONS

There are several very important concepts, values, and situations that involve dangers to the therapist that must be discussed.

There is no profession, employment or work situation that is worth damaging the individual or the individual's family and/or friends.

This concept cannot be emphasized enough. Some therapists, due to individual personality traits or past experiences, cannot deal with this particular group of clients (survivors) without suffering serious effects after each and every session. These effects include: anxiety, depression, nightmares, increased drinking or eating, and many other types of somatic and psychosomatic symptoms. These reactions, on the part of some therapists, can relate to treating *any individual* in the entire group of survivors or only to a *particular type* of survivor. It may also occur due to the *circumstances* surrounding a specific sexual abuse case. An example of each will clarify.

- DOUG, *a 30-year-old clinical psychologist at the master's level, was trained in the specialty of child psychology. He had recently completed an internship in a state facility, treating mildly to severely behaviorally disturbed young children and adolescents. His mentors graded him "highly efficient, professional and personable."*

*Upon completion of his internship, the institution offered "Doug" a full-time job. They had just begun a special unit for treating children who had been sexually abused. These were boys who were unable to adjust to either their homes or their schools, and had become serious community behavioral problems. "Doug" jumped at the chance to work with this special group of survivors **although he had had no training in this area nor had he been in treatment himself.***

Less than two weeks into the new program, "Doug" began calling in sick on a fairly regular basis. His complaints were mostly of migraine headaches and gastro-intestinal difficulties. A complete medical workup could find no physical etiology for his symptoms.

"Doug's" attitude and demeanor had also abruptly changed. He tended to be extremely quiet (the opposite of his old outgoing and effervescent self), isolated a great deal and no longer spoke enthusiastically about his groups or his work with sexually abused boys. Complaints also began coming in from the parents of the children that "Doug" was being dictatorial, screaming angrily at the children and either showing up late for his appointments or cutting them off in ten to fifteen minutes, rather than his usual hour or more. The children were now afraid of their old, kind and comforting friend.

When confronted by his supervisor with the changes noted by staff members and the complaints of the parents and the children, "Doug" angrily offered his resignation. The supervisor referred "Doug" to a sex therapist colleague of mine and the following discovery was made.

*"Doug," when ten years old, had been molested by a neighbor who was a close friend of the family. Whenever "Doug's" father went on a business trip, he took "Doug's" mother with him and "Doug" was left with the neighbors. A familiar scenario developed, with the "mister" of the house, taking "Doug" hiking, fishing and camping **and molesting him along the way.** This went on for several years (ages 10-13) until "Doug's" family moved out of town. **"Doug" never told anyone.***

When "Doug" went to the university for his clinical psychology degree, the university he chose had eliminated the old requirement for clinicians to be involved in at least one year of psychotherapy of their own as a requirement for the clinical degree (a tragic and serious decision, in my opinion). "Doug" often wanted to talk about his molestation with one of the psychologists at the school but felt (and was told by other graduate students) that if he revealed having any emotional problems, he would be weeded out of the clinical degree track and put into a research, education or industrial psychology track. "Doug" chose to remain silent.

*As he began to conduct group therapy with and to interview sexually abused children who discussed their molestations with him, the "old tapes" began to play and "Doug" relived his own **shame, guilt, feeling dirty, and fears of being gay,** with each child he treated. He also experienced unwanted **erections** when listening to the stories of the abused boys and began fearing he would become homosexually active, possibly with the children at the institution. "Doug" also supervised gym activities and that included locker room and showering supervision.*

As each new symptom occurred, "Doug" unconsciously punished himself with physical problems, starting with the migraine headaches and then adding the gastrointestinal problems (all unconsciously).

Once the story of his own molestation was revealed to his therapist, the physical symptoms slowly but steadily disappeared and "Doug" was soon physically ready *to return to work. The therapist, with "Doug's" permission, met with his supervisor and they both agreed to allow "Doug" to return to work **slowly**, beginning with a three-day week and with minimal therapy assignments.*

*Within six months of continued sex therapy, "Doug" was again given his original group of abused boys and decided to tell them of his own molestation. With the "ice broken" in that manner, the group responded positively and "Doug" once again felt like his old self. He became an effective and very well-liked and respected member of the institution's sexual abuse treatment team, and remains there to this day. All of the problems "Doug" encountered could have been avoided had he had his own treatment **before** becoming involved with sexually abused boys.*

A different type of problem for therapists in this field follows.

• KEITH *had been a Ph.D. clinical psychologist in his own practice for over ten years. A local referring agency sent him a 14-year-old girl,* NOELLE, *who had been raped by a stranger, while hitchhiking through the local area. In their first contact, "Keith" thought the girl looked familiar but said nothing about it. That night it bothered him and he was preoccupied with trying to identify where he knew her from.*

The same night, his own 14-year-old daughter, ELLEN *asked to talk to him privately in his study and proceeded to tell him that one of her closest friends at school had been raped by a stranger and that she did not know how to act around her. Without asking, "Keith" knew that his daughter was talking about "Noelle" and that he must have seen the two of them together, either in his own home or in the school area. "Keith" counseled his daughter, especially about her discomfort around "Noelle," without telling her that he was treating her friend and classmate.*

In his next session with "Noelle," "Keith" found himself feeling "uncomfortable" around her but he couldn't understand why. At times he was curt, almost angry with the young girl; something he had never done with any client before. His mind would not work. He didn't know where to go with the case and couldn't concentrate on what "Noelle" was saying. All he knew was that he wanted the session to be over with as quickly as possible.

That evening, "Keith" called me and asked if he could drop over for a chat. When he arrived, it was obvious that he was disturbed about something. He easily and quickly told me what was going on and that he was confused and not sure if he should continue with the case. Since "Keith" worked in a group practice, I suggested transferring the case (there had only been two contacts and no serious rapport had been established at that point). An excuse was manufactured, revolving about work schedule overload and this was accepted by both "Noelle" and her family.

*Over the next few months, "Keith" dropped in several times to discuss the case since it still bothered him and he still felt bad about dropping "Noelle" from his caseload. Slowly but surely what emerged was "Keith's" fear that it could have been "Ellen" who was raped. He had recently been working many late hours to make things better for his family and often, when "Ellen" called for a ride, he told her to walk or to ride her bike. "Ellen," however, had learned to hitchhike from "Noelle," who did it all the time, and "Keith" knew this but did nothing about it. Now the source of the problem was clear. "Keith" was **angry** at "Noelle" for putting his daughter in jeopardy. It was now clear that he could not work with "Noelle" and that the decision to transfer her to another therapist was the correct one.*

PERSONALITY CONFLICTS BETWEEN THERAPIST AND SURVIVOR

As long as therapists are *human,* there will be *personality conflicts* that are not caused by anyone or anything on a conscious level. When we are at a party or other group gatherings, and suddenly a new person enters the room, we will experience one of three possible reactions.

- 1. We will immediately be *attracted* to the person.
- 2. We will immediately *dislike* the person.
- 3. We will remain *indifferent* to the person.

Commonly, this response behavior is referred to as an initial or first impression. If, at that moment we were to be put on the spot and asked what our reaction was and then to *logically* explain the reason for our reaction, the majority of us would be unable to do so without a great deal of thought and contemplation. *Knowledge and information* about the person may or may not change this initial impression. Whoever or whatever we associate this new person to can be a positive memory association of any degree or a negative memory association of any degree. The *stronger* the association, the *greater* the impact.

For most therapists, there will be some survivors and other clients whom they will simply not like or not want to become involved with, for unknown reasons. These are the cases that should be considered for transfer to another therapist *once the reaction occurs regardless of whether or not the reasons for the dislike are identified or understood.* Too many therapists function under the erroneous and damaging belief that because they have a degree and training, and are professionals, they should be able to treat anyone, regardless of who they are or what they have done. This belief is not only an untrue and unreasonable attitude or value to hold but also bodes danger of damage for both the therapist and his/her client. Survivors have been damaged enough without having to be treated by an individual who has a *hidden agenda,* especially if the associations being made are extremely negative.

A well-known philosopher once said "Know yourself and the rest of life becomes easy!" (A loose, not literal translation.) This certainly should apply to professionals as well as the rest of the population.

An example will clarify and introduce an important staff activity, *peer supervision.*

Soon after the treatment program I was associated with opened, a decision was made to begin *peer supervision* once a week for an hour or two. Peer supervision was a meeting of all of the treatment staff, wherein no one had any authority over anyone else. Strict confidentiality was a condition of the meeting and anyone could say whatever he/she wanted to without fear of repercussion.

During one of the first peer supervision sessions, I brought up a case that had been assigned to me only a week or two before. From our first contact, the client and I literally *hated each other* and the sparks flew. For the life of me, I could not explain my immediate dislike of this individual and I doubt that he could explain his dislike of me. I told the staff that if someone else did not trade this case with me, I did not know what would happen since, whenever I was with him, I wanted to punch him in the mouth or worse.

The staff was shocked at my reaction but in a moment or two another therapist volunteered that he also had a similar problem with a particular new case and that his feelings were almost identical to mine. We agreed to *trade* cases and to everyone's surprise, I did extremely well with his offender and he related excellently with my old offender. Had we both acted in a so-called "professional manner" (in the wrong sense of the phrase), we would have had problems and neither of the offenders would have really profited from therapy. Clients, especially survivors, *know* when the therapist does not like them. When this occurs, they believe that the therapist does not want to help them or that they will never get well. This situation also confirms all of their own negative, judgmental feelings about themselves that brought them to therapy in the first place.

FIVE INDICATORS OF NEGATIVE THERAPIST REACTIONS

In supervising therapists for more than 20 years, I have observed the following indicators that there was some form of *negative reaction* occurring between the client and the therapist.

- 1. The therapist had fewer contacts with that particular client than with the rest of his/her caseload.

- 2. A consistent confrontation existed between the therapist and the client and few or no positive results came from the therapy.

- 3. There was less eye contact between the therapist and the client and vice-versa.

- 4. The therapist showed an absence of interest in the client and his/her problems during supervision.

- 5. The therapist had a tendency to write reports about the client that emphasized negative traits and qualities rather than a balance of both positive and negative ones.

THE DANGER OF BECOMING TOO INVOLVED

Just as *exaggerated negative association* towards a survivor can produce disastrous results for both the survivor and the therapist, too much of an *exaggerated positive association,* the "Halo Effect" can produce the same negative results. When a "Halo Effect" occurs, only the positive and good things about a person are seen and their failings, negative traits and damaging behaviors are either glossed over or ignored. The therapist also becomes an *advocate* for the survivor and loses his/her *objectivity.* Parents, friends, relatives, and lawyers can also fall prey to this problem. While the Halo Effect results in a very pleasant setting and atmosphere for both the survivor (or any other client) and the therapist, painful and sensitive issues are avoided or ignored and therapy becomes more of a social encounter than treatment.

As stated continually throughout this work, therapists and counselors need to maintain a *distance* from the survivor, especially where feelings and emotions are involved. With children and adolescents, the danger of becoming a *substitute-parent, best-buddy, protector,* etc., always exists. The more damaged the child, the more serious this danger may be. The therapist needs to take time to sit back and evaluate where he/she is going with each survivor and to evaluate what his/her role in the last several sessions has been. There is also a need to have some form of *objective* supervision to expose what the therapist may defensively have blocked out. This leads to the next topic.

KNOWING WHEN TO ASK FOR HELP

There are two specific situations where knowing when to ask for help becomes especially important.

- The first situation involves cases where no progress is being made.

Rather than face weekly frustration on both the part of the survivor as well as the therapist, asking for a *consultation* from a colleague, who is trained in and has years of experience in survivor treatment, is not only appropriate but is the only course of action that makes sense.

Some therapists feel that they should be able to handle any situation and that asking for help is a sign of some form of *deficiency* on their part. Nothing could be further from the truth. The opposite is true. Asking for help is a sign of a mature and well-trained therapist who is in touch with his own skill limitations and whose primary concern is the welfare of his client. At times, the therapist is *too close to the problem* and does not see what is going wrong, what options to consider, or what alternative treatment modalities to introduce. A *second opinion,* when this occurs can avert tragedy or failure.

- The second situation occurs when the survivor presents a problem or dysfunction with which the therapist has had no prior experience or training.

No therapist in the world can know everything. There will always be occasions when a survivor reveals a problem, question, or dysfunction that baffles the therapist. An example will clarify.

- *In dealing with* DENNIS, *(discussed in Chapters 6 and 12) an aspect of his masturbatory practices was revealed that I had never heard of before. "Dennis" could only masturbate by simulating intercourse on a towel that was placed on his bed sheets* **without lubrication.** *All attempts to masturbate with his hand failed. Although he did get an erection and some pleasurable sensations, he could not reach orgasm that way, regardless of the amount of time involved or the fantasy used. Logic dictated that there had to be some special meaning or significance to his technique, and all possibilities were explored over a period of several months, with no success.*

    In complete frustration, I discussed "Dennis" with a colleague who also was a certified supervisor, sex therapist, and had worked with survivors of sexual abuse for over 20 years. After telling him the details of the problem and the attempts I had made, his very first question was "Have you considered masochism? Surely, what he does must be painful!" I hadn't even thought of masochism or the obvious pain this practice was causing.

*In the next therapy session, I gently probed and explored that area and found that the results of this masturbation technique were **always** irritation and skin damage to Dennis's penis. **Pain** was a necessary element in his masturbation and manual stimulation did not provide that pain. In fact, "Dennis" volunteered that on several occasions, he ended up with "a raw and bleeding penis." Pain led to a discussion of self-punishment for both his homosexual and pedophillic obsessions and fantasies, and opened a whole new area of therapy. The consultation certainly paid dividends for both the survivor and the therapist.*

TRANSFERENCE AND COUNTERTRANSFERENCE

The first danger that should be discussed is that of the phenomenon of *transference,* a major danger in any therapy situation. A working definition, at this point, is essential.

The patient transfers his or her past emotional attachments to the [therapist] . . . The [therapist] is a substitute for the parental figure. Transference may be either positive or negative. In positive transference the patient loves the [therapist] and wishes to obtain love and emotional satisfaction from the [therapist]. In negative transference the patient views the [therapist] as an unfair, unloving, rejecting parental figure, and projects all of: Reliving of hostile feelings toward parents or parental substitutes in a psychotherapeutic setting and experiencing hostility toward the psychologist . . . (Wolman, 1989)

From the above definitions alone, the problems for the therapist become obvious. When, and if, the survivor becomes *more than normally friendly* and verbally becomes *highly personal,* especially with compliments, the therapist must immediately clarify his/her role and that of the survivor. Hoping this situation will pass and letting it go as a one-time occurrence only gives the survivor encouragement in his/her emotionally laden transference feelings. While compliments are certainly pleasant and make the therapist feel good, they also may be indicators of danger, when they become *too strong or too frequent.*

Any indication of *sexual innuendo* or *direct sexual reference* (concerning the therapist and the client) must also be dealt with *as it occurs,* regardless of the potential that the survivor may get hurt or feel rejected.

An example of the problems that can occur for the therapist will clarify.

- TANYA *was a 16-year-old girl sent to the old diagnostic center for evaluation and recommendation, following being charged with juvenile delinquency in that she was apprehended in flagrante delicto (the court's phrasing) prostituting with older men. From the first contact that I had with "Tanya," she was seductive, manipulative, and overly complimentary. It was obvious that she was looking for something more than therapy from me but was clever enough to bide her time until she felt I was "hooked" (her term).*

The center, where this occurred, had a no smoking rule for anyone under the age of 18 and apparently "Tanya" had been a compulsive chain-smoker at home. On the occasion in question, she came to her weekly therapy session in her usual short dress, a blouse with buttons open, and an overtly seductive manner. Within five minutes of her arrival, she brought up the question of the smoking rule and asked to be allowed to smoke during our sessions with the door closed, stating that "I'll make it well worth your while!" I explained that rules were rules, that I agreed with them, and would not consider violating them. I also explained that I believed that smoking at her age was unhealthy and a bad habit.

The following incident occurred almost immediately. "Tanya" got up from her chair, began yelling at the top of her lungs for me to "leave her alone and to stop trying to rape her." During this time, she was tearing off her own clothing. Within minutes, several social workers and other staff members arrived at the office to find her partially undressed, in tears, and pleading with them for protection from my attempting to rape her. Unfortunately, the arriving staff were too ready to believe the girl with out even asking me what happened. Fortunately for me, I had suspected that something might happen and left the door to the adjoining office partially open, asking another social worker, who occupied that office, to monitor my session with "Tanya." At that point, I simply went over to the door, opened it and asked the social worker to step into the office. Everything became immediately clear and the staff members apologized for their impulsive and unfounded suspicions.

What might have happened to me had I not sensed the danger in seeing "Tanya" alone and had not taken those precautions? Several therapists, who are colleagues of mine, have had the same kind of experience but with disastrous results.

One therapist, here in the USA, was seeing an alcoholic female after the regular treatment hours for his clinic when no one else was in the building. After her third attempt to seduce him, he informed her that he was transferring her to a female therapist in the same clinic. She became enraged and stormed out of the office, cursing and threatening. Two days later, he was arrested for rape on a complaint of the same client and, although the case was dropped, was forced to resign from his position at the clinic. He also lost his professional credentials.

In Europe, a social worker who was operating a crisis telephone line, for both physically and sexually abused boys and girls, uncovered a pedophile ring, composed of very powerful and influential individuals, some from the government and others from law enforcement. Out of a clear blue sky, he was arrested for raping one of his young female clients, age 15. Six police officers came to his house to arrest him and then ravaged the house and his home office, confiscating all of his confidential records that *included all of the names, dates, and all of the additional evidence that he had accumulated on the pedophile ring.* A day later, the rape charges were dropped. The crisis phone lines stopped ringing once the newspapers printed the story of all of the records of the crisis line being confiscated and held by the police. Both the counselor and the crisis line no longer exist and he is now driving a lorry (truck) for a living.

It was later discovered that the girl who accused him of rape had a father who was involved with the pedophile ring. The police and other authorities had failed to even investigate the girl's statements that her father was the one who had actually raped her. Whether this was deliberate can only be speculated upon. *Only proper training, acute observation and reasonable precautions can prevent disasters of this type.*

COUNTERTRANSFERENCE ISSUES

A working definition of *Countertransference* is necessary at this point.

Unconscious feelings evoked in the [therapist] by the patient which may adversely affect the necessary objective attitude to the patient and interfere with the treatment. (Wolman, 1989)

Therapists and counselors of all professional backgrounds must be trained in *introspection* and *self-evaluation* techniques in order for them to know when they are losing objectivity and beginning to have more than the usual feelings and attractions for their clients. Once any client becomes personally related to the therapist in the therapist's own mind, treatment ends and a social or personal relationship begins.

Therapists and counselors are *human* and can fall in love with clients, over identify with clients, place clients in the role of sibling or child and thus become parent, brother or sister, and not therapist.

Once this occurs all objectivity is lost and the *ex-therapist,* now friend, relative or parent, becomes a survivor advocate and cannot fault, criticize or confront the survivor when necessary. Through the "Halo-Effect," (mentioned earlier in this chapter) the survivor is canonized a saint, can do no wrong, has no faults or problems of his/her own and all the negative behaviors become completely someone else's fault. No effective treatment can take place under these circumstances.

Regular supervision or *case discussion* with a colleague (also trained in sex therapy and experienced with survivor types) can help to identify these situations and prevent damage or harm to both the survivor and to the therapist. To do this on a regular basis requires self-confidence and self-esteem, on the part of the therapist, at a level where *criticism* is not taken as a putdown or insult but as positive professional help. Case discussion is especially necessary in long-term cases, (those in treatment for over a year or more), where some progress has been made but promotion to self-sufficiency has not seriously begun.

Countertransference also accounts for many therapists keeping survivors and other clients in therapy for year after year. One survivor who transferred to my caseload, in explanation for changing therapists, said to me, "Every time I finished dealing with a list of problems that he gave me, he came up with another list. — I began to feel like I would never get better and would be in therapy for the rest of my life."

FEAR-OF-FAILURE PROBLEMS

Supervision is necessary to prevent this type of therapeutic abuse. When the supervisor sees that the therapist has not promoted the survivor after a lengthy period of therapy (1 year of weekly sessions or more), a supervisory session should be held to evaluate the progress of *both the survivor and the therapist. Usually in these sessions, the supervisor can easily pick up indicators of countertransference problems or fear-of-failure problems on the part of the therapist.*

Therapists who are insecure, especially new therapists to this field, whose confidence has not yet been established, often fear promoting or releasing clients, especially survivors, since they fear that *if the survivor fails, they have failed.*

Once identified as a fear-of-failure problem, the supervisor can *share* in the decision to promote or release making it a less threatening process. This sharing is appropriate only in the early stages of supervision and only with the first one or two survivor cases that the therapist treats. *Emancipation of the therapist* is also part of the supervisory process and the danger of a new therapist becoming overly dependent on the supervisor for all of his/her decisions is a very real one.

PREVENTING DAMAGE TO THE THERAPIST

The following list of therapist precautions has worked for me and for many of my colleagues in this field over the past 30 years.

- 1. Know your patients and their needs. A careful workup, including psychological tests, will help accomplish this goal.

- 2. Stay observant and wary of the survivor's affection or anger toward you during therapy sessions.

- 3. If treating someone of the opposite sex or someone involved in long-term sexual abuse or prostitution, be sure someone else is in the vicinity of the therapy area, employ video monitoring (without audio) or at least audiotape all sessions.

- 4. Provide adequate security where all records are concerned.

- 5. At the first feelings of discomfort working individually with a survivor, consider a group milieu or a co-therapy situation with a colleague, preferably of the opposite sex.

- 6. Confront the survivor as soon as you feel that he/she is becoming too personal, too friendly or seductive or he/she is too frequently using sexual references or innuendoes.

- 7. Always discuss cases of this type with a colleague, including all concerns, worries, and suspicions.

- 8. Maintain a proper distance from the case and be acutely aware of possible transference or countertransference issues.

FINAL THOUGHTS

In this work, I have attempted to share with the reader 30 years of personal experiences in treating the survivors of sexual assault and sexual molestation. In no way is this presentation considered definitive or the last word. To write a book that would take into account every possible condition, situation and problem in working in this field would require volumes.

This work should be seen as a *guideline* to be supplemented by the best possible source of knowledge in this field, i.e., personal experience. Each new survivor will be a teaching aide, bringing something new, unique, and different to the total experience that the therapist accumulates. As I stated before, after all of these years and the hundreds of survivors that I have worked with, I am still learning and meeting new challenges and problems daily. When enough new information accumulates, a revision and expansion of this work will be forthcoming.

This volume has dealt almost exclusively with treatment of the victim — in essence, with the repair of the damage once it has been done. But the larger issue of *prevention* has been touched upon only superficially. It is toward prevention that this writer has turned in another manuscript intended for parents, teachers, and child care givers to be entitled, *Not MY Child!* and covering such topics as How to Prevent Your Child from Being Sexually Abused; How to Recognize If Your Child Is Being Abused; and How to Cooperate and Aid the Therapist in Treating Your Sexually Abused Child.

APPENDIX

 *TRAINING PRE-TEST AND REFERENCES*

☐ 1. What is the most important personality trait in a prospective therapist needed to qualify for work with survivors of sexual abuse? (ANSWER = His/her personal COMFORT WITH SEXUALITY). *See* Chapters 7 & 15

☐ 2. What is the ONLY really effective type of group therapy that works with survivors of sexual abuse? (ANSWER = A Self-Help Group with other Survivors who can Network) *See* Chapter 15

☐ 3. What is the FIRST major factor that must be dealt with in therapy with the survivor of sexual abuse? (ANSWER = CONTROL) *See* Chapter 9

☐ 4. What is the major prerequisite to DISCLOSURE in the survivor of sexual abuse? (ANSWER = Self-Acceptance)

☐ 5. Name the major BLOCKING-FACTOR to treatment in the survivor of sexual abuse? (ANSWER = GUILT)

☐ 6. Of all the elements in a sexual molestation, name the one that is most often overlooked and yet can be the MOST DAMAGING one! (ANSWER = The WORDS used by the offender, the police, medical personnel, parents or the survivor themselves.) Chapter 2 and throughout book

☐ 7. Name the best indicator, in non-reporting children or adults, of either present or past sexual abuse. (ANSWER = Unwanted sexual thoughts, fantasies or behaviors.) *See* Chapter 10

☐ 8. Name the FIRST and MOST IMPORTANT consideration with survivors before any real treatment can take place. (ANSWER = READINESS) *See* Chapter 7

☐ 9. In INCEST, name the most frequently overlooked problem. (ANSWER = AMBIVALENCE) *See* Chapter 12

☐ 10. Define "IMPRINTING" and its effects on survivors of sexual abuse. *See* entire Chapter 5

REFERENCES

Abel, Gene. 1991. *National Institute of Mental Health Study of Sexual Dysfunctions and Offenses.* Washington: The Institute.

American Heritage Dictionary, Second College Edition. 1985. Boston: Houghton Mifflin.

American Psychiatric Association. 1987. *Diagnostic & Statistical Manual of Mental & Emotional Disorders, Third Edition, Revised.*Washington: The Association

Araoz, Daniel L. 1982. *Hypnosis and Sex Therapy.* New York: Brunner/Mazel.

Bach, Marcus. 1961. *Strange Sects and Curious Cults.* New York: Dorset.

Beacon Foundation. 1991. *The Beacon Foundation Information Pack.* Rhyl-Clwyd, Wales: The Foundation.

Brancale, Ralph, & Ellis, Albert. 1956. *The Psychology of Sex Offenders.* Springfield, IL: Charles C. Thomas.

Briere, John, Evans, Diane, Runtz, Marsha, Wall, Timothy. 1988. Symptomatology in Men Who Were Molested As Children: A Comparison Study. *American Journal of Orthopsychiatry,* 58, 3.

Behavioral Science Research Unit, Federal Bureau of Investigation. 1991. *A Statistical Report on Crime and Sexual Offending.* Washington: The Bureau.

Burgess, Ann, Groth, Nicholas, Holmstrom, Carl, & Sgroi, Michaelangelo. 1978. *Sexual Assault of Children and Adolescents.* Lexington, MA: D.C. Heath.

Davies, Maureen. 1991. *Helping Individuals and Agencies to Deal with Problems of Ritual Abuse.* Rhyl-Clwyd. Wales: Beacon Foundation.

Diamond, Vera. 1992. *Satanic Ritual Abuse Syndrome.* London: Unpublished Paper, Cornelian Trust.

Elliott, Diana M., & Briere, John. 1992. Ruminations about matters of urgent concern. *Medical Aspects of Human Sexuality,* 2, 23-37.

Finkelhor, David. 1984. *Child Sexual Abuse: New Theory & Research.* New York: The Free Press.

Finkelhor, David. 1992. *Parent to Parent: Talking to Your Children about Preventing Child Sexual Abuse.* New York: Vera House.

Hartman, William E., & Fithian, Marilyn A. 1987. *Body/Self Image.* Los Angeles: Sensate Media Service.

Kahaner, Larry. 1988. *Cults That Kill.* New York: Warner Books.

LaVey, Anton Szandor. 1969. *The Satanic Bible.* New York: Avon Books.

LaVey, Anton Szandor. 1989. *The Satanic Witch.* Los Angeles: Feral House.

National Center on Child Sexual Abuse Prevention. 1992. *Statistical Report on Child Sexual Abuse.* Washington: US Government Printing Office.

National Criminal Justice Reference Service. Washington: Bureau of Justice Statistics.

Oke, Isaiah. 1992. *Blood Secrets: The True Story of Demon Worship and Ceremonial Murder.* New York: Prometheus Books.

Otter, G'Zell, Editor. 1989. *Witchcraft, Satanism and Occult Crime: Who's Who and What's What.* Los Ippilotos, CA: Green Egg.

Pallone, Nathaniel J. 1990. *Rehabilitating Criminal Psychopaths: Legislative Mandates, Clinical Quandries.* New Brunswick, NJ: Transaction Books.

Pazder, Lawrence. 1980. Survivors of sexual abuse. Paper presented at the American Psychiatric Association Convention, New Orleans.

Prendergast, William. 1991. *Treating Sex Offenders in Correctional Institutions and Outpatient Clinics.* New York: The Haworth Press, Inc.

Ross, Colin, & Gahan, Pam. 1988. Cognitive Analysis of Multiple Personality Disorder. *American Journal of Psychotherapy,* 42, 2, 57-79.

Turkas, Joan A. 1991. Psychotherapy and Case Management for Multiple Personality Disorder: Synthesis for Continuity of Care, *Psychiatric Clinics of North America,* 14, 19-91.

Wolman, Benjamin B. 1989. *Dictionary of Behavioral Science,* Second edition. New York: Academic Press.

Zeig, Jeffrey K., Editor. 1982. *Eriksonian Approaches to Hypnosis & Psychotherapy.* New York: Brunner/Mazel.

Index of Names and Topics